WALKING LOCH LOMOND AND THE TROSSACHS

43 WALKS, INCLUDING 21 MUNRO SUMMITS

Katie Featherstone

JUNIPER HOUSE, MURLEY MOSS,
OXENHOLME ROAD, KENDAL, CUMBRIA LA9 7RL
www.cicerone.co.uk

© Katie Featherstone 2026
Third edition 2026
ISBN: 978 1 78631 240 2
eISBN: 978 1 78765 252 1
Second Edition 2018 Ronald Turnball
First Edition 2009 Ronald Turnball

Printed in China on responsibly sourced paper on behalf of Latitude Press Ltd.
A catalogue record for this book is available from the British Library.
All photographs are by the author unless otherwise stated.
© Crown copyright and database rights 2026 OS AC0000810376

Cicerone's EU representative for GPSR compliance is Easy Access System Europe, Mustamäe tee 50, 10621 Tallinn, Estonia. Email gpsr.requests@easproject.com.

Updates to this guide

While every effort is made by our authors to ensure the accuracy of guidebooks as they go to print, changes can occur during the lifetime of an edition. Any updates that we know of for this guide will be on the Cicerone website (www.cicerone.co.uk/1240/updates), so please check before planning your trip. We also advise that you check information about such things as transport, accommodation and shops locally. Even rights of way can be altered over time. We are always grateful for information about any discrepancies between a guidebook and the facts on the ground, sent by email to updates@cicerone.co.uk.
 Register your book: To sign up to receive free updates, special offers and GPX files where available, create a Cicerone account and register your purchase via the 'My Account' tab at www.cicerone.co.uk.

Front cover: Climbing the south-east shoulder of Beinn Chuirn (Walk 23)

CONTENTS

Map key 5
Route summary table 7
Mountain safety graphic 10

INTRODUCTION 13

The national park 14
History, archaeology and culture 14
Geology 18
Conservation, wildlife, plants and fungi 18

Practicalities 22
Getting there and around 22
Camping and accommodation 24
Shops, food and drink and other practicalities 27

Walking 28
When to go 28
Walking conditions 29
Gaining experience 29
Safety and emergencies in the mountains 29
Adders, ticks, midges and other biters 31
Weather and snow 32
Maps and navigation 32
Using this guide 34

THE EAST 35

Part 1 The Trossachs 36
Walk 1   Ben Venue 37
Walk 2   Ben A'an 41
Walk 3   Menteith Hills 44
Walk 4   Doon Hill and Fairy Knowe 49
Walk 5   Ben Ledi and Benvane 52
Walk 6   Beinn a' Choin 57

Part 2 Callander and Strathyre 61
Walk 7   North Callander Circular 62

Walk 8	Three Callander bridges	67
Walk 9	Beinn Each	70
Walk 10	An Sìdhean	72

Part 3 Lochearnhead and Inverlochlarig ... 75

Walk 11	Stob a'Choin	76
Walk 12	Beinn Tulaichean and Cruach Ardrain	79
Walk 13	Stob Binnein and Ben More from the south	82
Walk 14	From Lochearnhead around Edinchip	86
Walk 15	Kendrum and Ogle Circle	89
Walk 16	Meall an t-Seallaidh and Creag Mac Rànaich	94
Walk 17	Ben Vorlich and Stùc a' Chroin	99

THE NORTH ... 103

Part 4 Killin and the far north-east ... 104

| Walk 18 | Killin and Loch Tay | 105 |
| Walk 19 | Meall Glas and Sgiath Chùil (from Glen Lochay) | 110 |

Part 5 Tyndrum ... 114

Walk 20	Glen Cononish	115
Walk 21	Beinn Odhar	118
Walk 22	Ben Lui via Dubhchraig and Oss	122
Walk 23	Ben Lui via Chuirn and Dubh	128
Walk 24	Beinn Challuim and Two Corbetts	133

Part 6 Crianlarich to Inverarnan ... 137

| Walk 25 | An Caisteal and Beinn a' Chroin Horseshoe | 138 |
| Walk 26 | Beinn Chabhair | 142 |

LOCH LOMOND ... 145

Part 7 Loch Lomond East ... 146

Walk 27	Ben Lomond	147
Walk 28	Ardess Hidden History Trail	152
Walk 29	Conic Hill	155
Walk 30	Inchcailloch and Balmaha	158

Part 8 Luss ... 162

| Walk 31 | Luss Hills: Beinn Dubh, Doune Hill and Beinn Eich | 163 |

THE WEST 167

Part 9 Arrochar Alps 168
Walk 32 Ben Vorlich and the Little Hills from Ardlui 169
Walk 33 The Cobbler 173
Walk 34 Straightforward Beinn Narnain and/or Beinn Ìme 177
Walk 35 Arrochar to Ben Vane and Beinn Ìme 180
Walk 36 Beinn Narnain and The Cobbler with optional extension to Beinn Ìme 185
Walk 37 A' Chrois, Beinn Narnain and The Cobbler 189

Part 10 Glen Croe to Loch Goil 193
Walk 38 The Brack and Ben Donich 194
Walk 39 Argyll's Bowling Green 198
Walk 40 Beinn an Lochain 202

Part 11 Cowal 205
Walk 41 Loch Eck and Beinn Mhòr 206
Walk 42 Puck's Glen 210
Walk 43 Kilmun to Strone Hill 212

Appendix A Munros and Corbetts by route number 215
Appendix B Access information 216
Appendix C Gaelic in the landscape 217
Appendix D The long routes 218
Appendix E Further reading 219

Route symbols on OS map extracts

 route

  alternative route

(SF) start/finish point

(SF) alternative start/finish point

  route direction

for OS legend see printed OS maps

SCALE: 1:50,000

GPX files
for all routes can be downloaded free at
www.cicerone.co.uk/1240/GPX

WALKING LOCH LOMOND AND THE TROSSACHS

Descending north towards Rest and be Thankful from Ben Donich (Route 38)

Acknowledgements

Thank you, firstly, to my legs, who've done the lion's share of work on this book. I'm also very grateful to Ronald Turnbull for the years of effort, inspiration and experience that went into the routes from previous editions; to Joe Williams for his faith in me; my editors, Nicole Spray and Felicity Laughton, and everyone at Cicerone for being such a pleasure to work with; and to my friend and colleague Peter Edwards for sticking his Meindl boot in the door for me.

Thank you to Luke Bailey for joining me on undoubtedly the most fun week of my research – for tackling long days of 'changeable' autumn weather, big green hills and all those soggy, boggy cols with admirable enthusiasm. Thank you to my parents, Mary-Ann and Nick, for dragging us on long walks when we were small, and my sister, Jenny, for enjoying them with me now; to Pauline Short, Jan and Rod de Maine, and Bryony Welburn for their ongoing support; and, most of all, to my husband Dan – none of it would be possible without you.

ROUTE SUMMARY TABLE

Walk	Name	Start	Distance	Ascent	Time	Page
1	Ben Venue	Ben Venue car park (Loch Achray)	12.1km (7.5 miles)	675m (2210ft)	5hr 30min	37
2	Ben A'an	Ben A'an car park (Loch Achray)	3.8km (2.4 miles)	330m (1080ft)	2hr	41
3	Menteith Hills	The Lodge (Aberfoyle)	14.8km (9.2 miles)	485m (1590ft)	6hr	44
4	Doon Hill and Fairy Knowe	Aberfoyle village	6.3km (3.9 miles)	120m (390ft)	1hr 30min	49
5	Ben Ledi and Benvane	Little Druim (Loch Venachar)	22km (13.7 miles)	1275m (4180ft)	8hr 45min	52
6	Beinn a' Choin	Stronachlachar	16.4km (10.2 miles)	835m (2740ft)	8hr	57
7	North Callander Circular	Callander	12.5km (7.8 miles)	385m (1270ft)	4hr	62
8	Three Callander Bridges	Callander	8.6km (5.3 miles)	210m (690ft)	2hr 30min	67
9	Beinn Each	Ardchullarie More (Loch Lubnaig)	6.8km (4.2 miles)	660m (2170ft)	3hr 30min	70
10	An Sidhean	Strathyre	4.7km (2.9 miles)	385m (1260ft)	2hr	72
11	Stob a'Choin	Inverlochlarig	14.2km (8.8 miles)	825m (2710ft)	5hr 30min	76
12	Beinn Tulaichean and Cruach Ardrain	Inverlochlarig	12.7km (7.9 miles)	1010m (3310ft)	6hr	79
13	Stob Binnein and Ben More from the south	Inverlochlarig	17km (10.6 miles)	1510m (4950ft)	8hr	82
14	From Lochearnhead around Edinchip	Lochearnhead	9km (5.6 miles)	125m (410ft)	2hr 30min	86
15	Kendrum and Ogle Circle	Lochearnhead	22.3km (13.9 miles)	575m (1890ft)	6hr 30min	89

Walk	Name	Start	Distance	Ascent	Time	Page
16	Meall an t-Seallaidh and Creag Mac Rànaich	Lochearnhead	17.9km (11.1 miles)	1115m (3660ft)	8hr	94
17	Ben Vorlich and Stùc a' Chroin	Ardvorlich, Loch Earn	14.8km (9.2 miles)	1100m (3610ft)	5hr 30min	99
18	Killin and Loch Tay	Killin	7km (4.3 miles)	50m (160ft)	2hr	105
19	Meall Glas and Sgiath Chùil	Glen Lochay car park	21.5km (13.4 miles)	1150m (3800ft)	8hr	110
20	Glen Cononish	Tyndrum	7.3km (4.5 miles)	125m (410ft)	2hr	115
21	Beinn Odhar	Tyndrum	13.7km (8.5 miles)	765m (2510ft)	5hr 15min	118
22	Ben Lui via Dubhchraig and Oss	Dalrigh, near Tyndrum	23.6km (14.7 miles)	1515m (4970ft)	9hr 30min	122
23	Ben Lui via Chuirn and Dubh	Dalrigh, near Tyndrum	24km (14.9 miles)	1450m (4750ft)	9hr 30min	128
24	Beinn Challuim and Two Corbetts	Auchtertyre Farm, near Tyndrum	17km (10.6 miles)	1345m (4410ft)	7hr 30min	133
25	An Caisteal and Beinn a' Chroin Horseshoe	Keilator, near Crianlarich	14.7km (9.1 miles)	980m (3220ft)	6hr 30min	138
26	Beinn Chabhair	Beinglas Campsite, Inverarnan	13.4km (8.3 miles)	1010m (3310ft)	7hr	142
27	Ben Lomond return	Ben Lomond car park, Rowardennan	12.4km (7.7 miles)	925m (3030ft)	5hr	147
28	Ardess Hidden History Trail	Ben Lomond car park, Rowardennan	3.1km (1.9 miles)	70m (230ft)	1hr	152
29	Conic Hill	Balmaha	6.3km (3.9 miles)	340m (1110ft)	2hr 15min	155
30a	Inchcailloch	Balmaha	3.1km (1.9 miles)	100m (330ft)	1hr 30min	158

ROUTE SUMMARY TABLE

Walk	Name	Start	Distance	Ascent	Time	Page
30b	Balmaha	Balmaha	4.1km (2.5 miles)	65m (210ft)	1hr 15min	160
31	Luss Hills: Beinn Dubh, Doune Hill and Beinn Eich	Luss	20.1km (12.5 miles)	1430m (4690ft)	8hr 30min	163
32	Ben Vorlich and the Little Hills	Ardlui	12.5km (7.8 miles)	1040m (3420ft)	6hr	169
33	The Cobbler	Glenloin car park 2, Arrochar	11.5km (7.1 miles)	840m (2760ft)	4hr	173
34	Straightforward Beinn Narnain and Beinn Ìme	Glenloin car park 2, Arrochar	17km (10.6 miles)	1260m (4130ft)	8hr	177
35	Arrochar to Ben Vane and Beinn Ìme	Loch Long head, Arrochar	20.2km (12.6 miles)	1455m (4770ft)	9hr	180
36	Beinn Narnain and The Cobbler	Glenloin car park 2, Arrochar	11.4km (7.1 miles)	1140m (3740ft)	6hr	185
37	A' Chrois, Beinn Narnain and The Cobbler	Glenloin car park 2, Arrochar	15.2km (9.4 miles)	1245m (4080ft)	7hr 30min	189
38	The Brack and Ben Donich	Car park off B828, near Rest and Be Thankful	13.2km (8.2 miles)	1085m (3560ft)	7hr	194
39	Argyll's Bowling Green	Ardgartan (Loch Long)	15.6km (9.7 miles)	655m (2150ft)	5hr	198
40	Beinn an Lochain	Car park off B828, near Rest and Be Thankful	6.6km (4.1 miles)	635m (2080ft)	3hr 30min	202
41	Loch Eck and Beinn Mhòr	Benmore Gardens (Cowal)	19.7km (12.2 miles)	880m (2890ft)	7hr 30min	206
42	Puck's Glen	Benmore Gardens (Cowal)	5.7km (3.5 miles)	225m (740ft)	2hr	210
43	Kilmun to Strone Hill	Kilmun	7.2km (4.5 miles)	380m (1250ft)	3hr	212

Mountain safety

Every mountain walk has its dangers, and those described in this guidebook are no exception. All who walk or climb in the mountains should recognise this and take responsibility for themselves and their companions along the way. The author and publisher have made every effort to ensure that the information contained in this guide was correct when it went to press, but, except for any liability that cannot be excluded by law, they cannot accept responsibility for any loss, injury or inconvenience sustained by any person using this book.

International distress signal *(emergency only)*
Six blasts on a whistle (and flashes with a torch after dark) spaced evenly for one minute, followed by a minute's pause. Repeat until an answer is received. The response is three signals per minute followed by a minute's pause.

Helicopter rescue
The following signals are used to communicate with a helicopter:

Help needed: raise both arms above head to form a 'Y'

Help not needed: raise one arm above head, extend other arm downward

Emergency telephone number
999

Weather reports
The Mountain Weather Information Service (MWIS) www.mwis.org.uk

Last light over Ben Lomond, seen from the west (Route 27)

PREFACE

With this third edition of *Loch Lomond and the Trossachs*, the baton has passed from the indomitable Ronald Turnball – who's previous two editions have guided many walkers, both new and experienced, to the very best of the Trossachs National Park – to Katie Featherstone.

Ronald's love of the Scottish landscape; its crags and glens, lochs and summits, history, geology and wide, wild moors, fuelled decades of exploration and writing. It's a passion that Ronald shared with so many others through his many Scottish guidebooks. His effortless turn of phrase, humour, and "weakness for bleakness" encouraged many others to strap on their boots, pack their waterproofs, and head off into the hills.

After two editions of *Loch Lomond and the Trossachs*, Ronald decided it was time for another pair of hands to take the book forward into its next iteration. I'm delighted that Katie Featherstone, author of Cicerone's *Short Walks in the Trossachs* and co-author of *Rùm and the Small Isles* has stepped in and prepared this wonderful new book.

Katie is based on Islay and brings a rich writing experience and love of the Trossachs to this guide, having walked the length and breadth of the national park in its creation. Looking at the stunning photography on display, she also clearly has great luck in picking clear and sunny days to go for a walk – so walkers venturing out with this guide should be aware that this won't always be their experience!

Ronald, in finding a new home for Loch Lomond, rashly claimed that he was signing off from any new guidebooks. He's since written two more for us – nicely illustrating that the allure of those Scottish forests and glens (and, yes, the bogs too) never goes away.

Maddy Williams, Cicerone Press, October 2025

Heading towards the pointed summit of Ben A'an (Walk 2)

INTRODUCTION

Ben Vane, Loch Lomond, Loch Arklet and Loch Katrine from Glas Bhealach (Walk 35)

With its green hills to the north, forest-fringed eastern lochs, and far western peninsulas stretching towards the sea, the breadth and extent of Loch Lomond and The Trossachs National Park is barely encompassed by its rambling title.

Divided nearly in half by the eponymous body of water, this sprawling region covers 1865km² of hillside, woodland and freshwater, containing 22 substantial lochs, 50 rivers and – of particular interest to readers of this book – no less than 40 mountains over the height of 2500ft (762m).

The national park's 21 Munros (mountains above 3000ft/914m) and 19 Corbetts (2500–3000ft/762–914m), 16 of which are covered in this book, mark the beginning of the Scottish Highlands – geographically for most people, but also in terms of the difficulty encountered climbing them. Instead of looming crags and exposed, rocky ridges, here the majority of hills can be accessed via a network of narrow winding paths, which weave their way up through scattered boulders and between rocky outcrops. Hillwalking in the Highlands is never easy nor free of risk for anyone, but Loch Lomond and The Trossachs' big, green hills make for a comparatively benign introduction.

That's not to say all of this book is suitable for beginners. The routes include a combination of rewarding, popular walks alongside more imaginative, rambling circuits, where the challenge lies in rough, pathless ground and navigation, but where you'll have the massive landscape to yourself. Along with the length, ascent and terrain synopsis given at the start of each route, any major challenges are explained in the route introductions; if you're looking to gain hillwalking experience or climbing your first Munros, a collection of straightforward routes are included especially for you (see 'Gaining experience', in the Walking section of this introduction).

Ben Lomond seen across Loch Lomond (Walk 27)

THE NATIONAL PARK

At the geological and societal divide between Highland and Lowland, the history, landscape and culture of the area now encompassed by the national park is difficult to discuss as a whole; the region is connected through glens and mountain passes, and along the waterways and lochs that also pose as a divide.

HISTORY, ARCHAEOLOGY AND CULTURE

Prehistory

The earliest inhabitants were groups of semi-nomadic hunter-gatherers who had arrived by about 7000BC; their presence is known from chance discoveries of worked flint and red deer antler.

In the succeeding Neolithic period, from c.4000BC, more settled communities were established, characterised by farming and a new range of tools, including pottery and polished stone axes. From these early millennia the evidence is predominantly artefacts rather than dwellings, but there are also archaeological sites related to funerary and ritual practices. The stone circle at Killin (Walk 18) is thought to be late Neolithic, while several cairns contain the ruins of stone burial chambers – see: Auchenlaich (Walk 7), which is the longest in Britain, or a smaller example at Edinchip (Walk 14).

Evidence from the Bronze Age also consists mostly of burial monuments (predominantly round cairns) and occasional bronze artefacts, but settlements of later prehistory are relatively common including forts, duns, brochs, small dwellings and crannogs – you can climb Dunmore Fort near Callander (Walk 8) to admire the view from this once defensive position.

In the first century AD, after the Romans' victory at Mons Graupius, forts and camps were constructed just south of the Highland Boundary Fault, at mouths of Highland glens (see Bochastle Fort, Walk 8).

Medieval times

By c.600AD, the region was a frontier zone between the Britons of Strathclyde in the south, the Gaelic kingdom of Dál Riata to the west and the Picts to the east, with Viking raids bringing further instability from the western sea lochs in the ninth century.

Christianity arrived around the 6th century. Many places have traditional associations with early saints, including St Kessog in Luss; St Fillan with Killin and Strathfillan (see Holy Pool near Tyndrum, Walk 21); and St Kentigerna with Inchcailloch. In the 12th century parish churches began to appear, with many sites retaining religious significance throughout the following centuries (see Inchcailloch, Walk 30, and Kirkton Church, Walk 4).

In later medieval times, the region was ruled by clans. Castles first appeared during the 12th century with many undergoing later adaptions; islands in Loch Lomond provided additional strength for some strongholds. Walk 18 visits the atmospheric ruins of Finlarig Castle.

From the Jacobite rebellions to the railway

The Jacobites staged a series of rebellions in Scotland in the late 17th and early 18th centuries, attempting to oust the House of Hanover from the British Crown and restore the House of Stuart. In The Trossachs, this period is associated with folk hero Rob Roy MacGregor who was born at Loch Katrine, ruled the area as clan chief and later went on the run as a Jacobite outlaw.

The Highlands were poorly served by roads during the Jacobite rebellions, which made it difficult for the government to control the area. In response, more than 250 miles of road were built under the command of General Wade, with a further 800 miles added by his successor, Caulfeild. These linked forts between Fort William and Inverness with the road network in southern Scotland. Many of these routes are still in use now, while the traces of others are retained as walking paths; notable sites include Rest and Be Thankful (see Part 10), Stronachlachar to Inversnaid (Walk 6) and a section near Edinchip in Walk 14.

Up to the late 18th century, agriculture was predominantly based around multiple-tenancy farms with the resident population's houses clustered together into on-site townships. Fields were generally unenclosed except for a turf or stone head-dyke, which created a boundary and protected crops from livestock grazing higher up the hill. In the Highlands, cattle were taken to more remote pastures (shielings) during summer for additional grazing; some members of the community would accompany them there, living in shieling huts. The population of Highland areas reached a maximum in the late 18th century, which was followed by a dramatic decline known as The Clearances. People were ousted by landowners who wanted the glens for sheep, while others moved for economic reasons after poor harvests in the early 19th century or the attraction of industry employment further south.

Rural industry continued with sheep farming, deer stalking and forestry, while many of the national park's villages were rebuilt by their landowners into something similar to the present day. Up to the 19th century, Gaelic was the region's predominant language, but its usage declined along with the population (see Appendix C, Gaelic in the landscape).

The next major development was tourism. Romantically known as Rob Roy Country, The Trossachs and the outlaw himself were brought into public imagination by the popular works of early 19th-century writer, Sir Walter Scott. *The Lady of the Lake*, *Waverley*, *Rob Roy* and *A Legend of*

Edinchip Viaduct (Walk 14)

HISTORY, ARCHAEOLOGY AND CULTURE

Pier Road in Luss (Walk 31)

Montrose all use specifically named and identifiable places as settings for his fictional scenes. Late Georgian-era visitors, captivated by Scott's evocative descriptions, soon flocked towards Loch Katrine, earning The Trossachs its frequently used title, 'the birthplace of Scottish tourism'. A gateway from Lowlands to Highlands, The Duke's Pass – now a section of the A821 – was originally built by the 19th-century Duke of Montrose, but was later upgraded to accommodate Victorian tourists wanting to get from Aberfoyle to Loch Katrine.

Steam propulsion – firstly along lochs, then railways – made the area more accessible, with settlements like Strathyre springing up beside new stations. The now-defunct Callander to Oban railway line left us with impressive viaducts and sections now converted into walking paths (see: Walks 14, 15, and 18 particularly).

The formation of the national park

While the post-World War II era saw ten national parks created across England and Wales, nowhere in Scotland received the same status until 2002. In that year Loch Lomond and The Trossachs was designated the first Scottish national park, followed by the Cairngorms in 2003. As of 2025, these two remain the only national parks in Scotland, despite extensive discussions, campaigns and counter-campaigns about establishing more.

The present day

Politically, the national park is now split under the council areas of Stirling (covering the majority of the east), Argyll and Bute (the west), West Dunbartonshire (south of Loch Lomond) and Perth and Kinross, which catches some of the far north-east. Today there are just under 15,000 people living within its boundary, with

Callander (population 3000) being the only town. Picturesque villages are sporadically dotted across the region, regularly occupying the land at the head of lochs.

GEOLOGY

The Highland Boundary Fault, which runs diagonally south-west to north-east across Scotland, divides the country's Highland from Lowland. The vast majority of the national park falls on the Highland side of this divide.

Highland Loch Lomond and The Trossachs consists of Dalradian metamorphic rock. This was sedimentary bedrock – laid down at the bottom of the ocean more than 600 million years ago – which was subjected to faulting, folding and metamorphism during a mountain-building cycle called the Caledonian Orogeny (490–390 million years ago). There are also some younger igneous rocks intruding to form dykes, sills and plutons.

Along the Highland Boundary Fault itself – which runs in a line from Callander to Aberfoyle, Balmaha and Loch Lomond – metamorphosed rocks are grouped as the Highland Border Complex. These date from the early Cambrian to late Ordovician age, around 485 million years ago. The extreme northern edge of the Lowlands is formed of a layer of tough conglomerate (puddingstone) rocks, bent into an upright position by the movement of the Highland Boundary Fault; these form the abrupt ridgelines of Callander Crags (Walk 7), the Menteith Hills (Walk 3), Conic Hill (Walk 29) and four of the islands in Loch Lomond including Inchcailloch (Walk 30).

The south-east extremity of the national park, on the Lowland side of the Highland Boundary Fault, is based on Old Red Sandstone. This younger sedimentary rock is from the Devonian Period (419.62 to 358.86 million years ago) and part of a wider band which runs across Scotland.

Subsequent processes affecting the landscapes' geology include glaciation from the ice ages. Loch Lomond, for example, was formed when glaciers flowed north to south during the last ice age between 2 million and 10,000 years ago. The Cobbler's (Walk 33) current form was shaped by ice melting about 11,500 years ago; rock faces that had been contained by ice were then exposed, resulting in collapse and slope failure leaving dramatic rock peaks. The last ice sheet also transported boulders, then dumped them on the land surface as it melted; when these rocks are different from their surroundings (like Samson's Stone near Callander, Walk 8), they are known as 'glacial erratics'. Erosion from weather and water continues to sculpt the rock to this day.

CONSERVATION, WILDLIFE, PLANTS AND FUNGI

In additional to its national park status, certain parts of Loch Lomond and The Trossachs are covered by additional

CONSERVATION, WILDLIFE, PLANTS AND FUNGI

Damp, mossy forests provide ideal conditions for fungi

protections. There are 73 designated special nature conservation sites, 60 Sites of Special Scientific Interest (SSSIs) and two National Nature Reserves (NNRs). The first NNR, simply called 'Loch Lomond', covers a small area in the south-east of the loch including the wetland areas around the River Endrick and several of the islands – visiting Inchcailloch (Walk 30) is one of the best ways to enjoy this special habitat.

In 2015, an area stretching between Callander and east Loch Lomond, called The Great Trossachs Forest, also received NNR status. This ambitious NNR has a 200-year plan, aiming to restore and diversify monoculture conifer plantations and heavily grazed hills; within the first 10 years more than 2.5 million native trees have been planted, creating and expanding varied habitat for wildlife. Key wildlife species include black grouse, whose UK population is now below 5000 breeding pairs, and the now-rare pearl-bordered fritillary butterfly, which was considered extinct within The Trossachs before new survey methodology was adopted in 2017. Look out for black grouse on the hill slopes around Glen Finglas (Walk 5).

Within the wider national park, other birds to look out for include: golden eagle in mountain areas; osprey, which fish off the east bank of Loch Lomond during summer; dippers, little brown birds with white chests recognisable for their distinctive bobbing head movement, often spotted perching on riverbank rocks; large black and white (male), or brown (female), eider duck found around the saltwater lochs at Ardgartan (Walk 39) and Holy Loch (Walk 43); and both pink-footed and Greenland white-fronted geese, which overwinter in the south-east of Loch Lomond. Listen for croaking, camouflaged rock ptarmigan in mountain boulder fields, particularly Ben Lomond (Walk 27).

The most iconic mammal is probably the red squirrel.

Non-native grey squirrels arrived from North America in the 1870s, carrying a disease that only affected their native red cousins – since then, the grey species has dominated much of the UK, but red squirrels are reclaiming ground in Scotland. The national park is at the front line of this struggle, with red squirrels now dominating. The easiest place to see them is in The Lodge wildlife hide near Aberfoyle (visited on Walk 3), but gardens and woodlands around Callander, Killin and the south end of Loch Lomond are also good bets. The region's elusive pine martin help control the numbers of grey squirrels, which are larger and easier to catch than the nimble reds.

The park has three species of deer: red, roe and fallow. The largest species, red deer, are a common sight across all mountain and moorland areas. Spotty fallow deer can be seen around east Loch Lomond and its islands, while the smallest species – roe – is most commonly found in low-lying areas in farmland and forest.

If you're out on a summer evening, look out for bats, which feed on midges at the edge of woodland, around buildings and near streams. Adders, Scotland's only native snake, come out of hibernation in March and can occasionally be seen basking in sunny spots around moorland or hills (see 'Adders, ticks and other biters'). There are also strategically important populations of certain fish species, including Atlantic salmon and powan – a rare freshwater fish native to only Loch Lomond and Loch Eck.

Atlantic oakwoods, found particularly to the east of Loch Lomond and in The Trossachs, support mosses, ferns and a whole range of wildlife – one mature tree can support 600 different species. Woodland floors glimmer purple with bluebells in May; some of the best places to see them include Inchcailloch (Walk 30) and Callander (Walk 7).

The Trossachs and east bank of Loch Lomond are strongholds for mature oak woodlands

CONSERVATION, WILDLIFE, PLANTS AND FUNGI

Some enjoy the bogs more than others

More important habitat is created by the ancient Scots pine, which was among the first species to colonise the Highlands after the last ice age. Along with rowan, birch, oak, aspen and juniper, it formed the ancient Caledonian pine forest that once covered much of Scotland. Now only small remnants remain, with protected sites such as Coille Coire Chuilc (Walk 22) ecologically important for native wildlife, plants, lichens and fungi species.

While unappreciated by walkers, mountain bogs provide vital habitat for frogs, dragonflies and other insects. Layers of sphagnum mosses also build up over time absorbing and storing large amounts of carbon dioxide; across Scotland, these 'carbon sinks' store ten times the carbon of all Britain's forests combined. Colourful mosaics of moss, swaying bog cotton and purple heather make up for many a damp foot.

Found above 350m, mountain ringlets are the UK's only truly alpine butterfly species – the first to recolonise after the last ice age. Look out for their brown and red wings on sunny days around grassy mountainsides and gullies.

PRACTICALITIES

GETTING THERE AND AROUND

The southern end of Loch Lomond and The Trossachs National Park is only 30km north-west of Glasgow or 100km west of Edinburgh (both with international airports), with Stirling providing another main entry point from the south-east. These cities provide transport links between the national park, the rest of the UK and further afield. Key locations within the national park include Callander, Aberfoyle, Lochearnhead, Tyndrum, Arrochar and the villages around southern Loch Lomond (Balmaha and Luss). Over half of this book was researched using public transport and a large proportion of the routes are accessible via bus or train, although this does require some planning.

Public transport

You might find the National Park Journey Planner (www.nationalparkjourneyplanner.co.uk) useful to work out which bus companies and railway lines operate certain routes. The safest method is to check your options there, then visit the individual companies' websites to confirm the route, time and whether you need to book in advance. Similar route planning services are offered by Traveline (www.traveline.info) and Google Maps (www.google.com/maps, none of which are foolproof.

Trains

ScotRail (www.scotrail.co.uk) operates the famously scenic West Highland Line, which travels from Glasgow to Oban or Fort William/Mallaig via Arrochar and Tarbet, Ardlui, Crianlarich and Tyndrum.

Buses

Citylink (www.citylink.co.uk) 'Glasgow to Campbeltown' runs via Luss, Tarbet, Arrochar, Ardgartan and Rest and Be Thankful (although the latter is excluded in winter). 'Glasgow to Oban' follows Loch Lomond before travelling through Crianlarich and Tyndrum. Book in advance.

McColl's (www.mccolls.org.uk) serves the south. Bus 305 travels from Balloch to Luss; 309 runs from Balloch to Balmaha. Buy tickets on the bus (card or cash, but no change given) or online.

Trossachs Explorer (www.lochlomond-trossachs.org) summer-only bus pilot scheme is running for its second year in 2025, now operated by McColl's. Stops include Aberfoyle, The Lodge, Ben Venue, Loch Katrine, Ben A'an, Brig o'Turk, Kilmahog and Callander. Hopefully this continues.

Stirling Council (www.stirling.gov.uk) S60/C60 services run via Callander, Kilmahog, Strathyre and Lochearnhead – pay cash or by card on the bus. There's also

Demand Responsive Transport from Killin to Crianlarich and Tyndrum or Inverarnan – book at least 2hr in advance either online or by calling 01786 237800.

Ember (www.ember.to) electric buses along the east and north (Edinburgh to Fort William) stop at Callander, Strathyre, Lochearnhead, Crianlarich and Tyndrum; 'Glasgow to Fort William' visits west Loch Lomond plus Crianlarich and Tyndrum. Book in advance.

Garelochhead Coaches (www.garelochheadcoaches.co.uk) 302 service (Helensburgh to Carrick Castle) stops at Luss, Inverbeg, Tarbet, Arrochar, Rest and Be Thankful and Lochgoilhead. Buy tickets on the bus (card or cash, but no change given).

West Coast Motors (www.westcoastmotors.co.uk) serves Cowal. Pay driver with cash or card, or get discounted open tickets online/via app.

Boats
Cruise Loch Lomond (www.cruise-lochlomond.co.uk) offer fairly limited summer services, Balmaha Boatyard (www.balmahaboatyard.co.uk) run a tiny passenger ferry from Balmaha to Inchcailleach Island, while a 2hr steamship cruise (www.lochkatrine.com) travels up Loch Katrine from Trossachs Pier to Stronachlachar and back.

Luss Pier and Ben Lomond; Cruise Loch Lomond run some summer services across the loch

Travelling to Cowal from Glasgow, a Western Ferries (www.western-ferries.co.uk) vehicle and passenger sailing runs between Gourock and Dunoon.

Driving

For drivers, the national park is connected by several A roads, some of which are fast and busy. More remote areas are served by narrow, single-track roads, which can prove tricky for the unaccustomed; always pull into passing places (on the left side of the road) when faced with oncoming traffic or to allow a vehicle behind you to pass – you might need to reverse. Parking is often pay and display, ranging from reasonably priced to extortionate and payable via cash, card or (often irritating) app, depending on the site – it's a good idea to carry some change for this purpose.

Cycling

On a longer trip, walking routes can be connected by cycling. National Cycle Network Route 7 (NCN 7) takes a scenic route up the east of the national park from Glasgow to Killin, while West Loch Lomond cycle path runs from Balloch to Tarbet via Luss. There are also cycle routes along Loch Katrine, Loch Eck, Loch Ard and around Balquhidder and Strathyre.

CAMPING AND ACCOMMODATION

Wild camping, Camping Management Zones and campervans

According to the Scottish Outdoor Access Code (www.outdooraccess-scotland.scot), wild camping is permitted in small tents, well away from buildings and roads and avoiding enclosed fields of crops or livestock. The national park is subject to specific restrictions from the 1 March to 30 September: Camping Management Zones cover popular loch- and road-sides. These bylaws mean a permit is required for tents and campervans, with specific sites set aside for the purpose. The fee charged is small, but sites should be booked online in advance as they do fill up at busy times of year. Permit sites do not usually have facilities like toilets or drinking water. Some are tent-only, while others accept campervans. Further information/bookings: www.lochlomond-trossachs.org/things-to-do/camping.

For self-contained campervans/motorhomes, the 'Stay the Night' scheme run by Forestry and Land Scotland (www.forestryandland.gov.scot/stay-the-night) offers affordable overnight space in several national park car parks. There are other similar schemes run by different organisations, some with and some without services. One option is Loch Katrine (www.lochkatrine.com/motorhomes), which has a site at Trossachs Pier

Camping and accommodation

The basic, but beautifully situated Sallochy Campsite on the east bank of Loch Lomond is run by the National Park Authority

and another at Stronachlachar Pier (Trossachs Pier has much easier access, but the car park is large and busy, while Stronachlachar Pier is comparatively peaceful with access down a long single-track road).

Wherever you camp, be sure to leave no trace of your visit.

Campsites

The National Park Authority runs basic, affordable campsites at Loch Chon, Loch Achray, Inchcailloch and Sallochy (www.lochlomond-trossachs.org/things-to-do/camping). All beautifully situated on loch shores, these sites have toilets (often compost), but no showers and should be booked in advance. Loch Chon, Loch Achray and Sallochy provide drinking water and the option of (pre-booked) parking, but Inchcailloch does not.

Additionally, there are various private campsites across the park. Many request advance booking. The friendly By The Way (www.tyndrumbytheway.com) hostel and campsite in Tyndrum, and Beinglas Campsite (www.beinglascampsite.co.uk) in Inverarnan are predominantly used by people walking the West Highland Way, but provide good access for some of the routes in this book.

Two friends stopping for lunch on the summit of Stùc a' Chroin (Walk 17)

Elsewhere, sites often feel better set up for caravan holidays and campervans, but the following do accept tents: Glenloin House Campsite (tel 07810 194259), which is conveniently placed for the Arrochar Alps and very affordable for tent campers; and Luss Campsite (www.lusscampsite.co.uk), which is just north of the village. The Lochearnhead, Balquidder and Inverlochlarig area is lacking in conveniently placed facilities, but there is Immervoulin (www.immervoulinpark.co.uk), in Stathyre, and Cruachan Farm (www.largoleisure.co.uk), north of Killin. Cobleland Campsite (www.coblelandcampsite.co.uk) is a few kilometres south of Aberfoyle, while Keltie Bridge (www.keltiebridge.co.uk) is east of Callander.

Accommodation

Beyond the previously mentioned By The Way in Tyndrum, conveniently placed traditional hostels are few and far between. Rowardennan Lodge Youth Hostel (www.hostellingscotland.org.uk/hostels/rowardennan/) is well placed for Ben Lomond, as is Ben Lomond Bunkhouse (www.nts.org.uk/holiday-accommodation/bunkhouses/ben-lomond-bunkhouse). There is also Crianlarich Youth Hostel (www.hostellingscotland.org.uk/hostels/crianlarich/).

Other accommodation – including B&Bs, hotels, cabins, pods and self-catering – is listed by Visit Scotland (www.visitscotland.com), as well as on the usual sites such as www.booking.com.

SHOPS, FOOD AND DRINK AND OTHER PRACTICALITIES

Food shops are limited to the villages, with nothing available in the central national park. Small Co-op supermarkets are located in Aberfoyle, Callander and Killin, while most other villages have an even smaller village shop. Notable exceptions include Lochearnhead (whose shop has sadly closed) and Kilmun (shops on the opposite side of Holy Loch). Cafés, pubs and restaurants have a similar distribution pattern with the highest concentration in the south and south-east.

An increasing number of drinking-water refill stations, provided by Scottish Water, are popping up around the country, with some useful locations in the national park. They provide a map of all taps: www.yourwateryourlife.co.uk/find-my-nearest-tap/.

You should never rely on having mobile phone signal in the hills, but be aware that it's particularly patchy around The Trossachs, Lochearnhead and Tyndrum.

Looking down Callander Main Street towards Ben Ledi (Part 2/Routes 5, 7 or 8)

WALKING

WHEN TO GO

Scottish weather is hard to generalise, but late spring and early autumn provide some of the most rewarding conditions. April can still be winter on the summits, but May and June are enjoyable at all altitudes. The leafy Trossachs are at their most vibrant as new leaves break out and bluebells bloom in May. Midges come out at the end of May and stick around until the first frost, usually in September. July and August can be hot and humid, as well as busy in more popular locations. Low-level routes are also excellent in October as the birch leaves turn gold.

Winter is a time of short days and foul weather. Snow can lie on the high tops from December to April. Well-equipped walkers skilled in navigation and with ice axe/crampons love the winter most of all, for the alpine-style ascents of Ben Lui and the 100km views through the winter-chilled air.

Walking near Lochan a' Chlaidheimh in winter (Walk 34)

WALKING CONDITIONS

The aim across this book is to find the most rewarding and interesting routes that will suit a range of abilities. The national park's 21 Munros are all covered, as well as 16 of its Corbetts, but there's also a collection of worthwhile smaller hills and easier low-level walks. While some routes are fairly direct, others are more of a rambling exploration.

Lower-level walks explore the region's lush woodlands, peaceful loch shores and special points of interest – these areas are popular with wildlife and sprinkled with interesting historic sites. The region's rewarding mid-level hills rise rockily from beautiful lochs with helpful, followable paths.

Among the mountains, generally, it's the Munros that are pathed and peopled, making them often easier than the slightly lower Corbetts. For those experienced in hills further south, such as Snowdonia (Eryri) or the Lake District, these are only slightly larger but noticeably more rugged. Each of the Munros has its well-worn standard route, which usually travels up and down the same way. While these are used and pointed out where applicable, they aren't always described; if your main aim is to tick off the summits as fast as possible, perhaps buy Cicerone's *The Munros Vol 1 – Southern, Central and Western Highlands*, by Steve Kew.

GAINING EXPERIENCE

For the Munros, with its wide path and spectacular views, Ben Lomond (Walk 27) is a great place to start; Ben Vorlich by Loch Earn (Walk 17) also has a well-maintained path; and in the Arrochar Alps, Beinn Narnain and/or Beinn Ìme (Walk 34) provide straightforward returns. Simple Corbetts are less common, but Beinn Each (Walk 9) in the national park's east has an uncomplicated out-and-back route, as does The Cobbler (Walk 33), despite its dramatically rocky appearance. Smaller, but worthwhile simple hill routes include Conic Hill (Walk 29) above Loch Lomond, the return routes for Ben Venue (Walk 1) and Ben A'an (Walk 2) in The Trossachs, An Sìdhean (Walk 10) from Strathyre, Beinn Dubh (Walk 31) in the Luss Hills and Strone Hill (Walk 43) in Cowal.

SAFETY AND EMERGENCIES IN THE MOUNTAINS

Safety and navigation in the mountains are best learnt from companions, experience or, when in doubt, a paid instructor. Mountaineering Scotland (www.mountaineering.scot) run a range of relevant courses, while Scottish Mountain Rescue (www.scottishmountainrescue.org) provide advice about safety and emergencies online. There is no charge for Mountain Rescue in Scotland, which is provided by volunteers.

Walking Loch Lomond and the Trossachs

The trig point and cairn at Ben Vorlich's southern summit (Walk 32)

Preparation is key, including checking forecasts (see 'Weather and snow') and being kitted out with the correct clothing and equipment. Leave your route plan with a responsible person (and remember to tell them when you've returned): speak to your accommodation provider or keep a friend updated if you're wild camping.

If you're involved in an incident, remain calm, assess the situation and then decide what to do: check for immediate danger, give any necessary first aid, locate your exact position, keep warm and decide whether to descend, find shelter, remain where you are or call for help.

In an emergency, for Mountain Rescue, phone 999 and ask for Police and then Mountain Rescue. You'll be asked to provide your location (six-figure grid reference or named location – if you don't use GPS, the OS Maps app (free) pinpoints your exact location as a grid reference: download and try it in advance), the number of casualties, any injuries, size of group and their equipment, as well as your phone number and the numbers of any other mobiles in the group. Reception is good on most summits and ridges, as well as in an increasing number of other places within the national park.

Pre-register your phone to send emergency SMS texts (more likely to go through with limited signal) by texting 'register' to 999, then following the instructions; further information is available at www.emergencysms.org.uk.

Emergency satellite beacons, of which there are various types, provide the possibility of emergency call-outs without phone signal. Some are simply an emergency button sending your location to emergency services, while others provide the option to message contacts or track your route.

The international mountain distress signal is some sign (shout, whistle, torch flash etc) repeated six times over a minute, followed by a minute's silence. The reply is a sign repeated three times over a minute, followed by a minute's silence. To signal a helicopter for help, raise both arms above the head and then drop them down sideways, repeatedly. If you're not in trouble, don't shout or whistle on the hills, and don't wave to passing helicopters.

ADDERS, TICKS, MIDGES AND OTHER BITERS

Adders are Scotland's only venomous snake – they're grey or reddish-brown, with a dark zigzag stripe down their back. While bites to humans are rare and not usually serious, they should be checked and treated. If bitten, the affected part of the body needs to be immobilised – if near a road, call 999 and ask for an ambulance; in the hills, you'll need to call Mountain Rescue. See: www.nhs.uk/conditions/snake-bites/.

Ticks are unfortunately very common within the national park and they can carry Lyme or other diseases. Tucking trousers into socks can help prevent them, as can wearing a repellent like Smidge (www.smidgeup.com). Check yourself after any walk and extract any clingers-on with a tick removing tool as soon as possible. Be aware of any symptoms, which typically occur 3–30 days later and can include: an expanding rash, flu-like symptoms, fatigue, headache or muscle/joint pain. Search 'tick' at www.nhsinform.scot.

While other, generally non-dangerous, biting or stinging insects are present, midges are by far the most common. Thankfully, Scotland's midges are not dangerous (or we really would be in trouble!), but they can be a serious annoyance. Midges can't fly very fast, so you should easily outpace them and any breeze will blow them away. When stopping or camping in low, sheltered areas, the less exposed skin the better; a midge headnet can come in useful as well as repellent such as Smidge or Avon's Skin-So-Soft. Sometimes the only answer is to hide in your tent. For other biting insects or reactions, see: www.nhs.uk/conditions/insect-bites-and-stings/.

WEATHER AND SNOW

For mountain forecasts, see Mountain Weather Information Service (www.mwis.org.uk) and Met Office mountain forecasts (www.metoffice.gov.uk/public/weather/mountain-forecasts). For general area forecasts, it can be helpful to compare both Met Office and BBC (www.bbc.co.uk/weather).

The Scottish Avalanche Information Service (www.sais.gov.uk) issues snow and avalanche risk forecasts for Glen Coe. Conditions in Lomond and The Trossachs will usually (although not invariably) be rather less serious. They also produce an app.

MAPS AND NAVIGATION

The mapping in this book is from the Ordnance Survey's Landranger® series at 1:50,000. For lower-level walks this book's mapping might be sufficient, but for hillwalking it's advisable to have a larger map showing escape routes, diversions and the surrounding peaks for triangulation.

Map options are given at the start of each walk, mentioning both Ordnance Survey® (OS maps; www.shop.ordnancesurvey.co.uk/maps/) and Harvey Maps (www.harveymaps.co.uk). Harvey Maps are weatherproof, whereas OS maps come in standard or weatherproof versions. Use of either should be accompanied by a compass.

The 1:50,000 OS Landranger mapping covers the area on sheets 56 (*Loch Lomond & Inverary*), 57 (*Stirling & The Trossachs*), 50 (*Glen Orchy & Loch Etive*) and 51 (*Loch Tay & Glen Dochart*). Hills between Crianlarich and Inverlochlarig are awkwardly on the shared corner of all four.

For detailed exploration, a 1:25,000 scale is recommended. Harvey Superwalker maps are ideal for higher mountain walks; they're beautifully clear, legible and mark paths where they actually exist on the ground. They also overlap conveniently. Five sheets – *Arrochar Alps*; *Trossachs North (Loch Lyon & Crianlarich)*; *Loch Lomond & The Trossachs (Ben Lomond & Loch Katrine)*; *Ben Ledi (Hills North of Callander)*; and *Ben Venue (Loch Ard Forest & The Trossachs)* – cover most of the national park excluding Cowal and Loch Lomond's far south.

OS Explorer maps, also 1:25,000, are bulkier with less legible contour lines, but have more detail for the lower ground. While Harvey Maps mark fences and walls on the open hill, these features are absent from valleys. OS Explorer maps also include more detail on historic sites and man-made features, which are more common and interesting on lower-level routes. Sheets OL39 (*Loch Lomond North*) and OL46 (*The Trossachs*) cover the most ground, while other routes use OL38 (*Loch Lomond South*), OL37 (*Cowal East*), OL48 (*Ben Lawers & Glen Lyon*) and 377 (*Loch Etive & Glen Orchy*).

Harvey also offers a 1:40,000 scale: *British Mountain Map Southern*

A Shetland sheepdog enjoying the view (Walk 1)

Highlands that covers most of the national park, while the Ultramap series (*Loch Lomond & The Trossachs, Arrochar Alps, Trossachs North* and *Loch Earn*) includes everything except the far south and west.

Having two forms of navigation is the safest policy for hillwalking. Old-style GPS receivers should be set to the British National Grid. Satellite navigation devices are usually waterproof and don't rely on phone signal or your phone's battery.

For smartphone navigation, install an app (like OS Maps) with OS or Harvey mapping, be sure this works offline, and carry a backup battery pack as well as a paper map and compass. Relying on smartphone navigation alone seems convenient, but can make you vulnerable – batteries drain quickly at low temperatures, many phones aren't waterproof and technological issues can strike at inconvenient moments. Your first priority with a mobile phone is to ensure it will be there to contact emergency services if needed.

GPX tracks for the routes in this guidebook are available to download free at www.cicerone.co.uk/1240/GPX. A GPS device is an excellent aid to navigation, but you should also carry a map and compass and know how to use them. GPX files are provided in good faith, but in view of the profusion of formats and devices, neither the author nor the publisher accepts responsibility for their use.

A family looking over Loch Katrine from the summit of Ben A'an (Walk 2)

USING THIS GUIDE

This book begins in The Trossachs (the national park's central east) and works its way anti-clockwise around the north-east, north and north-west of the park as far as Inverarnan, just north of Loch Lomond. It then deals with Loch Lomond itself, starting on the east bank around Ben Lomond, before heading to the south-east and then west. Finally, the west of the park is covered starting with the Arrochar Alps before heading into Cowal.

Information boxes at the beginning of each route include a starting point with grid reference, the total distance and ascent, the maximum altitude, a quick synopsis of terrain encountered, possible maps and a suggested time. The times assume the pace of a fairly fit and determined walker – they're subjective and don't allow for much in the way of breaks. Always allow plenty of extra time before nightfall unless you're prepared to walk in the dark. Sometimes a shortcut, an extension to the main route or an alternative starting point is included, as well as parking or public transport details when necessary.

Appendixes include Munros and Corbetts by walk number, access information, some key words of Gaelic in the landscape, a list of long-distance routes crossing the national park and suggested further reading.

THE EAST

Descending from Ben Vorlich to Bealach an Dubh Choirein, with Stùc a' Chroin ahead (Walk 17)

PART 1 THE TROSSACHS

Along Loch Katrine from Beinn a' Choin (Walk 6)

Along the meadowed bank of the meandering River Forth, the attractive village of Aberfoyle provides the southern gateway to the world-famous, but surprisingly difficult to define Trossachs. At its most specific, the name 'Trossachs' refers to the region's leafy, green heart – a glen between the characterful, rocky peaks of Ben A'an and Ben Venue, with the outflow of Loch Katrine at its western border and Loch Achray to the east. The term can also be used to more generously encompass a larger area of forest, lochs and glens covering the central west of the national park but, for our purposes, this title covers Aberfoyle, The Trossachs proper and a tough hike up Beinn a' Choin from the west end of Loch Katrine.

WALK 1
Ben Venue

Start/finish	Ben Venue car park, Loch Achray NN 506 069
Time	5hr 30min
Distance	12.1km (7.5 miles); returning down the same ascent route is a bit further (14.6km/9.1 miles) but the going is much easier
Total ascent	675m (2210ft)
Terrain	Good rocky ascent paths and a very rough, pathless hill descent
Max altitude	Ben Venue 729m (2392ft)
Maps	OS Explorer OL46; OS Landranger 57; Harvey *Ben Venue*
Public transport	Seasonal Trossachs Explorer bus stop
Parking	Pay and display parking: cash, card or app

Ben Venue is from the Gaelic *A' Bheinn Mheanbh*, meaning 'Tiny Mountain.' (*Meanbh* is also Gaelic for midge, as 'very tiny fly', *meanbh-chuileag*.) The name fits. Venue is small but surprisingly rocky, and the second most popular hillwalk in this area after Ben Lomond. Views from the summit are nothing short of spectacular.

The straightforward return route following a well-maintained path through Gleann Riabhach is great in itself; an alternative descent to Loch Katrine, described here, is navigationally tricky and covers some very rough, steep ground. But perseverant hikers are rewarded with solitude and spectacular views over the tiny islets in The Trossachs' most famous loch.

The first 3km of this route are well signposted for Ben Venue. From the back of **Ben Venue car park**, take the path on the right, which climbs uphill. Follow it for about 500 metres to a junction, then turn right and walk downhill. The imposing north-east face of Ben Venue looms over the trees ahead. Keep to the path as it joins a wooden walkway, then follow it to a road junction with a small car park.

At the junction, turn left and walk down a private road, passing white gates and a sign for Loch Katrine Dam. Follow the road alongside a river for 550 metres until you reach a signposted left turn. Take this path and walk down to an arched footbridge over the tumbling **Achray Water**. Cross this and continue straight along

a track for a short distance, then turn right onto another track; follow this west for 350 metres, looking out for the 'Ben Venue' sign pointing left.

Take this turning, following a wide path as it rises up between tall trees. Look out for red squirrels. After 450 metres, ignore a left turn at a junction and continue uphill for another 250 metres. When you reach a T-junction with a forest track, turn left onto it and walk for 160 metres. As the track begins to bend left towards a bridge, turn right onto a narrower, indicated path which soon crosses a burn. Follow this path for 240 metres as it emerges from the mature forest to an area of young trees. When you reach a junction with a track, cross the track and continue walking uphill on a good path. The signposts end here, but follow this path as it heads roughly south-west above and following the course of the valley **Gleann Riabhach** for 1.6km with Ben Venue on your right.

Keep to the well-made path as it begins to bear right and climb north towards and past the slender Spùt Bàn waterfall. The path becomes less distinct as it climbs above and to the right of the waterfall with some exposed rock. After 150 metres, as the path dips into a wet, grassy col, look out for a continuation of the path on your left beyond a boggy area; rather than heading directly for this, take a wide, anticlockwise semicircle around to reach the path, crossing two small burns and avoiding the worst of the bog. Rejoining the path, keep to the most obvious strand as it splits, climbing for a further 300 metres, and emerges at a rocky cairn and junction at 580m elevation.

Turn right, following a steep, rocky path east north-east for 450 metres. When the path splits, just before descending steeply, with the highest point directly ahead, turn left onto a narrower path, which will take you to the true summit of **Ben Venue**. Follow it as it leads alongside a few rusty fence posts before climbing steeply (past more fence posts) to the summit cairn at 729m. A glorious view awaits.

To continue to the second summit, walk past the cairn and south-east along a path which descends a little. After 200 metres this path meets the larger bypass path; bear left onto this and climb its final rocky section to a broken trig point at 727m. There are great views over Loch Achray and Loch Venachar towards Callander.

By far the easiest descent route is to retrace your steps (the final section through the forest is well marked with signs for the car park). To continue to Loch Katrine, however, return north-west down the steep crag-base path for just 100 metres, to the col (NN 476 062) before Ben Venue's true summit. Now a little valley goes down to the right leading roughly north towards Loch Katrine; take this, finding a good line of descent north. Keep the small burn that runs down the valley on your right, then stay to the left of rocky crags in the middle of the valley as it begins to open out. After about 560 metres, as the gradient decreases and the rough ground starts to level out, cross the burn at a convenient place (NN 476 068). Bear right and head north north-east for 200 metres across the hags and slight rise at the base of Druim nan Sasunnach. On a clear day, Brenachoile Lodge and its pier can be seen up ahead on the opposite bank of Loch Katrine.

> Propelled to fame by Sir Walter Scott's 1810 poem *The Lady of the Lake*, picturesque **Loch Katrine** has been an enduringly popular visitor destination since late Georgian and Victorian times; Queen Victoria herself enjoyed a boat trip on its peaceful waters. However, very few people view the lake from this perspective.

Cross another stream (NN 476 070) an equal distance between two rowan trees growing on its bank (20 metres further downstream this joins the burn you were originally following, eventually feeding down into Allt Chroiteagan). A small path starts here, leading 200 metres east north-east to a wide, wet col just around the corner (NN 477 070).

Looking east from the col, two dips present opportunities of descent towards Loch Katrine and Loch Achray. The one on the left (the more northerly) is lower and steeper (a stream notch); but choose the shallower one on the right. Cross above the head of the more southerly dip (NN 479 071), aiming for Loch Achray briefly, then head down to an old metal fence post. A line of old fence posts leads

A broken trig point at the lower, south-eastern summit with Loch Achray and Loch Venachar beyond

east north-east steeply downhill (below you can see a fence running along the same line that meets Loch Katrine). Follow the general direction of the line of rusty posts, which are sometimes quite spaced out and difficult to see (when they disappear into trees, keep to the right) until you eventually reach a fence corner (NN 483 072) at the foot of the steep ground.

Go through a fence gap, to find a clear path running to the right below the side-fence. Follow this for 660 metres as it leads south-east, going below two large rocks popular with boulderers, then following a burn down into a little grassy valley. Follow the path as it leaves the burn, with another fence now on the left, then cross a ladder stile on your left, and turn right, initially downhill, on a path that bends round left to the dam of **Loch Katrine**.

Cross the dam, and take the tarred lane ahead, bearing right, near **Achray Water**; the lane becomes the one used at the start of the outward walk. Just before it joins a road, turn right on the boardwalk path with waymarkers. Where it divides, both branches lead quickly to the car park; take the right for an alternative view of dramatic little Ben A'an.

WALK 2
Ben A'an

Start/finish	Ben A'an car park, Loch Achray NN 509 070
Time	2hr
Distance	3.8km (2.4 miles)
Total ascent	330m (1080ft)
Terrain	Good but steep, rocky path
Max altitude	Ben A'an 454m (1490ft)
Maps	OS Explorer OL46; OS Landranger 57; Harvey *Ben Ledi*
Public transport	Seasonal Trossachs Explorer bus stop
Parking	Pay and display parking: cash, card or app

A miniature mountain, Ben A'an's rocky, conical summit rising from the forest is one of The Trossachs' most striking sights. Prior to Sir Walter Scott's Anglicisation, the hill's Gaelic name was *Am Binnean* meaning, appropriately, 'the pinnacle'. The only thing to beat looking at it, is to look out from it – the steep, rocky ascent rewards hillwalkers with unbeatable views over Loch Katrine, Loch Achray and Loch Venachar, as well as of the nearby Ben Venue and surrounding mountains.

From the car park cross the **A821** and go through wooden posts onto an uphill track with a sign for Ben A'an. This soon becomes a well-built path, as it ascends steeply (at one point splitting briefly before rejoining), then crosses the Allt Inneir by a footbridge. Continue as the path levels with Ben A'an looming directly ahead, looking to be the preserve of rock climbers from this angle (it isn't!).

Some 500 metres after the bridge, the path crosses a forest track. Ignore this and carry on straight, soon entering birch trees. Continue for another 400 metres to a clearing with large boulders. With a view of Ben Venue, this makes a good spot for a picnic.

From the clearing, follow the path as it ascends steeply up a series of rock steps beside a stream, then splits into vague branches to cross it. Keep going as it levels out, running to the right of the summit cone (ignore the eroded shortcuts on your left). Follow the path as it circles round to a col, before bearing left for the final ascent of **Ben A'an**'s rocky western summit (454m).

WALKING LOCH LOMOND AND THE TROSSACHS

From the western summit of **Ben A'an**, serpentine Loch Katrine snakes out west, while Ben Venue dominates the south-west; to the south-east Loch Achray and its larger neighbour Loch Venachar stretch towards Callander. On a clear day, you can see as far as the Arrochar Alps.

At the time of research, any alternative descent route was closed for flora protection, but it's no hardship to return the same way.

The old Trossachs Hotel beside Loch Achray

Walkers descending the path towards Loch Achray

Walking Loch Lomond and the Trossachs

WALK 3
Menteith Hills

Start/finish	The Lodge, just north of Aberfoyle NN 520 015
Time	6hr
Distance	14.8km (9.2 miles); starting in Aberfoyle adds 0.7km (0.4 miles) each way
Total ascent	485m (1590ft); starting in Aberfoyle adds 60m (195ft)
Terrain	Two-thirds paths and tracks, one-third rough ground over the hills
Max altitude	Craig of Monievreckie 400m (1312ft)
Maps	OS Explorer OL46; OS Landranger 57; Harvey *Ben Venue*
Public transport	Seasonal Trossachs Explorer bus stop at The Lodge; bus stop in Aberfoyle
Parking	Paid parking at The Lodge; free parking in Aberfoyle (Riverside car park)

The lumpy, diagonal ridgeline of the Menteith Hills is made of puddingstone – part of the Highland Boundary Fault. From its heathery, peaty vantage you look south across the Lake of Menteith to the Lowlands, and north across Loch Venachar to the Highlands.

You also have a view over the woods and plantations of Queen Elizabeth Forest Park. Well-laid trails around The Lodge provide a relaxing woodland start, with small waterfalls and a red squirrel hide. The junction of forest and hill here is also the joining point of Highland and Lowland, with a glimpse of the strange ocean-bottom rocks of the Highland Border Complex.

The Menteith Hills themselves are largely pathless, making this route tougher than you might expect if you consider the distance covered and metres climbed.

To reach The Lodge from Aberfoyle
Walk to Main Street Co-op and cross the road, walking up the pavement of the A821 following a sign for 'Trossachs Trail Forest Park Visitor Centre'. Follow the road up through houses for 400 metres until the pavement runs out. Shortly afterwards, there are some stone steps on the right – take these, then follow signs for

WALK 3 – MENTEITH HILLS

The Lodge along a well-made path. After 260 metres, you reach a junction: a shortcut ahead leads 100 metres uphill to The Lodge visitor centre (recommended) or you can turn right to join the main path and marked Lime Craig Trail (red markers at the time of research).

Main route

Starting from The Lodge, you can follow markers for the Lime Craig Trail (red at the time of research) as far as the disused Lime Craig quarry. Facing the entrance to The Lodge, walk around its right-hand side and down a 100 metres shortcut to the main path. Turn left onto the main path and begin to follow red markers.

When you reach two metal deer sculptures, turn left, then pass some interesting, mirrored human silhouettes. After 200 metres, you reach a river with pretty Little Fawn Waterfall on your left. Walk over the footbridge here and come to a junction. The route is straight ahead (second exit if the path junction was a roundabout). A short detour to a wildlife hide (marked with a binoculars sign) here is worthwhile for near-guaranteed sightings of red squirrels. Continue to follow the red markers, walking away from the river uphill. After 340 metres, turn left at a junction, following red markers and signs for the N.7 cycle route. Follow this track uphill for 470 metres to a second, 'secret' waterfall with a bench.

Continue along the track uphill for a further 470 metres until you reach a crossroads. Here, turn sharp right (south-south-west) and momentarily downhill, following a red waymarker and sign for 'Lime Craig Trail'. Walk along this track

Near The Lodge, Vestige by Rob Mulholland is intended as a reflection on past inhabitants of this place

WALKING LOCH LOMOND AND THE TROSSACHS

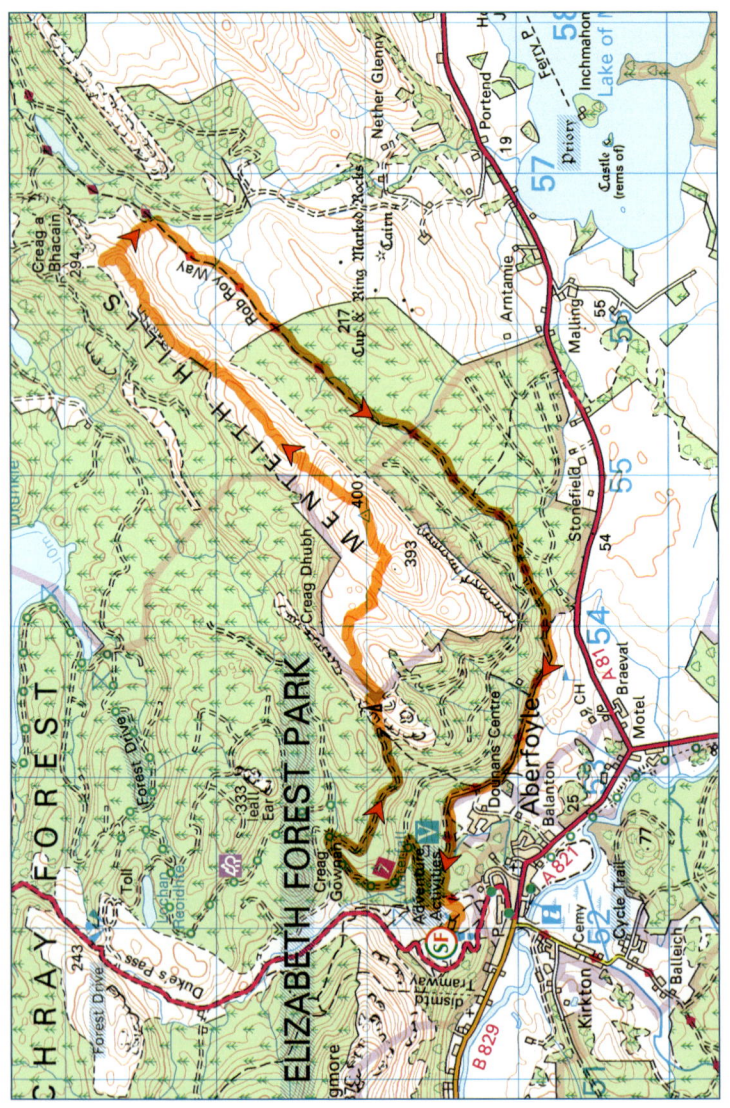

WALK 3 – MENTEITH HILLS

for 1.15km as it levels out for a while before climbing again through a mixture of young and towering coniferous trees – pass a viewpoint and information board about the Highland Boundary Fault, which you're standing on. From this elevated position, you overlook a contrasting Lowland landscape of farmland below.

When you reach a clearing encircled by boulders at Beallach an t-Suidhe, with the overgrown, rocky cliff of former Lime Craig Quarry up above.

LIME CRAIG QUARRY

This disused limestone quarry, cut into the very edge of the Lowlands, is a designated Site of Special Scientific Interest due to its unique geology. Fossils – including trilobites, brachiopods and ostracods – help to date the rock strata of the Highland Boundary Fault and show its links with Scandinavia and North America. The back wall is reddish conglomerate, whose cobbles, where broken, show discoloured quartzite washed out of a now-non-existent mountain range. The lower rocks, to left and right, are quite different: reddish black where weathered, pale green when freshly broken. This is serpentinite, originally a fragment of ocean bed snatched up between the two moving continental blocks.

Leave the red markers behind to take a narrower path uphill straight ahead, following a 'Path to viewpoint' sign. Follow this path as it climbs steeply above the treeline to a gateway gap above. A small mast and viewpoint bench looking over the hills to the east is on the right (worth a quick look), but to continue go left through a small metal gate and walk north-east on a faint, wet path that runs alongside an old fence on your left. Follow the path as it edges up right to follow a small ridge just above. After about 500 metres, before you reach the rounded high point of the lumpy, heathered **Creag Dhubh**, bear right (south-east) down a dip and up again towards the 360m plateau between Creag Dhubh and Craig of Monievreckie, walking between a small lone boulder and a single tree on the way. Head east-south-east down and across another shallow valley then climb a grassy path between the heathered lumps of the hill ahead. When you reach the saddle, turn left onto a small path which leads 300 metres north-east to the **trig point** (400m) and cairn on **Craig of Monievreckie**.

A path starts to the right of the cairn, leading north-east; follow this along the vegetated ridgeline as it descends to a fence corner in a dip at Bealach Conasgach. Cross the fence in front of you, walk across the dip and begin to ascend through bracken. Just above the first trees turn right to walk below rocky crags, then begin a steep ascent from the southern side back to the fenceline running along the ridge. Now continue north-east vaguely following the line of the fence across

Looking north-west towards Loch Drunkie and The Trossachs

rough, pathless terrain. Descend and ascend another dip at Bealach Cumhang and continue to the end of the ridgeline. With plantations ahead, the fence ends at the top of low crags.

Slant down left (north), crossing the fence where convenient, descend to the bottom of the hill, then turn right to walk along the foot of the crags. Step over the low point of an old stone wall, then head south-east downhill through patchy bracken – some of it unpleasantly thick – for 300 metres, to reach a well-used path; this is the **Rob Roy Way**.

Turn right onto the path and follow it as it runs back south-west, along the base of the ridgeline. After 1km, continue along the path following signs for the Rob Roy Way as it enters an area of managed forest. Forestry work is common in this area, but any diversions to the Rob Roy Way will be indicated. Continue as the path joins a track, then runs along the top of **Aberfoyle golf course**. Just past the golf course, a left turn through the **Dounans Outdoor Education Centre** would bring you out in the far east side of Aberfoyle, but to return to The Lodge, continue 600 metres along the track, soon picking up the red waymarkers of the Lime Craig Trail, which lead back to The Lodge.

Follow the waymarkers, taking an indicated side path on the left down to a bridge. Cross the bridge and at a fork take the path straight ahead, bearing slightly right, then turn right onto a larger path that rises uphill through oak trees beside the river. When you reach a junction, turn left (away from the river), soon passing some round-doored playhouses for children. At the next junction, turn right then, when you reach the deer sculptures from the beginning of the walk, turn left. From this path, follow signposts for The Lodge (or turn left onto a path marked for Aberfoyle to return to the centre of the village).

WALK 4
Doon Hill and Fairy Knowe

Start/finish	Aberfoyle bus stop and public toilets NN 522 101
Time	1hr 30min
Distance	6.3km (3.9 miles)
Total ascent	120m (390ft)
Terrain	Good paths, pavement and cycle route
Max altitude	Doon Hill 77m (253ft)
Maps	OS Explorer OL46; OS Landranger 57; Harvey *Loch Lomond & The Trossachs*
Parking	Free parking in Aberfoyle (Riverside car park)

Entwined with the story of a 17th-century, fairy-obsessed reverend, this meandering stroll ties together history with folklore and the natural with the supernatural. One of the most influential characters in the history of Scottish magical tradition, Reverend Robert Kirk (1644–92) was a Gaelic scholar, folklorist and author of *The Secret Commonwealth of Elves, Fauns and Fairies*, written in 1691. As minister of Kirkton Church from 1685 until the year he died, he's said to have learned the information for his book from his parishioners. In 1692, Robert Kirk dropped dead while on a walk. The story goes that he was taken by the fairies as a punishment for revealing their secrets and remains trapped in fairyland to this day.

Following good paths throughout, this route crosses the River Forth twice, climbs the 77m Doon Hill, where people still leave offerings for the fairies, and wanders through a north-eastern part of Loch Ard Forest, dense with oak trees, healthy moss and bluebells in spring.

From **Aberfoyle** bus stop and public toilets, walk south across Riverside car park, turn right and walk towards a road bridge. Cross this bridge over the River Forth and continue straight along the road heading south-south-west, passing the few houses that make up **Kirkton**. After 440 metres, the ruined Kirkton Church and its burial ground are on your left.

Built in 1744, **Kirkton Church** was built on the site of an older building where Robert Kirk served as minister. Two iron coffins by the entrance are mortsafes, used to protect corpses from early 19th-century body-snatchers. Around

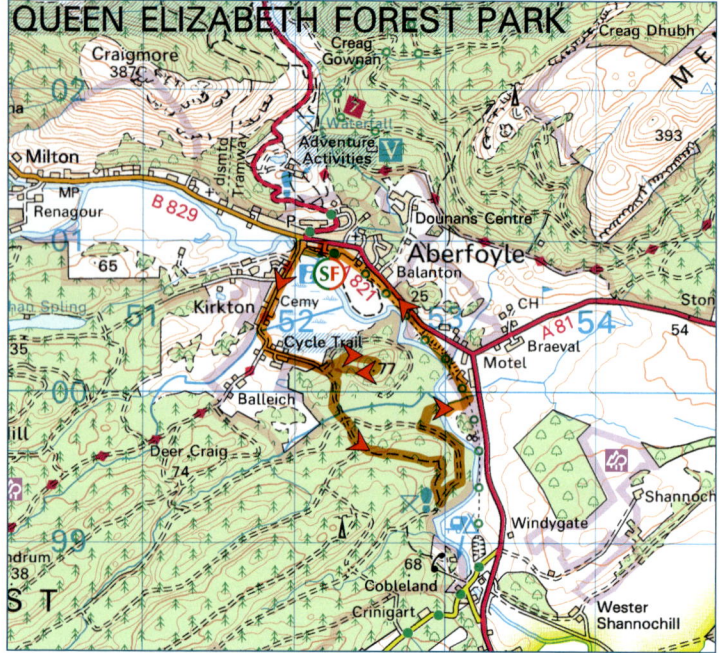

the back of the church is Robert Kirk's gravestone, with a carving of a thistle above a crossed sword and pastoral staff.

From the church, continue along the road and cross a bridge; 100 metres further, turn left onto a minor road, with a sign for 'Doon Hill Trail'. Follow this road past a few houses until it becomes a track and passes through a barrier. Some 20 metres beyond the barrier, turn left onto a smaller gravel path, then, after another 40 metres, turn right onto a path that leads uphill. Follow the path through mature oak trees, looking out for wooden carvings of mushrooms and other fairy-related sculptures along the route, to climb **Doon Hill**.

On the summit plateau, a singular Scots pine tree standing in a clearing among the oaks is known as **The Minister's Pine**, decorated with all manner of offerings to the fairies. It is sometimes said that Robert Kirk's spirit is trapped inside a fairyland within the tree.

WALK 4 – DOON HILL AND FAIRY KNOWE

To descend, retrace your steps across the clearing and, some 20 metres from the tree, find a path with a green marker to the left of your ascent path. Follow this downhill until you reach a T-junction, then turn left onto a track.

Walk along the track for 300 metres, cross a small bridge and go straight ahead at a track crossroads. Continue for another 230 metres until the track takes a sharp right turn, forming a second crossroads with two paths – here, go straight ahead, where there is a blue marker beside a path heading uphill. Follow this path over a slight hill in the woodland called Fairy Knowe until you reach a junction with a track after 860 metres. The native oak trees here support a rich ecosystem, with mosses, ferns and wildflowers carpeting the woodland floor.

Turn left onto the track and follow it for 720 metres, ignoring a blue way-marked path on your right, until you reach a junction signed for Aberfoyle. Take the right turn here and cross an arched bridge over the **River Forth**. Bear slightly left and follow a path north-east across a field until you reach a junction with a cycle path. Turn left onto the cycle path and continue for 800 metres, then turn left to follow a path along the bank of the River Forth back to **Aberfoyle** – the more direct route continues on the cycle path, but it's good to escape the traffic noise and wander through the meadows instead.

Looking towards Aberfoyle from the graveyard at Kirkton Church

WALK 5
Ben Ledi and Benvane

Start/finish	Little Druim Wood car park, Loch Venachar head NN 549 062
Time	8hr 45min; shortcut omitting Benvane: 7hr 30min
Distance	22km (13.7 miles); shortcut by Gleann Casaig omitting Benvane: 19.1km (11.9 miles)
Total ascent	1275m (4180ft); shortcut omitting Benvane: 1060m (3480ft)
Terrain	Hill paths and pathless hillside, track to return
Max altitude	Ben Ledi 879m (2884ft)
Maps	OS Explorer OL46; OS Landranger 57; Harvey *Ben Ledi*
Public transport	The walk in from Brig o'Turk (seasonal Trossachs Explorer bus stop) adds 1.4km (0.9 miles) each way

Between Stuc Odhar and Ben Ledi is a place of bilberry slopes and schist, a patch of wild country that few people visit; starting from Loch Venachar, this route climbs there by a pretty woodland path. The hillside above is only moderately rugged, and it's fun surprising people on Ben Ledi's busy southeast ridge path by suddenly arriving from somewhere else.

Although no Munro, Ben Ledi (879m) is the highest point of The Trossachs and gives an outstanding overview of the national park; on a *very* good day, you might be able to spot the sea on both sides of Scotland. Continuing along the knolly ridge creates a horseshoe with the second Corbett, Benvane (821m), finishing with a picturesque descent to Glen Finglas Reservoir.

Ben Ledi's infinitely more popular route starts from a car park south of Loch Lubnaig. This well-trodden path avoids some rough ground, but feels less adventurous and doesn't lend itself to creating a loop with Benvane.

From Little Druim Wood car park, which is signposted from the A821 (or Glen Finglas Visitor Centre car park 500 metres west), turn right out of the car park and walk on a path beside the main road (towards Callander) for 100 metres across a bridge. Then cross the road and go through a small wooden gate onto a pretty path up through woods. Keep to the path as it veers left, goes past an old shed,

WALK 5 – BEN LEDI AND BENVANE

The pathless terrain around Fuairn Fuaran south-west of Ben Ledi's summit

and passes through another small gate, following brown and blue arrows, before joining a wider track and running up through a larger metal gate near a bench. Continue as it bends briefly right then left to pass a cairn and another bench with a view over Loch Venachar – commemorating the Royal Mail Grove. Stick to the track as it bends to the right and slants up to a junction with the **Great Trossachs Path**. Here – 900 metres walk from the road, at 230m altitude – there is a wooden signpost: turn left, marked for 'The Glens'. After a further 400 metres, there is another bench with a slight descent to a burn just ahead. Look out for a blue arrow (NN 550 069) here, which points to a rougher, grassy path up to the right: take this.

The path is fairly clear, but boggy at times, with widely spaced blue waymarkers. It runs up to right of the burn, heading north-north-east for 600 metres to 360m elevation where it emerges from heather and bends left to cross the burn top (NN 552 073). After a further 120 metres, the path splits at a second burn; go right here, uphill, with the burn on your left until you reach a point where two waymarkers indicate where to cross it. Continue to climb roughly north for 600 metres on the rough, peaty path – follow an arrow pointing uphill (right fork)

where the path splits approaching another small burn – until you reach a ladder stile (NN 552 080); cross this, leaving the waymarkers behind.

Continue uphill north-east for 350 metres to the south-east ridgeline of Stuc Odhar at 594m. Now turn left and walk north-north-west, roughly following a line of old fence posts for 800 metres, to climb the ridge to the summit cairn of **Stuc Odhar** at 638m. Stuc Odhar, pronounced 'oh-arr', means 'Pointed Hill of Nondescript Dun Colour'.

Follow more old fencing, which guides down the northern ridgeline, skirting left of a ridgeline hump to a col just above the ridge foot (530m). Here, turn down right in a grassy hollow to cross the top of the **Milton Glen Burn**. Ahead now Ben Ledi is looking very big. A direct ascent leads up broken ground, so slant right, eastwards, across Fuairn Fuaran (a spring) and up a grassy ramp defined by the line of a small burn. You reach Ben Ledi's south-east ridge at the point called Meall Odhar (815m). Turn left onto a substantial, rocky path that leads up to **Ben Ledi's summit** (879m), passing a cross dedicated to a member of Killin Mountain Rescue Team.

From the summit cairn and trig point, take the pleasant ridge path leading north-west then north to Ledi's north top. Here, ignore the rocky path that heads steeply down ahead, and instead follow old iron fence posts that slant down north-west, with a clear path, to Bealach nan Corp. Follow both the fence and the path as they rise to pass the little **Lochan nan Corp**. Corp means 'corpse'; this pass was the line of an old corpse road.

Continue to follow the path and old fencing as they pass between another pretty lochan and the minor summit of Bioran na Circe. Over the next 1km the path undulatingly descends towards **Stuc Dhubh** (662m) and a peaty col at 604m. (Between Stuc Dhubh and this col you can take a shortcut track down left into **Gleann Casaig**; the track does not quite reach the ridgeline, so it's possible to walk past it – however, it is obvious when you glance back from the col just below.)

Continuing, there are some hags to deal with as you cross the col, before grassy slopes lead up to a point at 711m above **Creag Chaoruinneach**. The path and fence remnants now take a wide swing to the left over Meall a' Coire Dubh (753m), but you can contour forward, west, to cross a burn and head straight up to the summit of **Benvane** (821m). The Gaelic, A' Bheinn Mheadhain, means 'Middle Hill'.

Just down south-west from the summit are the old fence posts; follow the path beside them to Meall a' Coire Dubh. At the corner of the former fence, with three quartz boulders seen up to the left, keep ahead and walk down the gentle south ridge. Steep ground dropping right (west) appears transversely sliced, and is classic landslip terrain undermined by the ancient glacier of Gleann nan Meann.

Reaching the shore of Glen Finglas Reservoir

At its tip the ridge steepens around Sròn Achaidh na h-Airde; below, a fence crosses, with a wooden gate at a convenient point (NN 535 102). Find a good line down rough pasture to the gate, go through it and continue across lumpy grass to join a track rising from back down on the left. Follow this track down towards **Glen Finglas Reservoir**, where it meets the reservoir-side track beside **Allt Ghleann Casaig** (and the shortcut from Stuc Dhubh).

Turn left at the junction to go over the river bridge; the track now becomes a tarmac lane. Follow it for 1km, rising into woods above the reservoir until a gravel bike path turns up to the left (it has three boulders at its foot and a sign for 'visitor gateway' and Callander). Take this turn and follow the path as it climbs briefly to pass through a deer fence, then contours through woods above the fence. Continue as the path emerges onto open hillside for 1km, then dips into woods to a bridge. Shortly afterwards, a sign indicates a short detour on the right to a waterfall – worthwhile in winter when the trees are bare. In another 200 metres follow a signpost for the visitor gateway and **Brig o'Turk**, which points right and downhill; follow this, then ignore one left turn to pass a ruined farmstead, soon coming out at Glen Finglas Visitor Centre car park.

Turn left, walking through the car park, and join a woodland path alongside the A821 to **Lendrick Lodge**. Its driveway leads out to the Little Druim Wood car park.

WALK 6
Beinn a' Choin

Start/finish	Stronachlachar NN 404 102
Time	8hr
Distance	16.4km (10.2 miles)
Total ascent	835m (2740ft)
Terrain	Track to start and quiet road to finish, but the bulk of the route is very rough unpathed ground
Max altitude	Beinn a' Choin 770m (2526ft)
Maps	OS Explorer OL39; OS Landranger 56; Harvey *Loch Lomond & The Trossachs*
Public transport	You can catch the seasonal Trossachs Explorer bus to Trossachs Pier followed by a 2hr steamship cruise up Loch Katrine to Stronachlachar if you are wild camping. However, this would not be practical if you plan to walk the route and get back in one day.
Parking	Expensive parking (cash or card) with toilets and a café at Stronachlachar pier

The initial pathless ascent to Garradh on this route is a test of perseverance – it's steep and often deep with heather, tussocky white grass and bracken. The long, lumpy ridgeline from Garradh over Maol Mòr to Beinn a' Choin is also largely pathless, but the vegetation is lower and walking is much easier without the steep incline.

So, what is the attraction of this inconvenient Corbett? Uniquely positioned between lochs Arklet, Katrine and Lomond, the hike has spectacular views throughout: Ben Lomond dominates south, while the Arrochar Alps are laid out to the west; looking north, the bulk of the national park's Munros form a defensive line.

It's a walk for the experienced and determined: one to save for good weather, unless you're purposefully trying to test your navigation capabilities, and preferably outside of high summer when the bracken will be at its worst.

From **Stronachlachar pier** and car park, walk west back up Lochard Road ignoring turnings for a few houses. After 460 metres, turn right onto a path, which runs briefly on the left side of a gravel track, following a wooden sign for Inversnaid. Continue on a well-made path heading generally west past an information board.

WALKING LOCH LOMOND AND THE TROSSACHS

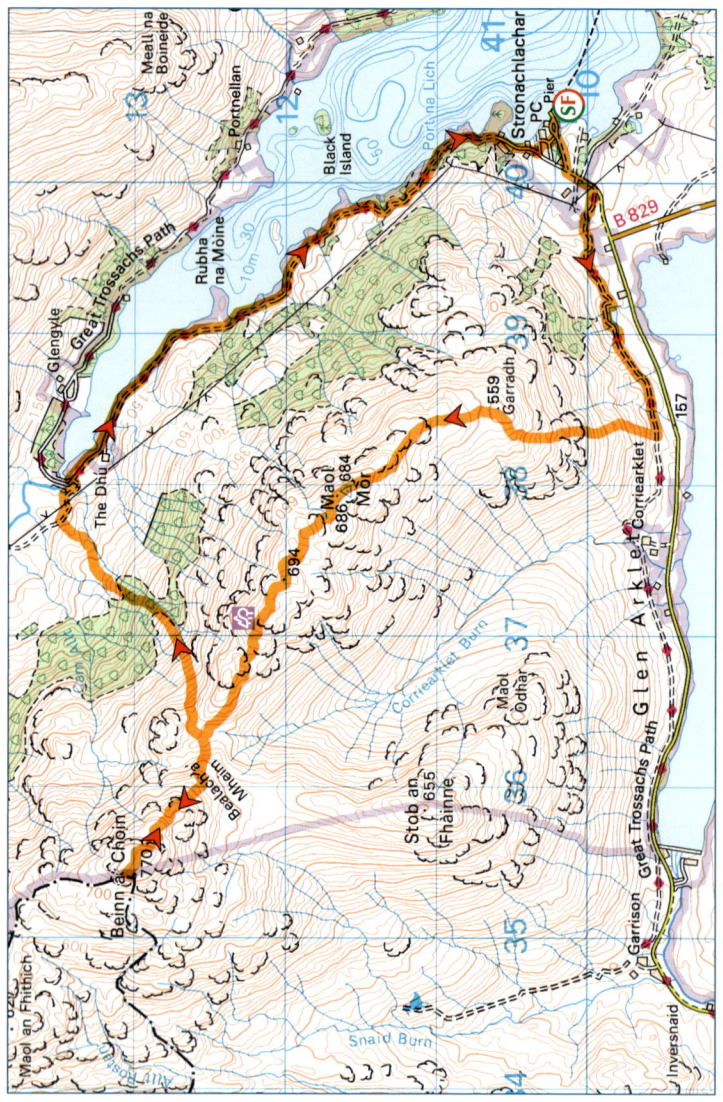

WALK 6 – BEINN A' CHOIN

This gentle section of the walk (part of the Great Trossachs Path) follows the route of an old military road, which ran from Stronachlachar to Inversnaid. **Inversnaid Garrison** was built in 1718 following the Jacobite uprising of 1715. Its strategic position overlooked two fords where the road from Inversnaid harbour connected with an important route from Dumbarton. This route ran via lochs Lomond, Katrine and Tay to join with the main road between Dunkeld and Inverness. The garrison was seen as a vital part of the Government's plan for restraining Jacobite sympathisers.

After 720 metres, ignore a left turn for Aberfoyle and continue past a tiny lochan with an overgrown jetty. Walk along the path for a further 820 metres past the lochan. The path goes over a burn then rises to a view of Ben Vorlich, Ben Vane and A' Chrois beyond Loch Arklet (and Loch Lomond, which you can't yet see). Just beyond the high point of the path, when **Corriearklet** boathouse on the shore of **Loch Arklet** is still 400 metres ahead, is the overgrown end of a fallen fence on the right (NN 383 095).

Here, leave the path and head north over very rough ground with heather and bracken. Climb 500m over the course of 1km, choosing the best line you can and avoiding small crags, to come upon the west side of a lump called **Garradh** (559m). Turn right (north-east) for the final stretch to the summit, which is marked with something of a cairn and a view of Loch Katrine. The worst of the ascent and

Descending to the bealach before Beinn a' Choin

difficult ground is now over, although the terrain continues to be rough and careful navigation is required along the lumpy ridge in poor visibility.

Head north for 250 metres to a gate and stile (NN 385 109); cross the stile (or climb the gate if the stile remains as rotten as it was at the time of research). Walk north-west for 1.2km – passing to the left side of a tiny lochan and the cragged hump just after, and keeping generally to the left side of the wide lumpy ridgeline – to the 684m point of **Maol Mòr**, which has a trig point (not at its true summit, which is further north-west). There are views of all the national park's north and north-eastern mountains, as well as the snake of Loch Katrine below.

Continue to weave along the ridgeline north-west, passing a lochan on your left and crossing Maol Mòr's lumpy summit; keep slightly left of the central ridgeline to avoid crags. Skirt left of crag-defended Stob a' Choin Dhuibh and descend to the bealach between Stob a' Choin Dhuibh and Beinn a' Choin. Look for a grassy track which ascends from the bealach up the left side of **Beinn a' Choin** – head up this, which soon fades, then continue north-west. There is one disappointing false summit, but from here you can pick up a small path. Pass little lochans on your right and left, cross a broken fence, and climb the final short distance to the summit cairn.

The descent is a doddle in comparison. Return to the bealach, picking up the grassy track on your way, then follow it over a dip between Maol Breac a' Bhealaich and Stob a' Choin Dhuibh. Keep to the track as it descends east and then north-east through a pretty scattering of trees. The track comes down to a gate in a deer fence (NN 374 132); go through this and continue along the track as it bends right past spruce trees. Keep going as the track briefly splits and rejoins, then goes around the left side of a fenced, forested quarry area. Eventually you will come to a gate; go through this and turn right onto a gravel track.

Follow the gravel track down to the quiet road that runs along the south-west bank of **Loch Katrine**. Follow the road south-east for 4.3km, passing the points of **Rubha na Mòine** and Rubha nam Mult, as well as **Black Island** across the loch. As you come into **Stronachlachar**, walk past a Scottish Water building on your left, then go through a gateway to cut across some grass. When you reach a road, go straight across, following a sign for the pier and café. Follow the road around to the left past a red barrier, then cross a road to return to the car park.

PART 2 CALLANDER AND STRATHYRE

Loch Venachar from the summit of Dunmore Fort (Walk 8)

Perched along the Highland Boundary Fault, the riverbank town of Callander provides a good base for exploration of The Trossachs and east of the national park. Heading north, gloomy Loch Lubnaig, with its steep slopes of Sitka spruce, leads up to the village of Strathyre. The strath – a wide river valley taking its meaning from the Gaelic word *srath* – provides a natural through-route. An early settlement here formed beside an old drovers' road. Then, in response to the 1745 Jacobite uprising, Major Caulfeild instructed the building of the Stirling to Fort William military road along the same line. The present village sprang up with the arrival of the (now defunct) Callander and Oban Railway in the 1870s, providing its picturesque Victorian buildings. Now strung along the A84, there are a couple of walks to detain you here if you're not zooming straight through. The old roads and routes continue up to Lochearnhead, which is covered in Part 3.

WALK 7
North Callander Circular

Start/finish	Callander War Memorial, Ancaster Square NN 628 079
Time	4hr
Distance	12.5km (7.8 miles). This route can be divided into several parts with straightforward shortcuts: Bracklinn Falls and Scout Pool circuit: 8.5km (5.3 miles); Callander Crags circuit: 6km (3.7 miles)
Total ascent	385m (1270ft); Bracklinn Falls and Scout Pool circuit: 240m (785ft); Callander Crags circuit: 285m (935ft).
Terrain	Good paths and tracks throughout with some steep sections
Max altitude	Callander Crags 344m (1129ft)
Maps	OS Explorer OL46; OS Landranger 57
Public transport	Bus stop in Callander
Parking	Callander, or else nearer Bracklinn Falls or Callander Crags

Starting in the town centre, this ambling route visits all the most impressive and interesting historical or geological sites to the east and north of Callander. It begins by following a disused railway line, covering ground shaped by glacial moraines, before passing a prehistoric, chambered cairn, thought to be the longest in Scotland, and an Iron Age hill fort. A couple of kilometres further, the route descends to the dramatic bridged gorge at Bracklinn Falls.

For expansive views, the final, clifftop summit of Callander Crags is the highlight. Part of the Highland Boundary Fault, standing here provides a dramatic perspective over Scotland's geological divide; the flat expanse of Callander and the Lowlands are spread out to the south-east, contrasting with the undulating hill country to the north.

Options for walking directly to Bracklinn Falls or Callander Crags, or returning to Callander after walking the east section or as far as Scout Pool are highlighted in the instructions below.

From **Callander War Memorial**, turn right onto Main Street and walk south-east for 430 metres, then turn left onto Bracklinn Road. Take the first right, signed as

WALK 7 – NORTH CALLANDER CIRCULAR

a cycle path and for 'Bridge of Keltie 1½'. Follow cycle path signs east through the quiet residential streets of Murdiston Avenue and Livingstone Avenue. At the end of Livingstone Avenue, cross the road and join a shared cycle path, following a sign for 'Keltie Bridge'. Keep to this cycle path for 1km as it follows the course of a straight section of disused railway and crosses Callander Terminal Moraine. The moraine is a bump running across the ground, left by an ice sheet's edge at the end of a cooling event around 12,000 years ago. Approaching **Auchenlaich**, where a few buildings stand beyond a picturesque duck pond ahead, you reach a path junction.

Turn left, following a sign for Bracklinn Falls. Head uphill, passing Auchenlaich Farm on your right and then a row of caravans (part of Keltie Bridge Campsite). Where a long, narrow field cuts between the caravans on your right, **Auchenlaich Chambered Cairn** runs under the track, stretching out to the north and south.

At 342m, **Auchenlaich** is Britain's longest chambered cairn. Thought to be 6000 years old, this Neolithic burial monument forms a noticeable ridge in the ground with some large protruding stones – these once formed part of the burial chambers.

Continue along the track for 200 metres, then take the sharp left turn up into mixed woodland – shimmering purple with bluebells in spring – for

Bracklinn Bridge over Bracklinn Falls

400 metres to reach a track junction. Bear right at the junction, following a sign for 'Bracklinn Falls ¾ mile'. A short distance after this, a post with an arrow indicates a side path to **Auchenlaich Hill Fort**. Follow this for 200 metres through mature oak trees to the summit of a small hill, where the fort once stood.

> Defended by a single rampart and external ditch, the 90m by 60m oval-plan **Iron Age hill fort** is now somewhat lost in woodland, but would have held a commanding position in Bracklinn Glen.

Once you're satisfied with your explorations, return to the main track and continue north, uphill. Keep to the main path when the way is occasionally obstructed by fallen trees; it veers gently to the left and then right, eventually emerging from the trees. When the path splits at a junction, bear right (signposted for **Bracklinn Falls**) and follow the most substantial path as it weaves down to Bracklinn Bridge over the impressive gorge and falls.

> An Anglicisation of the Gaelic name *A' Bhreac Linn*, meaning 'Dappled Pool' **Bracklinn Bridge** has long been a popular spot for both local and visiting walkers due to its dramatic gorge and naturally sculpted rocks.

Direct route from Callander to Bracklinn Falls

From **Callander War Memorial**, turn right onto Main Street and walk south-east for 430 metres, then turn left onto Bracklinn Road. Follow this for 900 metres to Callander Crags car park. From here, take the path indicated 'Bracklinn Falls 1 mile' on the opposite side of the road, which climbs gently through mixed woodland. As you approach Bracklinn Falls car park, a path bears right signed for **Bracklinn Falls**. Follow the path east as it slopes gradually downhill and keep to the main path as it weaves down to the river.

To return directly to Callander retrace your steps 250 metres uphill to the last junction and turn right, following a sign for 'Callander 1 mile'. Follow this path west for 1km, passing Bracklinn Falls car park on your right and continuing until you come out to Bracklinn Road opposite Callander Crags car park. Turn left onto the road and follow it back into **Callander**; when you reach Main Street turn right to return to the war memorial.

Main route

Cross the bridge, which gives a dramatic perspective over the gorge below – here the river flows through the base of Bracklinn (or Brackland) Glen – then turn left, now following signs for 'Bracklinn Falls Circuit'. Follow the path, climbing steeply through deciduous woodland, before joining a forest track. Follow the track as it

WALK 7 – NORTH CALLANDER CIRCULAR

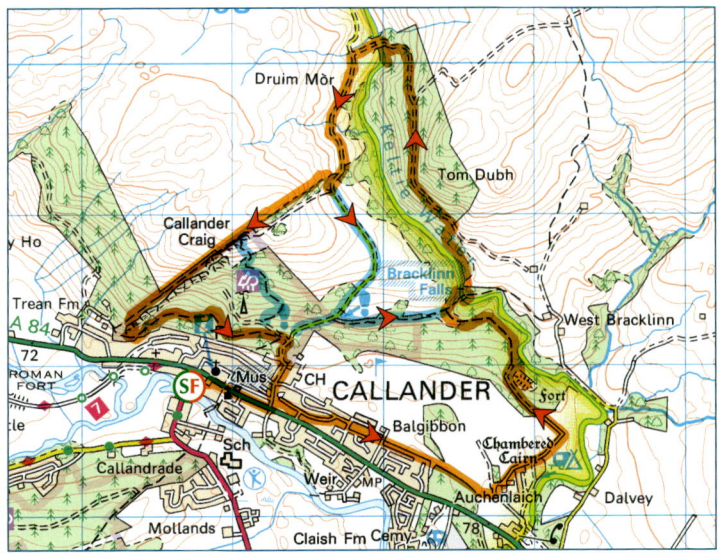

heads north-west and then north for 1km; it emerges from the forest approaching its high point, where it splits. Standing above Bracklinn Glen, you can see Ben Ledi and Ben Vorlich.

Take the left fork and follow the track downhill. As you reach a second bridge over a higher section of **Keltie Water**, don't cross it straight away, but turn left to leave the track onto a narrow, unmarked path beside the river. Follow the bank south for 200 metres to Scout Pool. Here, smooth, eroded rocks surround a calm pool in Keltie Water – a popular local swimming spot.

From Scout Pool, return to the bridge and cross it. Continue straight ahead for a short distance before turning left onto a minor road, signposted for Callander. To return directly to Callander, follow this road south for 2.85km.

Follow the road for 1km, passing a shallow well marked as Tobar na Cailleach (meaning 'Well of the Old Woman', or less politely, 'hag'), then look out for a path leading off into woodland on the right; it's marked by a sign for 'CRAGS' on a metal post, but this is facing the opposite direction, so is easy to miss. Follow this path as it climbs steeply through the trees, crossing some exposed rock as it ascends the north-east slope of **Callander Crags** (Callander Craig on some maps). Continue to follow the path until you reach the crags' highest point: the Queens' Diamond Jubilee Cairn at 343m.

QUEENS' DIAMOND JUBILEE CAIRN

The Queens' Diamond Jubilee Cairn

This conical stone cairn was built in 1897 and restored in 2000, now commemorating the diamond jubilees of both Queen Victoria and Queen Elizabeth II. It has spectacular views to Stirling and the Lowlands south-east, Loch Venachar and the Menteith Hills south-west, and the Highland peaks to the north and west. On a clear day, you can see Ben Ledi, Ben Vorlich and Stùc a' Chroin from here, as well as distant Ben Lomond beyond The Trossachs. The lumpy, exposed rock of Callander Crags is puddingstone from the Devonian Period.

Direct route from Callander to Callander Crags

From **Callander War Memorial**, turn right onto Main Street and walk south-east for 430 metres, then turn left onto Bracklinn Road. Follow Bracklinn Road for 500 metres to Callander Crags car park. Follow a forest track signed 'Callander Crags 2½ miles' through a barrier and walk down it for 200 metres, then turn right onto a narrower, but obvious path that climbs steeply through woodland. When you reach the top, turn right (indicated 'summit') and follow a path along the edge of the crags for 200 metres to the Queens' Diamond Jubilee Cairn. Retrace your steps for 200 metres to continue the route below.

Main route

Follow the path south-west along the top of the crags as it descends gradually alongside a fence. Keep to the path as it winds back down into the woods, eventually bearing left and starting to level out on the approach to **Callander**.

As you come to the northern reaches of town, bear left onto the Lower Woods Path – initially marked with red waymarkers – then stay on the most obvious, main path as it rises, weaving its way east through mixed woodland. It climbs gently to a small viewpoint, before descending gradually towards Callander Crags car park. From the car park, turn right to head down Bracklinn Road, then right again onto Main Street to get back to Ancaster Square.

WALK 8
Three Callander bridges

Start/finish	Callander War Memorial, Ancaster Square NN 628 079
Alternative start/finish	Bochastle/Ben Ledi car park
Time	2hr 30min
Distance	8.6km (5.3 miles)
Total ascent	210m (690ft)
Terrain	Good paths and shared cycle route throughout
Max altitude	Dunmore Fort 200m (656ft)
Maps	OS Explorer OL46; OS Landranger 57; Harvey *Ben Ledi*
Public transport	Callander bus stop
Parking	Callander or Bochastle/Ben Ledi car park

Following a lovely, meandering route along good paths through woodland and wide-open spaces, this easy, low-level walk visits several historic sites, a conspicuous glacial erratic said to have been thrown by a giant, and the small summit of Dunmore Fort, which provides great views over Loch Venachar and back to Callander town. There are good opportunities for spotting wildlife and bluebells are abundant in spring.

From Callander War Memorial, turn right onto Main Street for 120 metres, before turning right onto South Church Street. Pass the small Callander Community Friendship Garden and a restored sundial from 1753 and walk down to an old, metal-and-concrete bridge over the **River Teith**. From here there's a good view upstream to the red sandstone Callander Bridge. Cross the bridge, turn left (signposted for Coilhallan Wood) and follow a path, passing a rugby field on your right, down to the **A81**.

When you reach the road, turn right and follow the pavement for a short distance before crossing it and entering Coilhallan Wood between two stone pillars. Follow a path and signs west for 2km through mixed woodland and young birch trees to the edge of Coilhallan Woods car park.

Following signs for 'Dunmore Hillfort', turn left onto the road, walking through **Easter Gartchonzie**, then turn right to cross the arched Gartchonzie Bridge over **Eas Gobhain**. Follow the road 300 metres north-west to a T-junction. Cross the **A821** here and join a path on its opposite side.

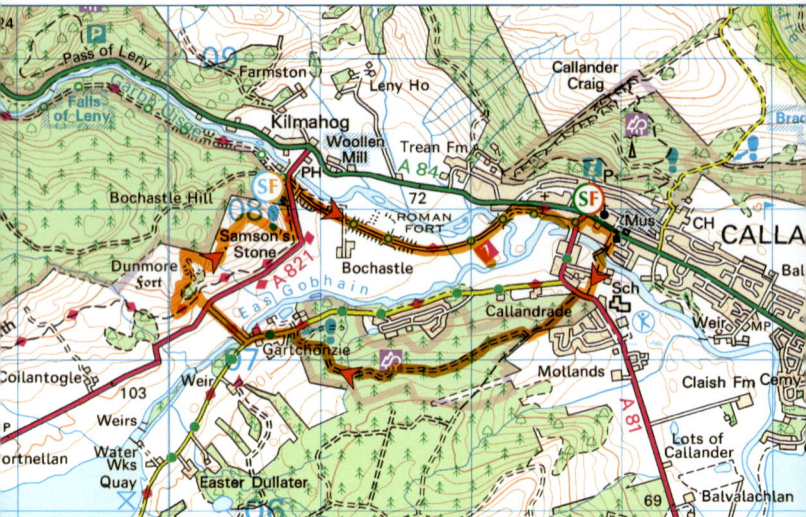

Continue straight on towards the wooded hill of **Dunmore Fort** until you reach a path junction, then turn left. After 200 metres, turn right onto a steeper, grassy path ascending the hill to its summit.

The remaining traces of Iron Age **Dunmore Fort** stand on a prominent puddingstone hillock. The harder rock here was more resistant to glacial erosion and was left, forming higher ground. The small hill has fantastic views over Loch Venachar to the south-west and Callander to the east.

From Dunmore, continue on the path down the northern side of the hill. When you reach a path intersection in front of a drystone wall, turn right downhill and walk for 200 metres until you reach a second path junction. Here, turn left to cross a small wooden bridge and follow blue arrows along a grassy path up the south side of **Bochastle Hill**, passing through a gate, to the giant boulder, **Samson's Stone** near the summit.

Samson's Stone is a metamorphic sandstone erratic, carried east by ice from the Highlands 12,000 years ago. According to legend, the giant Samson threw it from the top of Ben Ledi, proving himself to be champion of Scottish giants.

WALK 8 – THREE CALLANDER BRIDGES

Continue past the rock along the path and follow blue arrows through young oak trees, silver birch and hawthorn back to a junction with the main path. Turn left onto the main path and follow it north until you reach Bochastle car park. Here, follow signs to Callander, joining a path that runs beside the **A821** for a short distance, then crossing the road to join a cycle path heading east. Follow the cycle path, which runs along the line of a dismantled railway, towards Callander as it passes the grass-covered remains of **Bochastle Roman Fort** on the left, then Little Leny Burial Ground (traditionally used by the clan Buchanans of Leny) – 200 metres down a side path through Little Leny Meadows – on the right.

Bochastle Roman Fort, built about AD85, is an example of a 'Glen Blocker Fort'. Located strategically to control exits from valleys leading out of the Highlands, they were used only briefly before being abandoned.

Continue along the cycle path to reach the walk's third and final bridge, a rusty metal construction. Cross the bridge and after a further 130 metres, turn right onto a path (signed for Callander), which leads to Meadows car park, then walk along the bank of the River Teith to the peculiar, flat-topped lump of Tom ma Chisaig (Hill of Saint Kessog). This was probably a Medieval motte (castle mound) built to watch the bridge. Walk past Tom ma Chisaig and turn left onto Bridge Street, then take the first right onto Main Street and you'll soon be back at Ancaster Square.

The red sandstone Callander Bridge over the River Teith

WALK 9
Beinn Each

Start/finish	Lay-by off A84 at Ardchullarie More, Loch Lubnaig NN 583 137
Time	3hr 30min
Distance	6.8km (4.2 miles)
Total ascent	660m (2170ft)
Terrain	Forest path, track and hill path
Max altitude	Beinn Each 813m (2667ft)
Maps	OS Explorer OL46; OS Landranger 57; Harvey *Ben Ledi*
Public transport	No convenient bus stop

A straightforward up and down route for this popular Corbett with views south-west over Ben Ledi beyond Loch Lubnaig, as well as north to Stùc a' Chroin and south-east towards the Lowlands and the distant Firth of Forth. With paths the whole way and no notably difficult sections, fine conditions would make this walk a good starting point for people looking to get into hillwalking – or a quick leg stretcher for those who already are.

From elsewhere, Beinn Each is obscured: the hill isn't visible from any road, and even from surrounding peaks it's overshadowed by big Stùc a' Chroin or the tree-covered lump of Sgiath a'Chaise. The best place to see Beinn Each is from its own summit.

From the lay-by at **Ardchullarie More**, walk south a few metres over a weir in Ardchullarie Burn, then turn left following a sign indicating, 'Public footpath to Loch Earn via Glen Ample'. Follow the path as it climbs along the edge of woodland beside a fence. After 330 metres, follow the path bearing left across a burn. Continue for 220 metres until the path is intersected by a track; go straight ahead here, continuing to climb.

After a further 110 metres there is a junction with a forest track. Join this, keeping ahead/left, and walk north along the track for 230 metres to a high gate and a sign, 'To Loch Earn and hill routes via Glen Ample'. Continue ahead for 760 metres, ignoring a minor right turn at the edge of the forest and a track on the left which leads down over Ardchullarie Burn.

Just after the track crosses a ford, and before a stone ruin on the left, look out for a sign indicating, 'Hill route to Ben Each'. Turn right here onto a narrower, but

WALK 9 – BEINN EACH

obvious hill path. Keep to the path as it heads east and then bends to the left at a large boulder to continue north-east. After climbing quite steeply, continue as the path clings to the left of the summit plateau above steep slopes. The route remains clear over many false summits until you reach the real peak of **Beinn Each** (813m) and the Corbett's pathetically tiny cairn. The lumpy south face of Stùc a' Chroin is ahead, while the Lowlands stretch out south-east towards Edinburgh.

Return the same way, with great views of Loch Lubnaig and Ben Ledi ahead. Take care not to miss the junction back onto the smaller woodland path from the track.

The forested head of Glen Ample

WALK 10
An Sìdhean

Start/finish	Car park near Broch Café, Strathyre NN 560 169
Time	2hr
Distance	4.7km (2.9 miles)
Total ascent	385m (1260ft)
Terrain	Forestry tracks and paths, which can be boggy near the top
Max altitude	An Sìdhean 546m (1791ft)
Maps	OS Explorer OL46; OS Landranger 57; Harvey *Ben Ledi*
Public transport	Bus stop in Strathyre

This straightforward little walk climbs to a great viewpoint over the village of Strathyre, Strathyre Forest, Loch Lubnaig and the nearby mountains including Ben Vorlich, Stùc a' Chroin and Ben Ledi. The name Strathyre comes from the Gaelic *Strath Cor*, interpreted as 'Broad Winding Valley'; looked down upon from An Sìdhean, this makes perfect sense. The village nestles in a glen of the same name, which follows the course of the River Balvaig flowing out of Loch Voil and running south into Loch Lubnaig. Both sides of the strath are forested – emerging above them is a breath of fresh air.

Just south of the main village of **Strathrye**, take the turning off the **A84** marked for the Broch Café and a parking/picnic area. Instead of turning left to the café, go right and follow the road round to a car park at the back of a playing field where there is a recreated partial broch.

> Brochs were round, hollow-walled, drystone buildings constructed in the Iron Age. **Dun Lubnaig Broch Project** was built between 2004 and 2007 by the Drywalling Association of Great Britain, with the aim of demonstrating how a broch could have been built without using cement or modern tools.

Continue behind the car park, then turn left onto a cycle path. Cross a bouncy suspension bridge over the wide **River Balvag** and walk ahead, bearing right. After a short distance, turn right onto a gravel path following a sign for An Sìdhean. Continue for 100 metres to a junction with a minor road; bear right/ahead onto

WALK 10 – AN SÌDHEAN

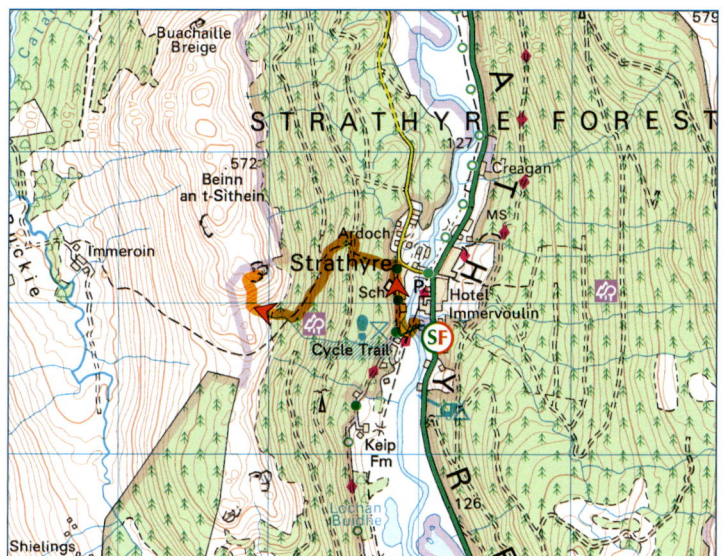

this and walk 260 metres. Just past Strathrye Primary School, a burn runs under the road – turn off onto a path running along the left side of the road immediately after this. Follow the path alongside the road for 100 metres, then turn up left through wooden barriers onto a forest path indicated for An Sìdhean.

Follow the path through moss-carpeted forest for 340 metres to a junction with a forest track. Turn right onto the track and walk north for 120 metres, then turn left onto a signposted path for An Sìdhean. Follow this path through forest as it climbs 100m over 330 metres to a viewpoint over the village of Strathyre, which has some handy boulders to sit on.

Strathrye village was established on the route of an old drove road, but was largely developed by the Victorians after the arrival of the railway in the 1870s.

Continue uphill (south-south-west) past a sign explaining that this is the end of the waymarkers. After about 450 metres, as the path veers west and the trees thin out; it becomes less distinct and boggy in parts. Continue along the wet path as it climbs west-north-west for 230 metres, then north for 180 metres. When you reach a junction, turn right and climb to the lump of An Sìdhean at 546m.

Dense forest on the ascent and descent of An Sìdhean

An Sìdhean, meaning 'The Fairy Hill', is a minor summit on the larger hill Beinn an t-Sìdhean (572m), 720 metres north-north-west. But An Sìdhean is the more satisfying viewpoint, being perched on the lip of the strath with extensive views.

Return to **Strathyre** the same way.

An Sìdhean and Beinn an t-Sìdhean (left) overlooking Strathyre and Loch Lubnaig

PART 3 LOCHEARNHEAD AND INVERLOCHLARIG

The pass between Creag Mac Rànaich and Meall an t-Seallaidh (Walk 15)

Lochearnhead, as the name suggests, occupies the western end of Loch Earn. Connected to Strathyre and Callander further south, the broad and deep Glen Ogle runs north, following the route of least resistance for historic roads and railways. The ways of past travellers make themselves known throughout these walks, with a couple of impressive viaducts, stretches of disused railway line, and a grassed-over military road.

The wider landscape provides classic Highland hillwalking. There are rough and pathless Corbetts and better-trodden Munros, with expansive views throughout. To the west, travelling up Balquhidder Glen, past Lochs Voil and Doine, through the Braes of Balquhidder to Inverlochlarig, you enter wild landscape with a feeling of remoteness that's uncommon within the national park. The Celts are said to have described this area as a 'thin place', where the divide between Earth and Heaven was less substantial than usual.

There's no public transport to Inverlochlarig and the 11km of narrow single-track road beyond Balquhidder should not be underestimated – reversing to a passing place is a likely necessity and it might well be around an oak tree-lined corner. Lochearnhead is more readily accessible at the junction between roads A84 and A85, as well as having a bus stop.

WALK 11
Stob a'Choin

Start/finish	Inverlochlarig car park NN 446 185
Time	5hr 30min
Distance	14.2km (8.8 miles)
Total ascent	825m (2710ft)
Terrain	Track, rough pathless ground and small hill paths
Max altitude	Stob a'Choin 869m (2851ft)
Maps	Split between OS Explorer OL46 and OL39; OS Landranger 56; Harvey *Loch Lomond & The Trossachs*
Parking	Free parking at road end

After a long approach – following a track winding up the mountain glen above the River Larig – this route tackles several challenges before summitting the standalone Corbett of Stob a'Choin: first there is the river itself, which you must leap across on boulders; then there's a complicated area of young trees and bog; before finally you climb 500m over 1.25km of steep, unpathed grass. A there-and-back walk by way of the descent described here would avoid some of the obstacles, but make for a less pleasing circuit.

Stob a'Choin, meaning 'Peak of the Dog', should not be confused with Beinn a' Chroin, on the north side of the glen, nor with Beinn a' Choin, 8km to the south-west. Then again, it also isn't Stùc a' Chroin, 20km to the east.

Start west along the track up the glen, passing over a bridge and between the buildings of **Inverlochlarig** and its farm. Rob Roy MacGregor spent his final years at Inverlochlarig and is buried at Balquhidder graveyard. Climb a stile beside a gate on the track 650 metres past the last buildings, then cross a ford; 500 metres beyond this is a footbridge on the left, below Stob a'Choin's steep northern slopes. This footbridge will be the return route. You will be crossing this same river, without benefit of bridge, a couple of kilometres upstream. If it's in spate, cross the footbridge, and use the descent route for the upwards walk too.

Continue up the track. After 1.5km a side-track leads to sheep pens; continue on the main track as it fords the sizable **Ishag Burn** that comes down off Cruach Ardrain (it's usually easier to head upstream a little to cross on small boulders). Continue along the track passing through a gate just after the ford.

WALK 11 – STOB A'CHOIN

Keep to the track for another 1.3km, then pass through another gate and cross a smaller ford just afterwards. Now leave the track to go through a wooden gate on the left, and cross the grassy valley floor and steep bank down to **River Larig**. In normal conditions this can be crossed on boulders, but it does require a bit of a jump.

Go through a gate on the opposite side of the river (NN 404 166) then cross a boggy area of fenced young trees south-south-east. When you reach another fence at the other side after 330 metres, turn right along it, heading roughly south for 400 metres up to the saddle between Stob an Duibhe and Stob a'Choin. Here, there is a fallen section of fence and a gate; cross it and turn left to head back along the fence (perhaps taking a wide berth of the bog) for 100 metres to another gate at a fence junction. Go through this gate and begin your ascent directly east towards the summit of Stob a'Choin.

The grassy slopes are steep, so take your time choosing the best line of ascent. At around 700 metres the slope is interrupted by small outcrops; weaving among these provides a grassy route at a gentler gradient. The main summit of **Stob a'Choin** (869m) is just 2m higher and 100 metres south-east of the small northern

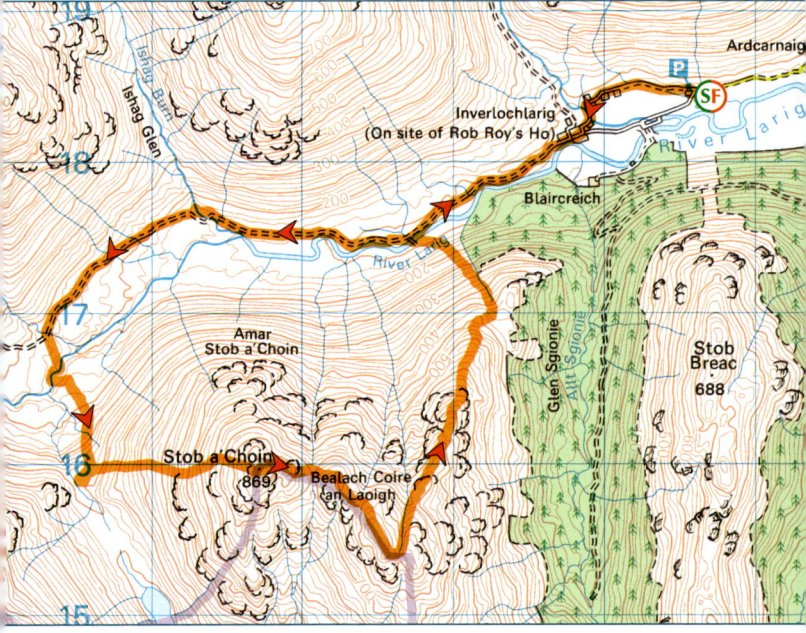

top; since the hard work is done now, it's worth visiting both for views right down into the glen.

Occasional iron fence posts arrive at the summit from the south and mark a way east down the next steep descent. Keep to the right of the main upper crag and weave among the smaller ones into the col **Bealach Coire an Laoigh**. Continue east as fence posts and a rough little path lead up the next steep rise to the 803m point. Rock exposed in the steep path is silvery phyllite. Head now south-east as the fencing leads to the right, over grassy humps of Meall Reamhar. Meall Reamhar means 'Fat Hump'.

Continue to follow the fence posts to a corner; turn left here and descend to a little valley (NN 426 154). Walk north down the little valley for 300 metres, then slope up right onto a lumpy ridgeline, which has more old iron posts to guide you. Descend north, soon on a well-defined ridge (Creag nan Saighead) with an intermittent path. Follow it down – with one steep step requiring care (take a few steps to the right if you arrive at crag tops here) – to the 460m contour. Here, follow the old fence down to the right to the head of a grassy valley, where it meets a tall deer fence. Turn left to continue your descent alongside the deer fence, passing through a gate at a fence junction. Now, slant down left, north-west, on grass and rushes, to the footbridge over **River Larig**.

Turn right and retrace your steps for 2.3km, past **Inverlochlarig**, to the car park.

Looking from the slopes of Stob a'Choin towards Beinn a' Chroin on the other side of the glen

WALK 12
Beinn Tulaichean and Cruach Ardrain

Start/finish	Inverlochlarig car park NN 446 185
Time	6hr
Distance	12.7km (7.9 miles)
Total ascent	1010m (3310ft)
Terrain	Hill paths (not always clear on the ascent and descent) and valley track
Max altitude	Cruach Ardrain 1046m (3432ft)
Maps	Split between OS Explorer OL46 and OL39; OS Landranger 56; Harvey *Trossachs North*
Parking	Free parking at road end

Starting deep in the Balquhidder Glen, this route summits two fine Munros connected by a narrow, winding path, which hardly loses any elevation. Part of the rambling range of mountains to the west of Ben More, they typify what the Southern Highlands are all about – there are no huge or intimidating crags, nor the endless grass slopes of Perthshire to the east, but the perfect mix of both. Small wiggly outcrops of schist interrupt steep-sided ridges, with a small path picking its way along the grass between the rocks.

Considering two Munros are climbed, this route is not particularly long or difficult, but the path is somewhat unclear on the lower section of Beinn Tulaichean's ascent and it is a bit steep at times.

Head west past the 'End of public road' sign and walk along the track for 750 metres to **Inverlochlarig Farm**. Keep to the track as it veers left (south) following a hand-made 'Hill Walkers' sign, then crosses a bridge over Inverlochlarig Burn. Just past the bridge, cross a stile on the right indicating 'Beinn Tulaichean, Cruach Ardrain, Crianlarich' on another handmade sign, then follow a path north-west with the burn on your right. After 160 metres, pass a small hydroelectricity building, then turn right/straight ahead onto a track, which heads north into Inverlochlarig Glen.

Keep to the track for 170 metres, then go through a gate. Continue for a further 220 metres, then, 20 metres before you reach a conspicuous white quartz rock, turn left at a small cairn onto a trodden path. Follow the path, which becomes less distinct, to the right of a large cairn on a grassy knoll, then continue west-north-west up grassy slopes. The path, which is difficult to follow near the

WALKING LOCH LOMOND AND THE TROSSACHS

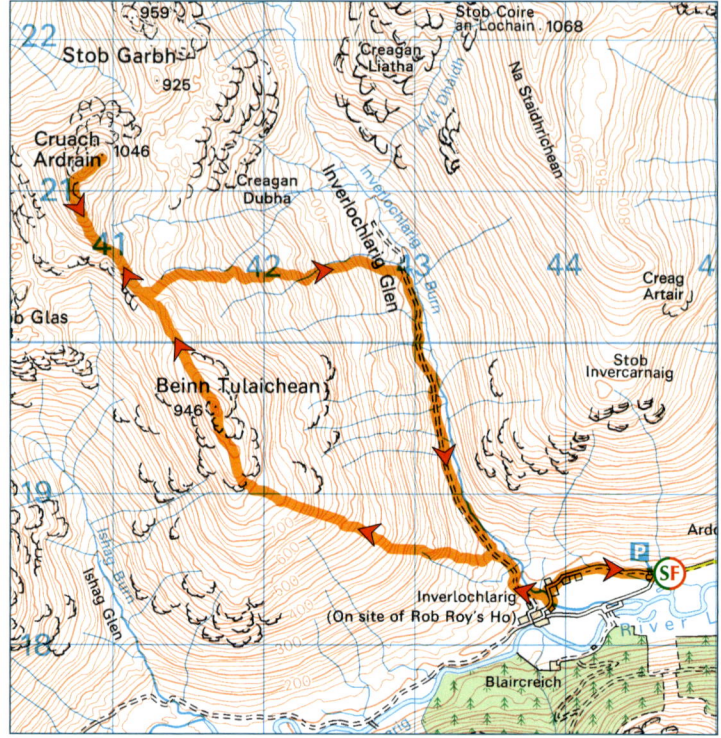

base of the hill, becomes more obvious as you ascend (if you lose it, try to spot it running up above).

Pass through a broken gate (NN 426 188) in a fence at 500m and continue west-north-west uphill along a trodden path. Keep to the path as it becomes more defined: from 700m the ascent becomes less steep, then veers north-north-west up onto the ridgeline. Continue along the gentle ridge to the rocky summit of **Beinn Tulaichean** (946m), which has a cairn.

Descend north-north-west to the bealach. After 800 metres, a small cairn at the lowest point marks what will be your descent route on the right. Continue ahead for another 770 metres to another small cairn at a junction; here, bear right, uphill, and keep climbing up to Cruach Ardrain's summit ridge. Walk north-east over one cairned false summit and descend a little before climbing the final rocky

WALK 12 – BEINN TULAICHEAN AND CRUACH ARDRAIN

section to the summit of **Cruach Ardrain** (1046m). There are spectacular views over the national park, with An Caisteal across the valley west and the mighty peaks of Stob Binnein and Ben More to the east.

Retrace your steps for 1.2km to the small cairn and a path leading down grassy slopes on the left. Follow this path, which is boggy at times, for 1.75km east down into **Inverlochlarig Glen**. When you meet the track running along the glen floor, turn right onto it and walk south alongside the burn for 2km. Walk through a gate, then join your outward route; keep an eye out for a 'car park' sign, which indicates where to leave the track and walk back past the small hydro station. Retrace your steps back to the car park.

Climbing the well-trodden path up Cruach Ardrain from the bealach

WALK 13

Stob Binnein and Ben More from the south

Start/finish	Inverlochlarig car park NN 446 185
Time	8hr
Distance	17km (10.6 miles)
Total ascent	1510m (4950ft)
Terrain	Grassy slopes and hill paths, quiet road to finish
Max altitude	Ben More 1174m (3852ft)
Maps	OS Explorer OL46; OS Landranger 57 and 51; Harvey *Trossachs North*
Parking	Free parking at road end

Ben More means 'Big Hill' and it is the highest in this book. It's not many people's favourite mountain, though; once you've climbed steeply up it, there's not much to do but go back down again. Ben More and its southerly neighbour Munro, Stob Binnein, are usually climbed from the north, giving you the opportunity to climb steeply up, steeply down, steeply up and then steeply down again.

The route suggested here is admittedly longer, but it starts from a lovely quiet glen by Loch Doine, later returning through peaceful green coires with pretty lochans popular with birds. The solitude of the seldomly frequented descent route here is a welcome relief after the crumbly, eroded Munro-bagger paths.

From the car park, return east up the road for 70 metres to a gate next to an oak tree marked with a sign for 'Am Binnein, Stob Coire an Lochain, Ben More'. Go through the gate and turn back left walking along a path beside a wall and the road for 70 metres to a small burn. Cross the burn then head uphill following a trodden path with the burn on your right.

Follow this path north, a bit eroded in places, for 800 metres, ascending 360m. At 550m, where a fence crosses, follow the path as it bends to the left – to meet a place where there was once a stile – then continue along it uphill. Keep to the path as it then veers a little right, the worst of this initial ascent's steepness now over. There is a last view down to the car park, and also along Loch Voil towards Ben Vorlich and Stùc a' Chroin (Walk 17).

Looking towards Stob Binnein (left) and Ben More (behind right) from Stob Coire an Lochain

Head up onto a shoulder called **Stob Invercarnaig**, with a steeper climb to the first false top (890m) where there is a cairn. Now follow a gentle and very pleasant ridge, **Na Staidhrichean**, which becomes quite narrow and leads to **Stob Coire an Lochain** (1068m), with another cairn. Na Staidhrichean possibly means 'the Staircase'. Continue north-north-west, with a steepish climb up the final cone to the summit of **Stob Binnein** (1165m).

Descend along a more substantial path, which leads down north, becoming rather steep – in early spring this spur can hold refrozen snow, unsuspected when the mountain is seen from the south. Cross the wide col **Bealach-eadar-dha Bheinn** (862m – the name translates, appropriately, as the 'Pass Between Two Hills') and continue up the Ben More ascent path opposite, which is initially again rather steep, a bit to the left of the direct line out of the col. At 1000m the slope becomes less severe. The final moment to the summit is defended (on the path line) by a 2.5m scramble up an inwards corner in a rock wall. It has good holds and is not exposed but is steep – a walk round to the right will avoid this step. A smaller scramble just beyond presents no difficulties. **Ben More** summit (1174m) has a trig pillar and, just beyond, a cairn overlooking Crianlarich.

Descend back to Bealach-eadar-dha Bheinn, then leave the path to the left to drop into the corrie to the east towards two tiny **lochans**. This section is steep and holds snow; the easiest line slants down south-east aiming between the lochans and crags of Creagan Dubha.

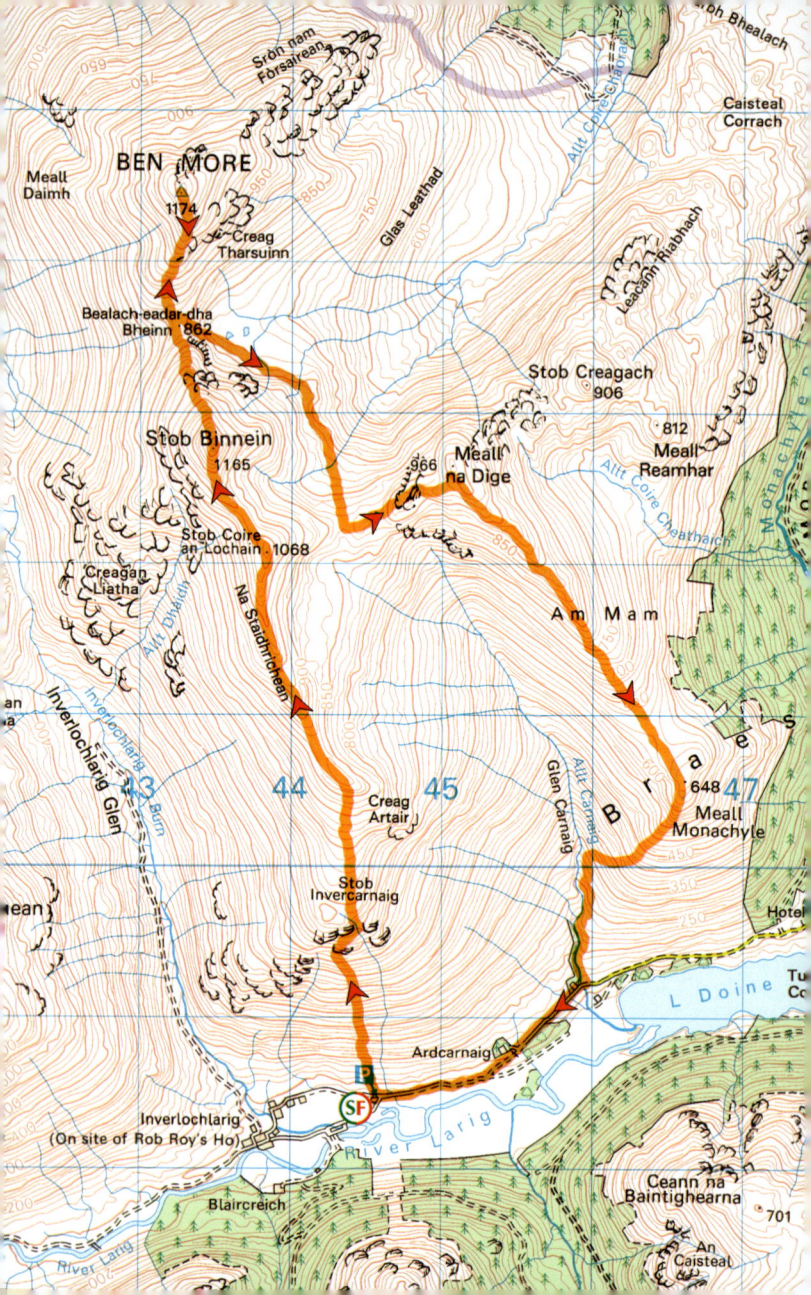

WALK 13 – STOB BINNEIN AND BEN MORE FROM THE SOUTH

Cross the corrie floor south-east below the rocky slope of Creagan Dubha – it's drier if you keep close under the crags. Then rise a little to cross the lumpy Coire Each south-south-east, cross a burn and gain the low shoulder east of Stob Coire an Lochain – aim for the low point of this ridge; shortcutting to Meall na Dìge leads to crags. At the wide crest, turn left (east) on a small path, which initially runs alongside an old wall, then to the left of a small pool, before threading among low outcrops to **Meall na Dìge**. The summit (966m) is just left with a small cairn.

From Meall na Dìge head south-east down a gentle ridge with a small path. At its end, it tips up to **Meall Monachyle** with a cairn at 648m. There are great views over Loch Doine between the River Larig and Loch Voil. Turn down south-west, around the rim of a small crag hollow on the right (Coire Buidhe). Descend steepish grass slopes, which become tussocky at the very foot. Aim for a gate at the corner of a fenced area of mixed young trees at Lag an Fhuarain in **Glen Carnaig** – don't go through the gate, but instead walk around the fenced area to the side of **Allt Carnaig** river. Turn left onto a path which follows the edge of the fence on high ground above the river. Follow this path and Allt Carnaig south, keeping outside a complication of fence junctions.

After 900 metres, you will come down to a gate. Go through the gate and turn right onto the road over a cattle grid. Continue west along the narrow road for 1.6km back to the car park.

The River Larig feeding into Loch Doine, seen from Meall Monachyle

WALK 14
From Lochearnhead around Edinchip

Start/finish	Lochearnhead car park at public toilets NN 593 238
Time	2hr 30min
Distance	9km (5.6 miles)
Total ascent	125m (410ft)
Terrain	Tracks, cycle path and trodden path
Max altitude	Old railway above Lochearnhead 194m (636ft)
Maps	OS Explorer OL46; OS Landranger 51; Harvey *Ben Ledi*
Public transport	Bus stop in village centre
Parking	Free parking

With views over Loch Earn, an impressive viaduct, pretty woodland and interesting historic sites, this easy ramble follows sections of the dismantled Callander and Oban Railway and an old military road – now covered by soft grass – to explore the peaceful landscape around Edinchip Estate, southwest of Lochearnhead.

Start at the large car park in **Lochearnhead** and turn right onto the **A85** to follow the pavement 430 metres, past the small police station and across **Ogle Burn** (footbridge slightly to the right of the road bridge), to the **A84**. Turn left onto the pavement of the A84 and, after 560 metres, at the end of the village, turn right – passing a small, metal sculpture of a dog – up a lane past the church.

Follow the lane for 440 metres to its top, passing a few houses. Just before a bridge over an old railway, turn off left down a path to join Cycle Route 7. When you reach a junction, keep ahead/left, following a sign for Baliquidder to walk along the old railbed cycle path. Continue for 700 metres as the cycle path passes through ash woods, then crosses a high viaduct, before reaching the **A84**.

Edinchip Viaduct was built between 1901 and 1905 to connect a section of the Caledonian Railway between Balquhidder Station and Comrie. The modern girder section was replaced in 1997 using funds raised by the parents of cyclist Nigel Hester who was killed on the A9.

Keep to the path as it runs roughly alongside the road for about 400 metres – crossing a side road to Edinchip Estate – then bends to the right, into pretty, mixed

WALK 14 – FROM LOCHEARNHEAD AROUND EDINCHIP

woodland. After 900 metres, when you reach a junction near Balquidder Station, keep ahead (right fork) following a sign for Cycle Route 7. At the junction immediately after, keep ahead. Then, after a further 170 metres, at the next junction (also marked for Cycle Route 7), turn right onto a quiet, old road with the remains of cat's eyes. Continue for 120 metres, then turn off to the right onto a narrower path (still indicated as part of Cycle Route 7), which leads onto moorland.

After 80 metres, the path crosses a cattle grid and small bridge; continue for another 140 metres and, as the cycle path bends left, turn off right through a broken field gate. Follow a grassy track – part of an old military road – as it runs north-north-east, crossing a burn, then passes to the left of a reedy **lochan** popular with ducks and geese.

After the Jacobite rebellion of 1745, **military road** building between Stirling and Fort William started in 1748. The new road ran by Callander, Lochearnhead, Tyndrum, Bridge of Orchy and the Devil's Staircase in Glencoe, and was part of an ongoing initiative intended to improve communications and increase the ability to mobilise troops across the Highlands.

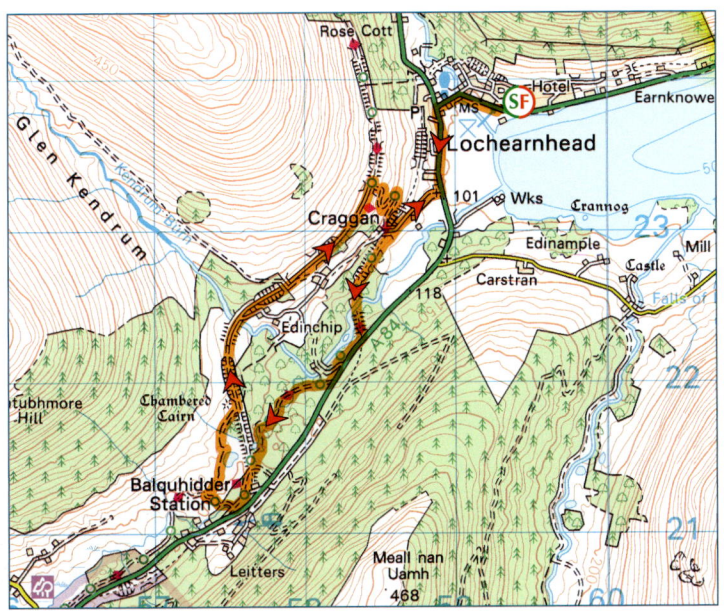

Just past the lochan, follow the now-indistinct track as it bears left around a small mound before bearing right again and passing between a few ruined stoned buildings, crossing another small burn. The track then reaches a gate to join a wider one at some derelict sheds and cattle feeders (NN 575 218). Just before you reach a gate, you can turn off the track left and walk over rough ground into the trees for 30 metres north-west to find an impressive chambered cairn. Go through the gate and bear left, onto what is the higher of Lochearnhead's two abandoned railway lines.

After 360 metres, keep straight ahead through two gates, and continue as the smooth track soon crosses **Kendrum Burn** and reaches a junction. Follow the railbed ahead through a gate and then under a decrepit ornamental footbridge. Another 150 metres further on, keep ahead (right fork) to pass under a more substantial stone bridge. Continue through a high gate in deer fencing, above a white house with a view of Loch Earn, and follow the old railway for another 600 metres (passing one broken, open gate) to another high gate.

Go through the gate and shortly afterwards turn right to follow the sharp zig-zags of the cycle path towards **Craggan**. After 700 metres, pass under a bridge to reach a junction; here, turn sharp left, following a sign to **Lochearnhead** and rejoining the walk's outward route. Continue ahead down the lane and past the church. Turn left onto the pavement alongside the **A84** and walk back into the village.

Along the old military road

WALK 15
Kendrum and Ogle Circle

Start/finish	Lochearnhead car park at public toilets NN 593 238
Time	6hr 30min
Distance	22.3km (13.9 miles)
Total ascent	575m (1890ft)
Terrain	Good tracks
Max altitude	Kendrum/Dubh pass 600m (1969ft)
Maps	OS Explorer OL46; OS Landranger 51; Harvey *Ben Ledi*
Public transport	Bus stop in village centre
Parking	Free parking

Equally suitable for mountain bikes or trail running, this long route follows good tracks throughout, with straightforward navigation and easy terrain. It climbs up Glen Kendrum and down Gleann Dubh – over a remote mountain pass between Corbetts Creag Mac Rànaich and Meall an t-Seallaidh – before traversing some forestry tracks and returning along the disused Callander to Oban railway line through Glen Ogle. The first half of the walk is wilder, a rare opportunity to get up in the hills without actually needing to climb them; in contrast, the second half descends Glen Ogle, parallel to the A85, which, although on the opposite side of the glen from the old railway, will still disrupt your peace at times. But crossing a mighty viaduct and the views down towards Loch Earn will provide decent compensation.

Start at the large car park in **Lochearnhead**, turn right onto the **A85** and follow the pavement for 430 metres, past the small police station and across **Ogle Burn** (on a footbridge slightly right of the road bridge), to the **A84**. Turn left onto the pavement of the A84 and, after 560 metres, at the end of the village, turn right, past a metal sculpture of a westie, up a lane towards the church. The sculpture, *Ewen, Westies of Craggan,* is by blacksmith and TV personality Kev Paxton).

Follow this lane for 440 metres to its top, passing a few houses. Just before a bridge over an old railway, turn off left down a path to join Cycle Route 7. When you reach a junction, turn right following a sign for Killin. Go under the bridge and walk uphill following a series of hairpin bends as Lochearnhead village and the loch come into view behind.

On reaching the top, turn sharp left, through a metal gate, onto a path along a second disused railbed. Continue for 830 metres, then 50 metres before the trackbed heads under a stone bridge ahead, turn off left through a rotting gate on a grassy track following an old sign for Glen Kendrum, and cross the bridge. At the junction just after, bear right and head uphill on a track.

With the cragged face of Creag Mac Rànaich ahead, follow the track up **Glen Kendrum** through a fertile landscape scattered with boulders and sheep. After 2.6km, continue as it fords a branch of the burn and slants up into the moorland pass between Creag Mac Rànaich and Meall an t-Seallaidh. Walk 16 follows the horseshoe route of these two Corbetts.

Follow the track north through the wide moorland col descending **Gleann Dubh**, with small waterfalls in Ardchyle Burn alongside on the left. Some 5km beyond the pass, the track bends left towards a ford, but here fork off right on a faint old track that stays to the right of the burn, which – after a waterfall – is lost in a deep slot.

Keep to the track as it crosses a smaller burn then, reaching a grassy junction, head left to a gate (NN 531 280). Go through the gate, entering an area of felled and young trees, and continue on a somewhat overgrown track for 100 metres to a junction; turn right here on a track running level which passes through an ugly felled area. The track is now rough from forestry trucks, but follow it around a sharp corner at the forest edge before entering trees where it soon becomes gravel.

WALK 15 – KENDRUM AND OGLE CIRCLE

The old railway line in Glen Ogle

After almost 2km through forest and felled areas, turn right at a junction onto a smooth, level-running track that is again the abandoned railway. This route now follows the old railway line for 7.2km.

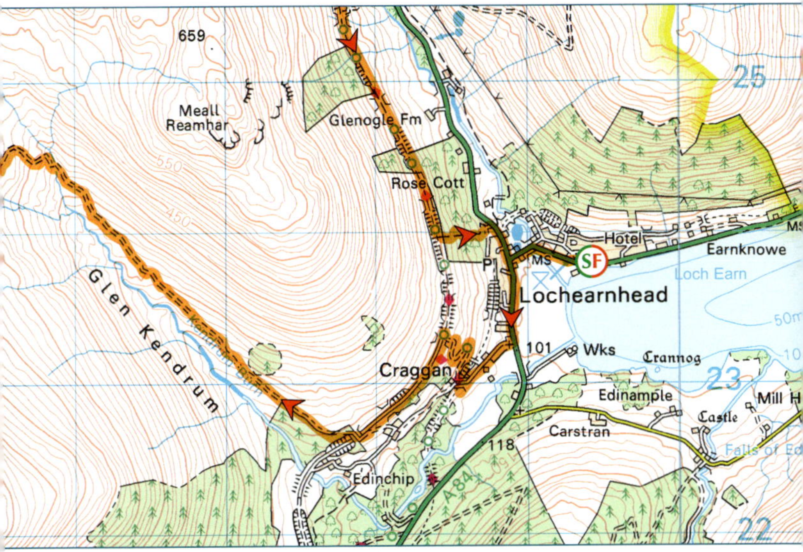

Glen Kendrum with Creag Mac Rànaich and Meall an t-Seallaidh ahead

Continue east and then south along the dismantled railway line, with old barriers and the odd hut giving some indication of the route's past life. At the top of Glen Ogle, the A85 is close enough to be noisy for a couple of kilometres, but continue alongside **Lochan Lairig Cheile**, with Route 7 cycleway now joining the railbed, and the old railway soon branches away from the road. When the track splits, go straight under a bridge as the path becomes tarmacked through a cutting.

At the northern end of Lochan Lairig Cheile, the disused railway passes the old **Glenoglehead Station**, with a cottage and an old brick ruin by the track. This intermediate station on the Stirling to Crianlarich portion of the Callander to Oban route was opened (as 'Killin Station') in 1870. It was renamed Glenoglehead Station in 1886 (at the opening of the Killin branch) and was further renamed Glenoglehead Crossing in 1891 before closing in 1916.

After 1km the railway line crosses a **viaduct**. In another 2.1km continue through a gate with a cattle grid; 55 metres further (200 metres before a second gate and cattle grid), a steep, unmarked path turns down left towards **Lochearnhead**. Take this turning and follow the zigzags down through birch woodland and scrub to a kissing gate; turn left here and follow a path down to reach **A85** at the northern edge of the village. Turn right and walk along the verge to return to the village.

WALK 15 – KENDRUM AND OGLE CIRCLE

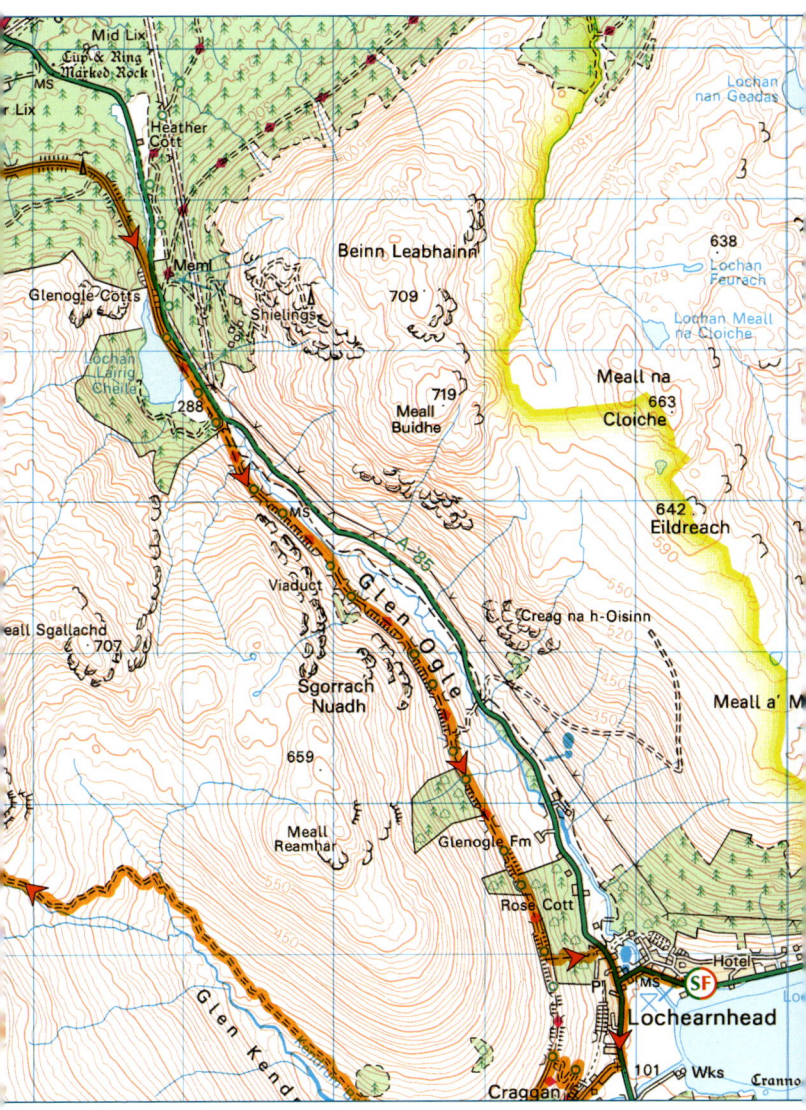

WALK 16
Meall an t-Seallaidh and Creag Mac Rànaich

Start/finish	Lochearnhead car park (free) at public toilets NN 593 238
Time	8hr; Meall an t-Seallaidh only: 6hr 15min; Creag Mac Rànaich only: 6hr
Distance	17.9km (11.1 miles); Meall an t-Seallaidh only: 17.6km (10.9 miles); Creag Mac Rànaich only: 16.4km (10.2 miles)
Total ascent	1115m (3660ft); Meall an t-Seallaidh only: 795m (2610ft); Creag Mac Rànaich only: 825m (2710ft)
Terrain	Some track, but mostly pathless grassy hillside and moorland
Max altitude	Meall an t-Seallaidh 852m (2795ft)
Maps	OS Explorer OL46; OS Landranger 51; Harvey *Ben Ledi*
Public transport	Bus stop in village centre

Meall an t-Seallaidh (852m) is the 'Hump of the Viewpoint' and Creag Mac Rànaich (809m) is the 'Craggy Hill of the Son of Rànaich'. It's unusual to find two hills of Corbett height (above 2500ft/762m) lying together in a natural horseshoe, but – like most Corbetts in the region – the route remains relatively unpopular with little in the way of paths. There is no escaping the fact that the initial, grassy ascent of Meall an t-Seallaidh is a slog and the lumpy ridgeline between Creag Mac Rànaich and Meall Reamhar is a bit arduous too, but you're rewarded with views over Loch Earn, down Loch Voil and north towards Killin. Ben Vorlich and Stùc a' Chroin (Walk 17) also look majestic just across Strathyre Forest.

This route can be split into two parts, utilising the good track through Glen Kendrum.

From the car park in **Lochearnhead**, turn right onto the **A85** and follow the pavement 430 metres, past the small police station and across **Ogle Burn** (footbridge slightly right of the road bridge), to the **A84**. Turn left onto the pavement alongside the A84 and, after 560 metres, at the end of the village, turn right, past a metal dog sculpture, up a lane past the church.

Walk 16 – Meall an t-Seallaidh and Creag Mac Rànaich

Follow this lane as it climbs for 440 metres. Just before a bridge over an old railway, turn off left down a path to join Cycle Route 7. When you reach a junction, turn right following a sign for Killin. Go under the bridge and walk uphill round a series of hairpin bends with Lochearnhead and the loch in view behind.

On reaching the top, turn sharp left, through a metal gate, onto a path along a higher disused railway line. Continue for 830 metres, then, 50 metres before the old railway heads under a stone bridge ahead, turn left through a rotting gate onto a grassy track following an old sign for Glen Kendrum. Cross the bridge and, at the junction just after, bear right and head uphill on a track. For Creag Mac Rànaich on its own, continue up this track through Glen Kendrum for 4.6km to its top at the pass between Meall an t-Seallaidh and Creag Mac Rànaich – skip three paragraphs below.

To climb Meall an t-Seallaidh, follow the track past plantation and woodland for 570 metres then go through a gate. Continue along the track for another 140 metres, looking out for a grassy track on the left, which leads down to an informal ford across **Kendrum Burn**. Take this and cross the burn on stepping stones, then begin a long, grassy ascent west-south-west. Aim initially to the right of a boulder perched on higher ground, then continue trudging in roughly the same direction for 2.3km. There are great views of Loch Earn behind.

Descending north from Meall an t-Seallaidh

WALKING LOCH LOMOND AND THE TROSSACHS

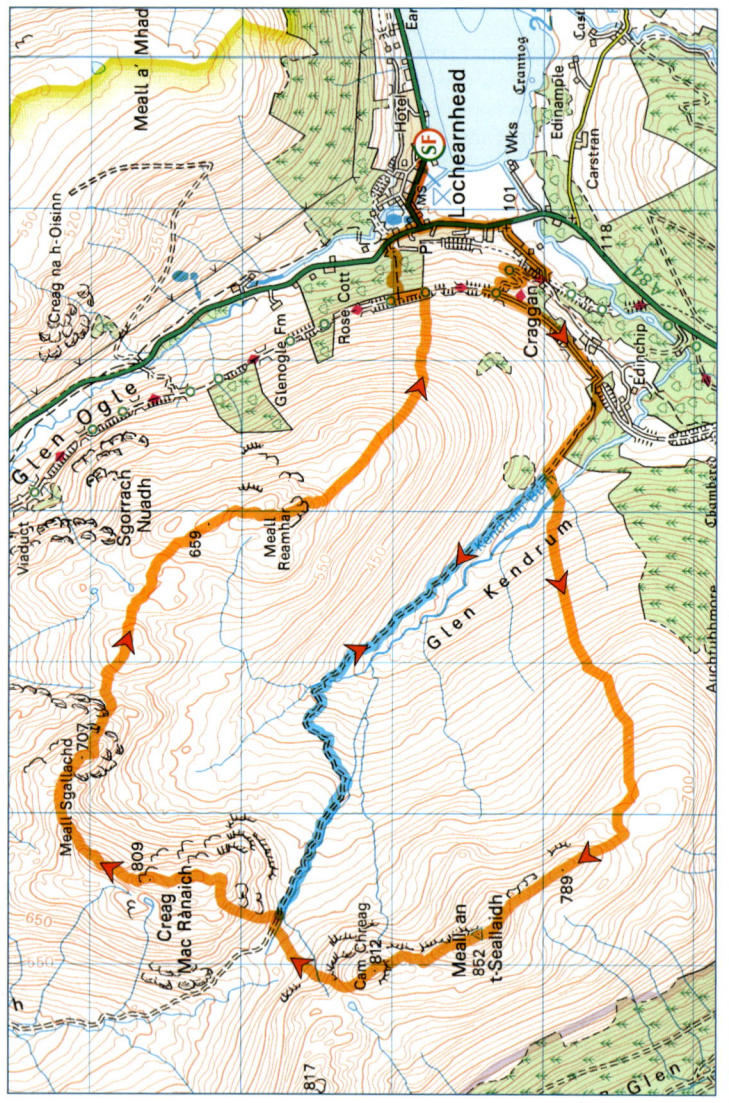

WALK 16 – MEALL AN T-SEALLAIDH AND CREAG MAC RÀNAICH

At the wide flat plateau, turn right and follow occasional posts of an old iron fence up the rising spur. Point 789 has a cairn with quartz lumps in it. Continue across a short descent, then follow the continuing rise to the trig point on **Meall an t-Seallaidh** summit (852m).

Follow the fencing gently downhill north-north-west to a col with a small pool, then climb a slight rise north to **Cam Chreag** (812m). From there, continue to follow the old posts north-west to a steep but grassy and short descent to a col (741m). From the col turn right, north-east, down a grassy hollow towards the pass between Meall an t-Seallaidh and Creag Mac Rànaich. From the foot of the steep ground, a trodden path leaves from the left side, but is hard to follow – slant out right, to minimise the moorland crossing, to the track that passes through the wide col between the two mountains. To take the shortcut down Glen Kendrum and back to Lochearnhead, simply turn right, down the track to rejoin the outward route. Those aiming for Creag Mac Rànaich on its own arrive up the track now.

While descending from Meall an t-Seallaidh, you will have surveyed your route up Creag Mac Rànaich; you probably want to turn right onto the track for a few steps going slightly downhill towards **Glen Kendrum**. Head up north where a stream trickles under the track (NN 543 248); 20 metres uphill is a pointed boulder with a mossy hat. Go up past this boulder.

Above are two crags – a smaller one on the left and larger on the right – go up to the left of the smaller one onto a steep grassy slope on the hill face. Pass up to the left of a rock tower and continue on the same line, to arrive at the summit plateau at a small col with a bog pool (NN 543 251).

Head up north-east to the south summit (808m), whose cairn has a rounded quartz boss alongside it. Then follow a small path, which leads north across a col with a small lochan and up a rocky step to the main summit of **Creag Mac Rànaich**, 1m higher (its cairn has a quartz streak running past it, but no rounded boss).

Follow the grassy ridge, with crag drops on the right, north-north-east over one hump, then north-east over another, and finally east to **Meall Sgallachd** (707m) with its small cairn. Meall Sgallachd means 'Bald-headed Hump'. Go down a few steps to a peaty col. The direct ridgeline ahead (south-east) leads to some crags, so turn left and descend grassy slopes east. As the angle eases, head back to the right to reach the peaty col before the moorland crossing.

Cross moorland humps south-east, until you can gain the grassy slopes around 650m. From here, follow fence posts to the cairn on **Meall Reamhar** and then down south-east, with a steep descent to the shoulder at 580m. Continue as the line of old fencing leads down towards Lochearnhead on slopes that get more heathery until the fencing dives into deep patches of bracken. Dodge around the bracken patches, but return to the same fence line. When the fence meets a

The cairns on top of Creag Mac Rànaich

junction with a wall, cross the wall at a low point on the left of the fence, then continue downhill following the same line of fence (soon fence and wall running together). When you reach a fence junction just above the old railway line shrouded by birch trees, cross a low point of the fence ahead and descend to the railway path.

Turn left onto the disused railway line, at once crossing a cattle grid. Continue north for 200 metres until an unmarked path leads steeply down to the right. Follow this as it zigzags through birch scrub to the northern edge of **Lochearnhead** village. Continue down to the **A85**, then turn right to walk along the verge then pavement. After 240 metres, turn left and continue back to the car park.

WALK 17
Ben Vorlich and Stùc a' Chroin

Start/finish	Ardvorlich, Loch Earn NN 633 232
Time	5hr 30min; Ben Vorlich only: 4hr
Distance	14.8km (9.2 miles); Ben Vorlich only: 10km (6.2 miles)
Total ascent	1100m (3610ft); Ben Vorlich only: 855m (2810ft)
Terrain	Straightforward path up Ben Vorlich; steep mountain paths for Stùc a' Chroin with some scrambling
Max altitude	Beinn Vorlich 985m (3231ft)
Maps	OS Explorer OL46; split across OS Landranger 57 and 51; Harvey *Ben Ledi*
Public transport	No convenient public transport
Parking	Lochside verge parking is limited along the single-track South Loch Earn road; arrive early and avoid blocking passing places
Note	This is the Ben Vorlich beside Loch Earn. For the Loch Lomond/Arrochar Alps Ben Vorlich, see Route 32.

In the far east of the national park, these two Munros above Loch Earn make for a fine mountain walk. With the exception of Ben Lomond, Ben Vorlich (985m) has the most straightforward route and best path of any of the national park's mountains, making it a great place for anyone looking to gain experience; if that's you (or some of your party), the recommended route is up and back down the same way. The views over Loch Earn and the surrounding hills are nothing short of spectacular.

Stùc a' Chroin (975m) means 'Peak of Danger' and – in comparison to Ben Vorlich's ascent – the name seems appropriate. The south-western descent from Ben Vorlich is steep and loose, an assault on the knees after the well-made path up, and the direct ascent of Stùc a' Chroin from the col requires some scrambling over bounders and some bare rock. If you have any scrambling experience at all, however, this is unlikely to present much difficulty.

Start at the bridge where the South Loch Earn road crosses **Ardvorlich Burn**, and go through stone gateposts on the river's east bank with a sign for Ardvorlich House. Follow a track south alongside the river for 240 metres, then take the right

WALKING LOCH LOMOND AND THE TROSSACHS

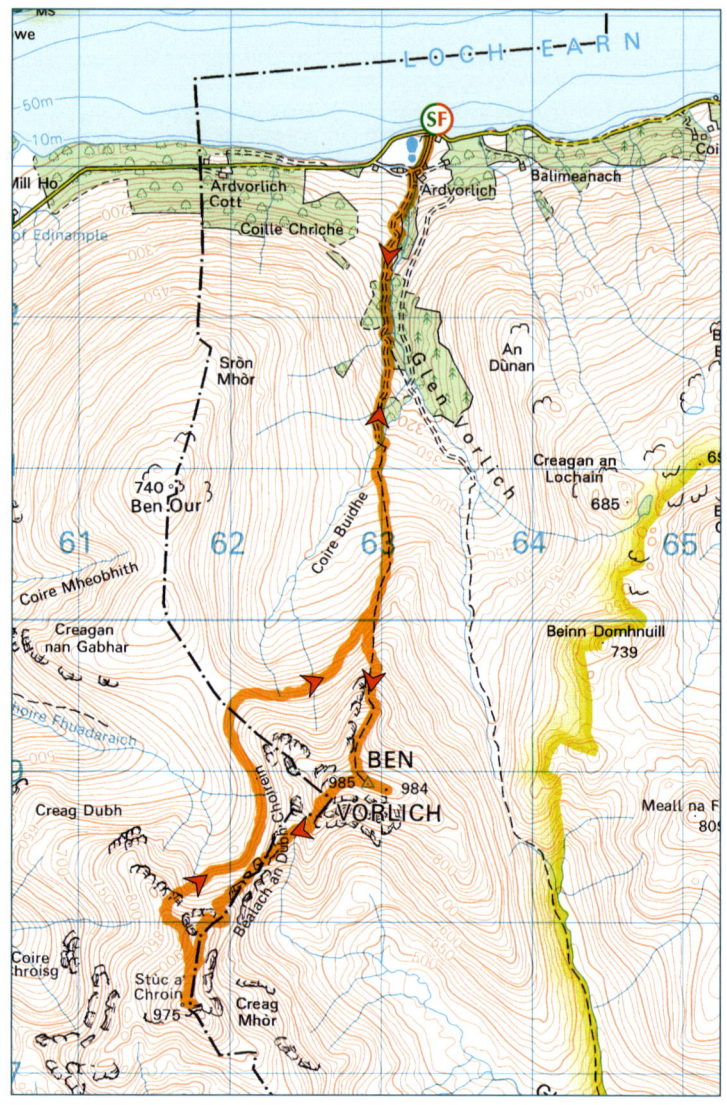

WALK 17 – BEN VORLICH AND STÙC A' CHROIN

fork at a junction which crosses the river towards Ardvorlich House. Walk over the bridge and at once, turn left onto a stony track with the river now on your left.

Keep to the track as it runs uphill, south, through a gate, and then carry on straight at a crossroads. Continue along the track for 1.2km, passing through three gates with stiles, and when the track splits at a junction, keep right on the more substantial, main track uphill. Continue south for a further 430 metres as the track gradually rises away from Ardvorlich Burn. Follow the track across a ford, and continue for another 220 metres to a bridge over a dam. Cross the bridge; here, where there is a grassy picnic spot by a large boulder, the track then becomes a well-built path onto open hill.

Continue south along the path, which is clear all the way to the final steepening and **Ben Vorlich**'s summit trig point (985m). The south-east summit 150 metres away is 1m lower according to OS mapping, but has excellent views. To climb Ben Vorlich on its own, simply return the way you came. The continuing route to Stùc a' Chroin is more challenging.

To continue to Stùc a' Chroin, return to the trig point and descend the south-west ridge, on a steep and loose, eroded path, weaving among small

The summit of Ben Vorlich

outcrops, to the levelling of the **Bealach an Dubh Choirein**. Walk across the bealach towards the steep rocky face of Stùc a' Chroin. (Before you begin the steep ascent, you could avoid the scrambling ahead by contouring out to the right on an indistinct path (starting at NN 620 182) to a more obvious path ascending south-west onto the north-western spur of Stùc a' Chroin. This option is not exactly easier, as the ground is steep and loose with erosion.)

At the foot of the steep section, the path bears left then deposits you at the bottom of a pile of small boulders. Climb up on the left side of these boulders to where the path reforms above. The path splits into several branches, with short scrambling sections on some. Keeping to the most obvious route, there is only one section which requires any upper body strength and it has good holds – the path is a little exposed at times, but not intimidatingly so in good, summer conditions. Continue up to the grassy plateau and cairned 951m north summit, which has an impressive view back to Ben Vorlich, then continue south following a line of old fence posts across a slight dip to the main 975m summit of **Stùc a' Chroin**. From here there are great views over Lochan a' Chroin towards Ben Ledi and The Trossachs.

Return north, retracing your steps along the crest for 200 metres to the dip before the rise to Stùc a' Chroin's north peak. Here, turn left (north-north-west) following a vague path past a small cairn toward a bealach on Stùc a' Chroin's north-western spur.

After 500 metres, another small cairn marks the descent towards **Bealach an Dubh Choirein** and Coire Fhuadraich on the right, which is loose and steep, but obvious. When you reach the bottom of the steep section, don't climb up to the bealach, but instead follow a path below it on its north-west side, heading roughly north at around 700m. Keep to this path, which is boggy at times, for 2.7km as it contours around the west side of Ben Vorlich, crossing the Munro's north-west shoulder then across the wide col above **Coire Buidhe**.

When you eventually meet the main Ben Vorlich path, turn left onto it and retrace your outward steps back to **Ardvorlich**. There are great views over Loch Earn.

THE NORTH

Ben Lui from the River Cononish (Walk 22)

PART 4 KILLIN AND THE FAR NORTH-EAST

Kinnell Park Stone Circle (Walk 18)

Killin is in the far north-east of the national park or, should you be coming that way, a gateway from the north. At the heart of the region of Breadalbane, this ancient village occupies the spit of land between the mighty rivers Lochay and Dochart as they form a confluence on their course to Loch Tay.

The region is rich in archaeology and historic sites, with prehistoric standing stones and crannogs, close connections with the eighth-century Irish Saint Fillan and remnants of the turbulent clan times when the area was wrestled between the MacNabs and the Campbells of Breadalbane.

With a population under 1000, Killin is popular with and well set up for visitors. One walk here explores the village's varied history and archaeology, while another leaves the national park entirely to travel up Glen Lochay, approaching two stubborn Munros from the north.

WALK 18
Killin and Loch Tay

Start/finish	Falls of Dochart south bank, Killin NN 571 324
Time	2hr; including Auchmore Circuit: 3hr 15min
Distance	7km (4.3 miles); including Auchmore Circuit: 11.4km (7.1 miles)
Total ascent	50m (160ft); including Auchmore Circuit: 125m (410ft)
Terrain	Paths, tracks and pavement
Max altitude	Killin 136m (446ft)
Maps	OS Explorer OL48; OS Landranger 51; Harvey Ultramap *Loch Earn, Glen Ogle & Killin*
Public transport	Bus stops throughout the village
Parking	Limited parking on roadside at walk start, car park in village centre, at McLaren Hall and Killin Cemetery – all free

In the far north-east of the national park, the picturesque village of Killin straddles the Falls of Dochart. A narrow, multi-arched, stone bridge connects the smaller south and main north parts of the settlement, which is central to Breadalbane, one of the traditional provinces of Scotland.

This varied and rewarding route explores the village and some of its historic sites, a ruined castle, old railway lines with a viaduct and the head of Loch Tay. It's an easy, largely level walk with good paths throughout. If you have time, the Auchmore circuit adds some peaceful woodland and a view over the Killin glen.

Starting at the **Falls of Dochart**, cross the bridge to the north side of River Dochart where a water mill with a restored wheel is on the left; turn right instead and walk along Main Street towards the village centre.

After 200 metres, just before you reach a chemist, turn left up Manse Road past a Freemasons' meeting house and an old manse. Take the second right onto Stewart Road, walk to a T-junction and turn right onto Fingal Road. Follow the road downhill through a residential area to a pond, then turn left onto a path. After 70 metres, Fingal's Stone is on your left.

The Bridge of Dochart and Killin

KILLIN

Inchbuie island, just north-east of the Bridge of Dochart, holds Clan MacNab's burial ground – its grand, stone entry archway and pillars are visible from the bridge.

The Old Mill, just north-west, is a 1840s building standing on a traditional site occupied by a succession of meal mills, the earliest of which is said to have been erected by St Fillan who came to Scotland from Ireland in AD717. The current building is home to the 'Healing Stones of St Fillan', as well as a local makers' market and is worth a visit if it's open.

In local legend, this prehistoric **standing stone** is the grave of Fionn mac Cumhaill, a hero in Celtic mythology. In 1830, the stone is said to have been moved from a field further up the hill, because crops were being damaged by the number of people visiting it.

Return to and continue along the main tarmac path. As you approach Breadalbane Park, turn right and walk around the edge of the playing field to an ornate gate. Exit through the gate and turn left onto Main Street. The route now follows this road for 700 metres. Pass the village post office, the Outdoor Centre, McLaren Hall and two churches, then follow the road and pavement north with the River Lochay on your right.

WALK 18 – KILLIN AND LOCH TAY

Made from corrugated iron, the white **Episcopal Church of St Fillan** with its green roof is an excellent example of a tin tabernacle. Erected in 1876 by the seventh Earl of Breadalbane, it was built as a private chapel for shooting parties earning it the nickname, 'Grouse Chapel'.

Reach a junction with Pier Road on your right, cross a road bridge over the River Lochay – and the north-eastern border of the national park – and continue for 340 metres. Pass Killin Cemetery and, 100 metres further on, a trodden path on the left leads up to the atmospheric ruins of **Finlarig Castle** (the masonry is unstable, so don't get too close).

Although there may have been an earlier castle on the site of **Finlarig Castle**, the present building dates from the early 17th century and was built under instruction from 'Black' Duncan Campbell (Donnchadh Dubh) of Glenorchy, the Clan Campbell chieftain. A stone-lined hole on the castle's north side is said to be a beheading pit – a punishment saved for nobles, while the common folk were hanged.

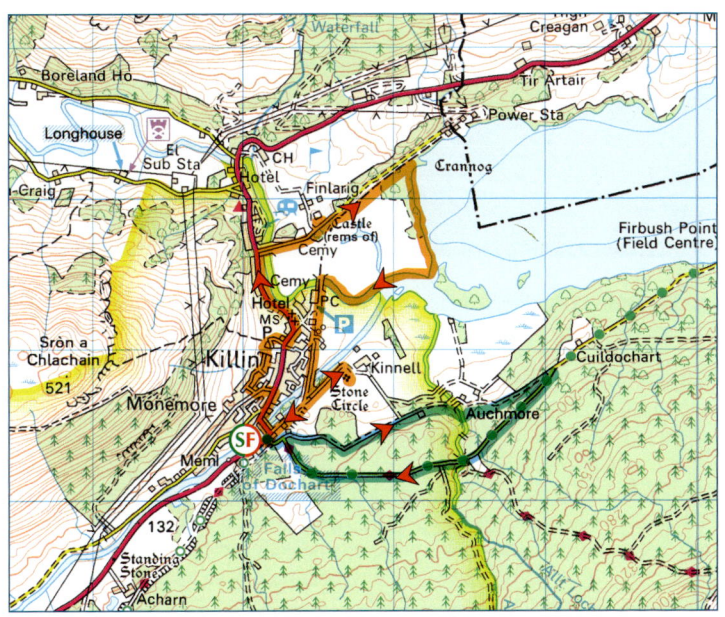

The 17th-century ruins of Finlarig Castle

Continue along Pier Road for 200 metres. Walk just past a metal bench with gold spheres on its posts, then turn onto a path which runs parallel with the road on its left, continuing in the same direction. This path runs through deciduous woodland, with bluebells in spring, along part of the disused Callander to Oban railway line. Continue north-east for 530 metres then, at a couple of old concrete pillars and a junction, turn right following a sign for Loch Tay.

Go through a gate and immediately over a small burn onto a dirt path along the shoreline of Loch Tay. The tied wooded islet to the left is a crannog called Eilean Puttychan or Eilean Sputachan. Continue along the path, which runs between the loch and an old, moss-covered wall, overhung with ancient oak trees. After 700 metres, the path reaches some sandy beaches overlooking a tree-covered island; follow it as it veers right around a corner and continues up the River Lochay.

WALK 18 – KILLIN AND LOCH TAY

After 840 metres, go through a kissing gate to rejoin the old railway line path beside a bridge. Turn left to cross the bridge over the River Lochay and continue south for 340 metres along the back of the village. At the end of the path, continue ahead/left onto the residential Lyon Road, then, after 50 metres, turn off left onto a track marked for 'Falls of Dochart' with a wooden sign. Continue south on the track for 240 metres to a viaduct over the River Dochart. *If you want a view of the viaduct from below, head down steeply on the left on its north side just before crossing – climb back up the same way.*

Completed in 1885, the **viaduct** has five arches. While the piers, spandrels and parapets were built from masonry, the arch-rings are concrete, giving the structure a claim to be Scotland's earliest concrete viaduct.

Cross the viaduct and continue ahead for 110 metres to a junction. *Carry on straight here for a quick return to the falls.* To visit **Kinnell Park Stone Circle** turn back, sharp left (north-north-east), soon passing between large stone pillars, and continue along a dead straight track lined with grand horse chestnuts. *This track leads to Kinnel House, once the seat of Clan MacNab who ruled the area before being usurped by the Campbells of Breadalbane.* After 360 metres, pass through a second pair of pillars (with carved lions on top), then turn right through a gate into a field. The stone circle is 80 metres south-east, as you will have noticed as you walked along the track.

Return the way you came up the horse chestnut-lined track, then carry straight ahead at the junction. Pass a couple of idyllically situated cottages, including one painted yellow, and continue ahead to rejoin the road at the **Falls of Dochart**.

Extension around Auchmore Circuit

From the Falls of Dochart, to add the extension around Auchmore Circuit, walk south along the A827 past the Falls of Dochart Inn, then turn left down a road indicated 'Ardeonaig South Loch Tay' on a large road sign and 'Auchmore Circuit' on a smaller wooden sign below. Follow this road for 130 metres around a left turn, at the next corner (when the road turns right) turn off left onto a track marked 'Auchmore'. Look out for red squirrels along this route. Continue along the Auchmore Estate track through woodland for 1.3km with views over farmland and Loch Tay. Cross Auchmore Burn via a stone bridge and immediately take the right fork onto a narrow track that climbs gently uphill. Continue for 670 metres through mixed woodland until you reach the South Loch Tay Road.

Turn sharply right onto the quiet road and continue straight ahead, back west, for 2.3km.

WALK 19
Meall Glas and Sgiath Chùil (from Glen Lochay)

Start/finish	Glen Lochay car park NN 477 368
Time	8hr
Distance	21.5km (13.4 miles)
Total ascent	1150m (3800ft)
Terrain	Tracks, paths and pathless grassy hill, some of which is very steep indeed
Max altitude	Meall Glas 959m (3146ft)
Maps	OS Explorer OL49; OS Landranger 51; Harvey *Trossachs North*
Public transport	No public transport
Parking	Free parking at Glen Lochay car park (10km/6.2 miles) west of Killin, just east of Kenknock Farm)

This pair of awkward Munros lie on the national park's northern border. To keep the walk within the boundaries of Loch Lomond and The Trossachs, you could approach from the south, but this involves precarious verge parking along the fast and busy A85 followed by an arduous, boggy approach. You might choose that option if you're in a real hurry to get round the Munros, as it's 6km shorter; but the route described here has much less frightening parking, as well as being generally more peaceful and pleasant. Glen Lochay lies at the heart of green and grassy Breadalbane; there's nothing particularly dramatic here, but the gentle slopes give way to replanted native woodland and tumbling riverbanks popular with wildlife.

This route includes a wide, unbridged ford, which is not usually deep, but could become problematic in spate. It also has some unpathed sections and a very steep, grassy descent and ascent between the two hills.

Head south-west down the track from the car park past **Kenknock Farm**. After 1.2km, go straight at a crossroads (the bridge on the left will be on the return route), continue through a gate and then cross a bridge over **Innisraineach Burn**. Keep heading south-west along the track for a further 1.7km heading up **Glen Lochay**. When you reach a junction where a gate leads down to a ford and a house (**Lubchurran**) on the south side of **River Lochay**, turn left through the gate and cross the ford.

Walk 19 – Meall Glas and Sgiath Chùil (from Glen Lochay)

Go through another two gates on the opposite bank and follow the track south around the right-hand side of the house (passing through two more gates). Follow the track as it climbs with **Lubchurran Burn** on the left and up past a small waterfall. Keep ahead as the track heads south for 2.2km, rising above Lubchurran Burn and passing through a gated area of native tree planting. Then continue for a further 800 metres as it swings round to the right, contouring west then north-west around the flank of Beinn Cheathaich. Gaining the wide, grassy northern ridgeline of Beinn Cheathaich, the track ends abruptly – continue along the trodden path ahead briefly, then follow it left to climb south.

The path is easily lost to mossy grass, but follow the ridgeline and you'll find it again higher up as the shoulder narrows. After 1.1km and 235m ascent, you'll reach the trig point at the summit of **Beinn Cheathaich** (937m). Turn right here and follow a small path south-west down to a bealach. Continue west along the path, which leads round the right-hand side of the ridgeline then climbs easily to the cairned summit of **Meall Glas** (959m).

Meall Glas means 'Grey Hump' and while it's not the region's most spectacular mountain, it does have good views of Beinn Challuim (Walk 24) to the west and Ben More (Walk 13) to the south, as well as across the endless grassy hills of further Breadalbane.

Crossing the River Lochay in dry conditions

WALKING LOCH LOMOND AND THE TROSSACHS

WALK 19 – MEALL GLAS AND SGIATH CHÙIL (FROM GLEN LOCHAY)

Fog at the summit of Meall Glas

Retrace your steps for 1.2km to the bealach below Beinn Cheathaich, then turn right onto a trodden path leading east. This path is soon lost, but continue east (passing south of Beinn Cheathaich's summit) and descend Beinn Cheathaich, avoiding crags on the right by picking your way down a steep, grassy gully (NN 445 325).

Meall a' Churain is ahead across the boggy pass of Lairig a' Churain. Pick up and follow a path weaving its way east around the worst of the bog, then bear left (north-east) to climb a lesser gradient of steep grass to arrive on the ridgeline north of Meall a' Churain. Once you've gained the ridgeline, turn right and pick up a path which leads south over **Meall a' Churain** (917m) and to **Sgiath Chùil** (921m) without any further difficulty.

From the summit of Sgiath Chùil, which has a cairn, retrace your steps back over Meall a' Churain, then continue north down a lumpy ridgeline, which soon becomes pathless. Descend north-north-east to **Allt Innis Daimh** with its rocky stream bed, cross the burn and continue north on its eastern bank.

After 760 metres, cross a joining burn and continue 150 metres to a point where Allt Innis Daimh tumbles into a deep gorge. Head around the east side of the gorge then continue until you meet a path at a small dam. Bear right and follow this path north-north-east for 300 metres to another hydro works and the start of a track.

Turn right onto the track via a gate or stile and follow it as it descends down a couple of hairpin bends. Cross the bridge over the **River Lochay** then turn right onto the track at the crossroads ahead. Follow your outward steps for 1.2km back to the car park.

PART 5 TYNDRUM

Ben Lui (left) and Beinn Chuirn (right) seen from the River Cononish (Walk 23)

In the far north-west is the tiny village of Tyndrum. It's endlessly popular with walkers who make pit stops in the pub, enjoy a hearty meal from the Real Food Café, or replenish their supplies from The Green Welly Stop shop. Spend a few nights at By The Way campsite, however, and you'll quickly discover that 95% of those walkers are trudging down the West Highland Way. There's talk of sore feet and heavy bags and whether a plastic poncho proved sufficient for the most recent deluge – but you're not there for all that. The hills around Tyndrum are big, green and grassy with expansive views; perhaps they lack the rocky drama of Arrochar Alps or the knobbly crags found further south, but these hills have a character of their own – it's one best enjoyed as clouds drift over the landscape, creating patches of shadow and light as wind blows ripples across the broad grassy slopes. Then there is Ben Lui, a different beast altogether and arguably the finest mountain in the whole region.

WALK 20
Glen Cononish

Start/finish	Tyndrum NN 329 306
Time	2hr
Distance	7.3km (4.5 miles)
Total ascent	125m (410ft)
Terrain	Forest roads and well-built paths
Max altitude	Forest south of Tyndrum 305m (1001ft)
Maps	OS Explorer OL39; OS Landranger 56; Harvey *Trossachs North*
Public transport	Bus stop and train stations in village
Parking	Free daytime parking at The Green Welly Stop

This walk is short, sheltered and easy underfoot. After some uneventful forest road, Glen Cononish is enjoyably wild, dominated above by Ben Lui and with some ancient Scots pines across the River Cononish. The woodland along the West Highland Way is also enjoyable, despite the rumble of the A82, and passes a pretty lochan associated with Robert the Bruce.

Start in **Tyndrum** centre. Head out north-west towards Fort William and Oban, crossing a footbridge alongside the **A82**, then turn left crossing the road onto a street signposted as the **West Highland Way**. Pass a few houses and just beyond the end of the tarmac turn right on a well-made path indicated, 'Cattle Creep Trail'. Follow this as it crosses bog and then a small wooden footbridge, to a bridge under the Oban railway. The cobbled stream bed, normally mostly dry, is the Cattle Creep, providing field-to-field access for farm animals.

Walk under the railway bridge and then follow a path, which heads up beside a stony stream: this is the sterile outwash from old lead mines on Sron nan Colan. The streambed contains chunks of quartz vein, and shattered faultline rocks bound with quartz.

After 100 metres a waymark points to the left (a path on the right zigzags up through the old workings onto Sron nan Colan). Take this wide path left, above the railway line, to a track above Tyndrum Lower Station. Turn right, signed for Ben Lui, away from the station just below. Keep to the forest track for 2.25km as it climbs gently, then descends to **Glen Cononish** where you come out at a gate.

WALKING LOCH LOMOND AND THE TROSSACHS

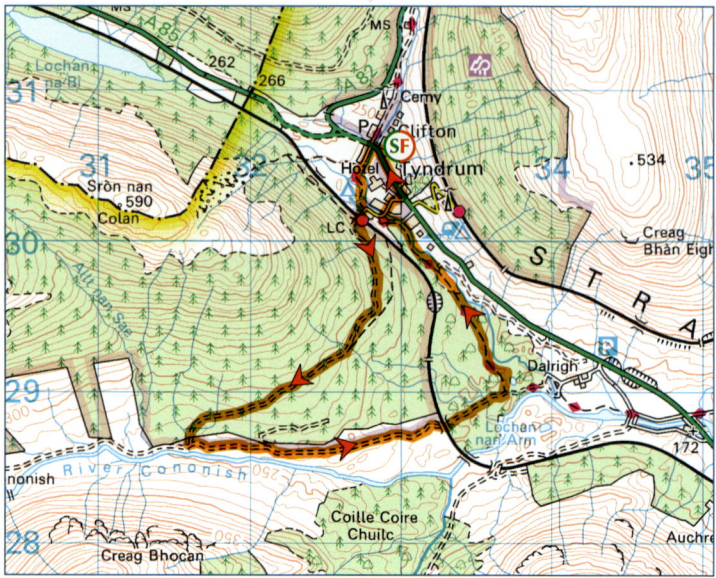

Go through the gate and at the track 'T' here, you could turn right and ramble up the glen for the views of Ben Lui, before returning downstream. Otherwise, turn left and follow the track down the valley for 1.75km to a **railway bridge**.

Pass under the railway into scrubby woodland, then after 450 metres turn left onto the well-made **West Highland Way** path. In 50 metres pass a small lochan, The **Lochan of the Lost Sword**.

> Legend tells that **The Lochan of the Lost Sword** is where Robert the Bruce threw away his long-sword when trying to escape from some MacDougalls of Lorne, who caught up with him anyway 10 minutes later.

Continue along the good path through regenerating Scots pine, birch and heather along an elevated ridge with a river below on the right, then follow it across a patch of bare stony ground poisoned by the ore-crushing plant of the lead mines. Go through a gate and ignore the cycle path on the right to continue ahead up a gravel path, which enters mature pines at the edge of **Tyndrum**. At the first street turn right, to the village centre.

An old dam by the Cattle Creep

WALK 21
Beinn Odhar

Start/finish	Tyndrum NN 329 306
Alternative start/finish	Dalrigh car park NN 344 291
Time	5hr 15min
Distance	13.7km (8.5 miles)
Total ascent	765m (2510ft)
Terrain	Grassy slopes, track and path
Max altitude	Beinn Odhar 901m (2986ft)
Maps	OS Explorer 377; OS Landranger 50; Harvey *Trossachs North*
Public transport	Bus stop and train stations in village
Parking	Free daytime parking at The Green Welly Stop

Another 13m (45ft) of altitude would make Beinn Odhar a Munro, with a hundredfold increase in visitors and an eroded path. But Beinn Odhar completely lacks rocky features and doesn't feel much like a mountain. From the north it's an impressive steep cone, but from Tyndrum the remains of an old path lead up reasonably angled grass; and the south ridge via Meall Buidhe is a splendidly gentle descent route. A stretch of the West Highland Way completes a day that feels far too gentle for something a few metres short of a Munro.

Start in **Tyndrum** centre. Head out north-west towards Fort William and Oban, crossing a footbridge alongside the **A82**, then turn right up the **West Highland Way** past the small grocers. Follow the lane, which becomes a track, passes a graveyard then crosses the railway after 1.3km.

Just over the bridge, turn off right up grassy slopes. Find an old grassy path leading up the spur above **Crom Allt** and follow this north-north-east. At just above 600m, follow the path as it slants out left onto the south-western spur, which it follows up to a shoulder at 750m. Here there is a small **lochan** and tiny stream. Head up a stony slope to the summit of **Beinn Odhar** (901m).

Descend south-east, quite steeply at first, to **Lochan Choire Dhuibh**. Pass to its right hand where the ridge eases to give fast, easy walking with a small path heading south. After another tiny lochan and a peaty col, climb a slight ascent to

Looking over Coire Thòin to Meall Buidhe and the Munros south-east, including Ben More and Stob Binnein

Meall Buidhe (653m). The ridge, now slightly rougher, continues south, with a swampy col leading to the final rise with **cairn** (534m).

Descend towards Strath Fillan south-south-east to a gate at a fence junction. Go through two gates – one metal and one wooden – then walk downhill inside the fence line aiming for Auchtertyre Farm ahead. A line of fence posts then guides you straight downhill to a footbridge over the **railway** (NN 350 293). Note: this bridge was blocked by a fence at the time of research; it's passable at your own discretion or you can follow the railway bank 460 metres east to cross there.

Having crossed the railway, follow another fence down to a gate on the right, go through this and cross a small burn, descending alongside a wall on your left-hand side to a metal gate, which brings you out onto a minor road; this is part of the **West Highland Way**. Here, turn right (west) towards the A82.

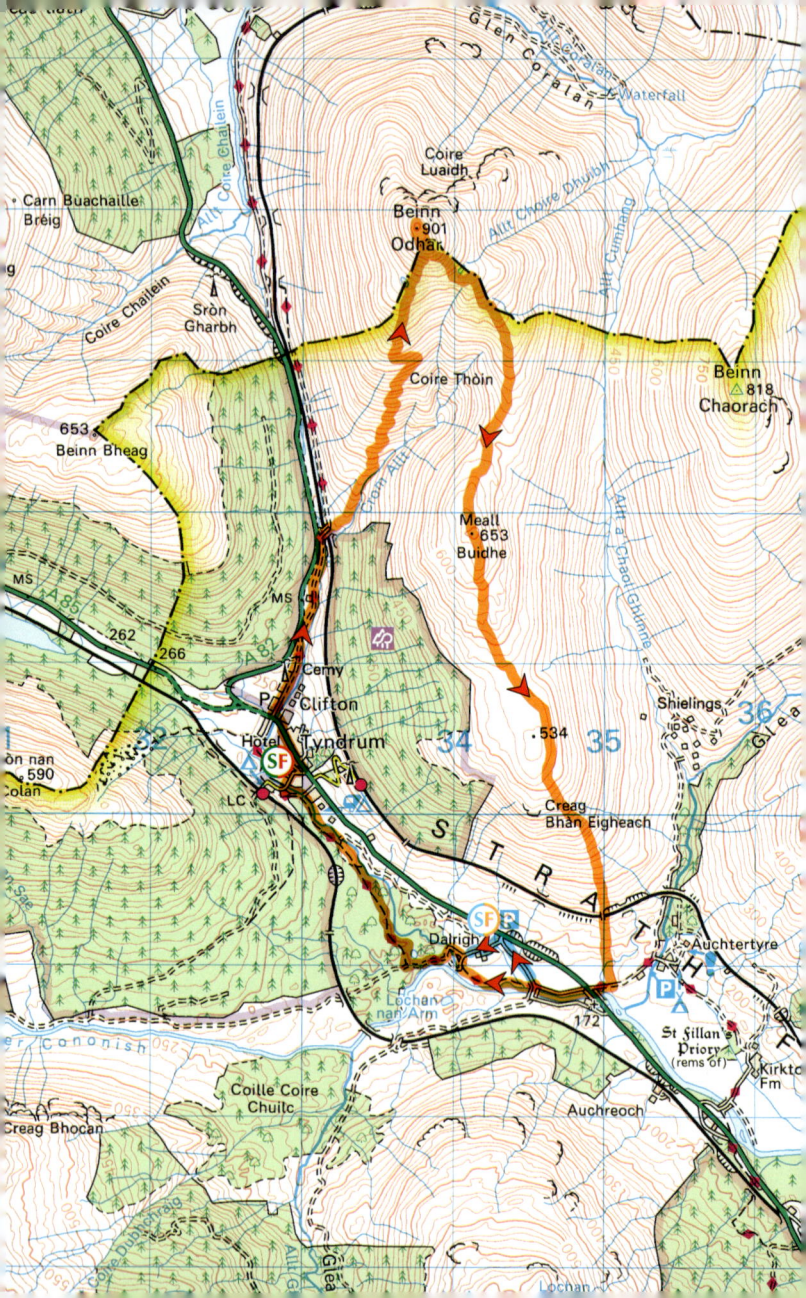

WALK 21 – BEINN ODHAR

Beinn Challium looming over Beinn Chaorach east of Meall Buidhe

As a minor detour, directly opposite a short path (choose the right fork, don't go over the stile) leads to the **Holy Pool**, used by St Fillan for baptisms, but in later centuries for magic dunkings that were believed to cure insanity. The waters are said to have lost their powers after a wild bull was thrown into them.

Coming out at the **A82**, dip left under the road to the tarred path of the West Highland Way that follows the River Fillan west to a tarred track at White Bridge (where a right turn leads to the **Dalrigh car park**, NN 344 291, an alternative start for the walk). Cross the tarred track but not the river, continuing along the north bank on waymarked West Highland Way path. Pass **Dalrigh battlefield**. Dalrigh is the site of a small skirmish involving Robert the Bruce in 1306. Dalrigh means 'Field of the King'.

Near Dalrigh houses, continue to follow the West Highland Way as it turns off left to join a new track, which crosses a wooded side-stream. After 350 metres turn right following indications for the West Highland Way, at once passing the Lochan of the Lost Sword.

Follow the good path, which continues a little up to the left of the stream through regenerating Scots pine and heather. It enters mature pine forest to reach the edge of **Tyndrum**. At the first street, turn right to the village centre.

Walking Loch Lomond and the Trossachs

WALK 22
Ben Lui via Dubhchraig and Oss

Start/finish	Dalrigh car park (free) off A82 south-east of Tyndrum NN 344 291
Alternative start	Walking in from Tyndrum via West Highland Way adds 1.5km (1 mile) each way
Time	9hr 30min; escape route excluding Ben Lui: 8hr; including Beinn a' Chleibh: 11hr 15min
Distance	23.6km (14.7 miles); excluding Ben Lui: 21.9km (13.6 miles); including Beinn a' Chleibh: 25.9km (16.1 miles)
Total ascent	1515m (4970ft); excluding Ben Lui: 1080m (3540ft); including Beinn a' Chleibh: 1644m (5390ft)
Terrain	Track and narrow paths with one unexposed scramble moment
Max altitude	Ben Lui 1130m (3707ft)
Maps	OS Explorer OL39; OS Landranger 50; Harvey *Trossachs North*
Parking	Dalrigh car park is free

This meaty hike summits three fine Munros connected by small paths along a high ridgeline. The highlight is Ben Lui: the mountain rises in five converging ridges to an airy peak, which towers above the rest and is visible from half the Highlands. While maps use the anglicised spelling, the Gaelic *Beinn Laoigh* is sometimes seen, with the same pronunciation. It translates as 'Mountain of the Calves' – a name which is more likely to refer to deer than cows. It's many people's favourite Munro within the southern Highlands.

If – through choice or necessity – you're leaving Ben Lui for another time, Beinn Dubhchraig and Ben Oss make for a very respectable day's walk on their own. The route described here also offers this possibility.

Beinn a' Chleibh is an awkward outlier, and actually 150 metres beyond the national park boundary, but to save a later ascent, the option to add this forth Munro is also included.

Leave **Dalrigh** car park south-east, turning left onto a track and going through a gate. Continue for 270 metres, then cross a bridge over the **River Fillan**. Turn right onto a track heading west-south-west, which soon runs alongside the railway.

After about 1km, cross the railway on a stone bridge, then turn right onto a smaller path heading west. After 300 metres, cross a curved wooden bridge over the **Allt Gleann Auchreoch** and bear left onto a path. Follow the path, which is boggy at times, south and then south-west as it rises through woodland, leaving the riverbank behind.

COILLE COIRE CHUILC

The trees here are native Scots pines and the woodland itself, Coille Coire Chuilc, is protected as an SSSI. A remnant of the former Caledonian Forest – a vast ecosystem dominated by Britain's only native pine tree that's estimated to have covered 1.5 million hectares at its largest point around 7000 years ago – Coille Coire Chuilc was isolated by early fragmentation of the forest and consequently the pines have developed a unique genetic structure. This ancient pinewood also supports a rich ecosystem including several rare invertebrates, including 11 nationally scarce species of beetle, for which it is also protected.

The path begins to follow the course of the **Allt Coire Dubhchraig**, passing above a waterfall on the left and crossing a ruined fence and ladder stile after 1.5km. Keep alongside this burn, crossing a couple of smaller burns as they join it, and follow the path as it climbs south-west for a further 2.5km. The route leaves the woodland and rises to the broad ridge north-west of Beinn Dubhchraig near some pools (NN 304 258). Turn left here and climb south-east for 500 metres (with only 50m of ascent) to the summit of **Beinn Dubhchraig** (978m) and its cairn, which has a fine view over Loch Lomond.

A pool in the Allt Coire Dubhchraig

WALKING LOCH LOMOND AND THE TROSSACHS

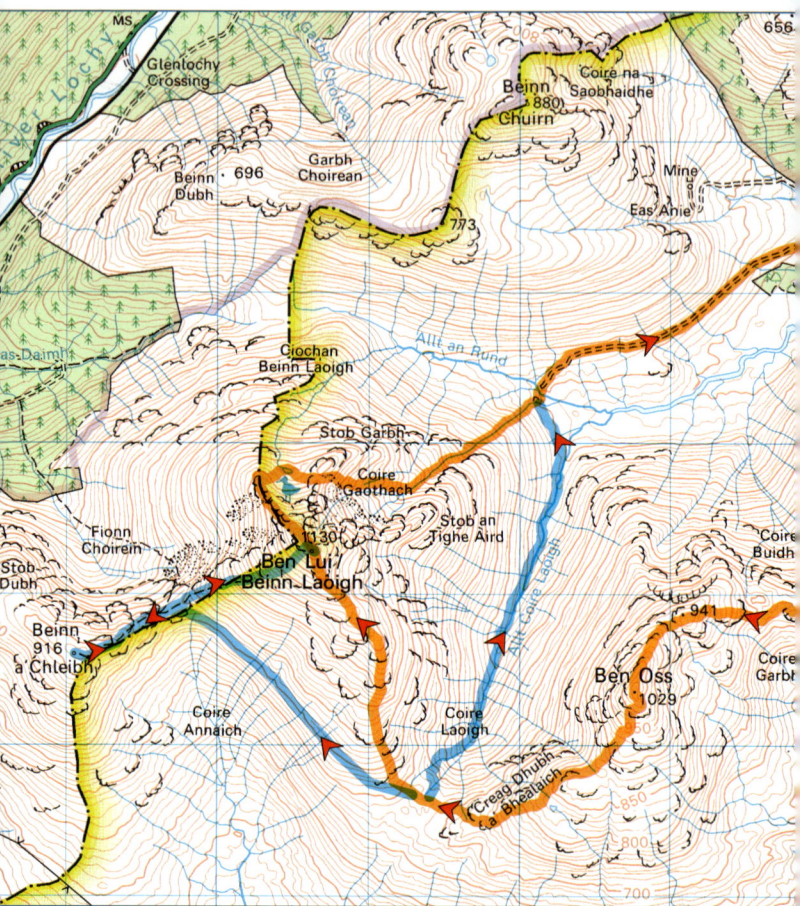

Return the same way to the pools, then turn left and descend to Bealach Buidhe. Here there is a great view over Loch Oss and the steep south-western face of Beinn Dubhchraig which gave the Munro, 'Mountain of the Black Rock', its name. As the path starts to plateau, look out for a junction with a tiny cairn (NN 296 258); turn right here onto a fainter path which climbs west to the 941m-high point on the ridge north of Ben Oss.

WALK 22 – BEN LUI VIA DUBHCHRAIG AND OSS

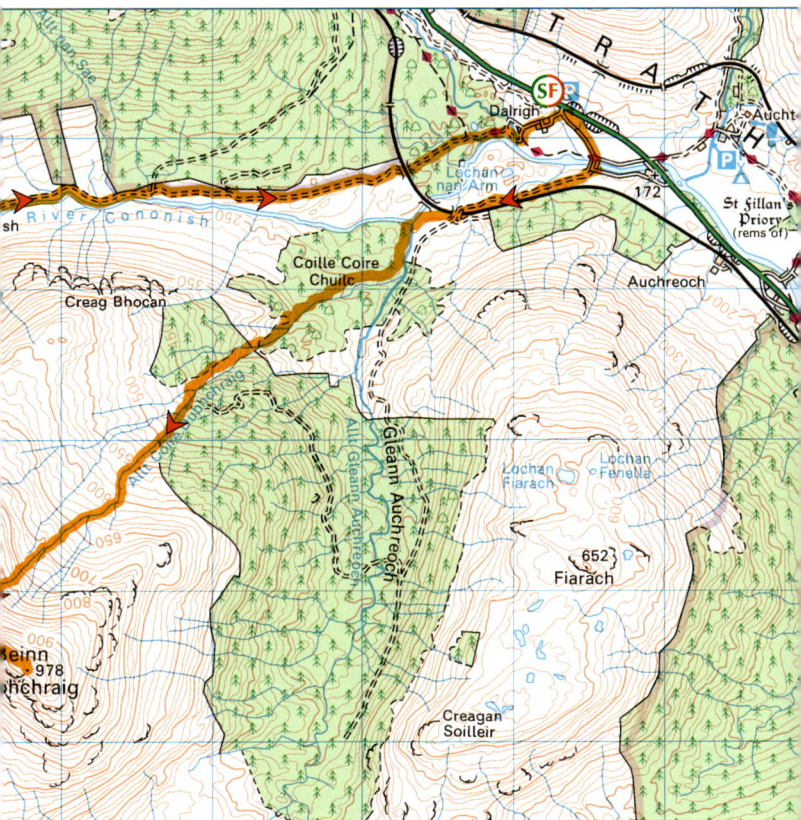

Head south-west then south-south-west for 650 metres along the broad ridge to the summit of **Ben Oss** (1029m), where there is a cairn. The imposing eastern face of Ben Lui dominates the scene to the west.

Follow faint paths down the wide ridgeline south, then bend south-west into the wide knolly col between Ben Oss and Lui.

In 2011, experts and surveyors from the Tay Western Catchments Partnership identified the **Allt Coire Laoigh**, which runs down from here, as the source of the Tay, the longest river in Scotland.

If conditions are unfavourable or your legs have had enough, you can make an escape from here to the track through Glen Cononish: walk down steeply on the west side of **Allt Coire Laoigh**, then skirt round the eastern foot of Ben Lui, passing a ruin and crossing **Allt an Rund** to join the track. Then follow the return described at the end of this route.

Adding Beinn a' Chleibh

Cross the Oss/Lui col, then contour out left onto the south-west slope of Ben Lui. It is steep, and grassy, and named Sgiath Dhubh (Black Wing) on some maps. Contour along it north-west for 2km, rising slightly towards the 776m col joining Ben Lui to Beinn a' Chleibh.

Note: Incised stream valleys run down Sgiath Dhubh, and in mist it is not easy to maintain a level route without a GPS or altimeter. If you do maintain your level, then it should be easy to recognise the change in the downslope from south-west (on the side of Sgiath Dhubh/Ben Lui) to south as you arrive below the Chleibh col. If you arrive too high, you'll have to watch out for the fairly clear intersecting path which descends from Ben Lui, and a more subtle change of slope.

Join a path, which follows the well-defined ridge across the Cleibh col and up to the 916m summit of **Beinn a' Chleibh**. A small pool decorates the summit plateau beyond the cairn.

Return across the Cleibh col and follow a reasonably clear path uphill east-north-east. It follows a poorly defined spur, to arrive on Ben Lui's summit ridge at the low point between its north-west summit and its main one. Turn right, crossing a short rocky slab (avoidable on the right) to the main summit.

Main route

To continue to Ben Lui from the Oss/Lui col, head up the grassy ridge north, then north-west as the ridge becomes more defined and a path forms, to the airy summit of **Ben Lui** (1130m).

Follow the pathed ridgeline north-west around the rim above Coire Gaothach, with one small rocky moment avoidable on the left. At the lowest point of the short ridge, a stony path heads down left for Beinn a' Chleibh, but continue ahead bending right, up to the north-west top – it's almost as airy as the true summit.

Continue around the corrie rim for about 30 metres, to where a steep spur down to the right is Coire Gaothach's northern ridge. Do not take this spur, but instead bear left down the pathed north-west ridge of Ben Lui. On the way down the ridge has a genuine scramble moment, on clean rock with good holds and not exposed.

At 960m the ridge becomes grassy and less steep. Turn down right, into Coire an Lochain with its pools (on Landranger maps this corrie is unnamed, but marked with a blue duck).

Ben Oss from Glen Cononish

Cross Coire an Lochain below the pools, and ease up right to a col on the ridge beyond (this is Coire Gaothach's northern ridge again). On the col, which has a small cairn, you meet a path coming down from the right. Follow it as it descends ahead in zigzags towards **Coire Gaothach**. Continue west across Coire Gaothach to a junction marked with a small cairn next to Allt Coire Ghaothaich – turn left here.

Follow the path as it runs down to left of the burn, dropping steeply out of the corrie. At the valley floor below, continue past a stone ruin and ford the **Allt an Rund** to the beginning of a track.

In 1741, lead was discovered in **Glen Cononish** by Sir Robert Clifton who extracted 1697 tons over the next four years until, in 1745, The Campbell of Argyll Militia occupied the mine on account of Clifton's Jacobite politics. An 18th-century plan of the lead mines depicts two buildings at the location of this ruin, naming them Moenlea.

Follow the track for 5.6km out along Glen Cononish, passing above Cononish farm and alongside **River Cononish**, to a railway bridge. Pass under the bridge, cross a stile beside a cattle grid, and continue for 640 metres, ignoring a sign-posted turning for the West Highland Way on your left (leading to the Lochan of the Lost Sword, Walk 20) and keeping to the track. At the next junction, take the right fork down to a bridge over the Crom Alt just above its confluence with the River Fallon. Cross the bridge, then turn left. Keep ahead for 200 metres, then continue around the left side of the houses at **Dalrigh** towards the A82. Before you reach the main road, turn off right to the car park.

WALK 23

Ben Lui via Chuirn and Dubh

Start/finish	Dalrigh car park off A82 south-east of Tyndrum NN 344 291
Alternative start	Walking in from Tyndrum via West Highland Way adds 1.5km (1 mile) each way
Time	9hr 30min; escape route excluding Ben Lui: 6hr 30min.
Distance	24km (14.9 miles); excluding Ben Lui 20.2km (12.6 miles)
Total ascent	1450m (4750ft); excluding Ben Lui: 740m (2430ft)
Terrain	Track, pathless hillside and narrow rocky paths with one unexposed scrambling move
Max altitude	Ben Lui 1130m (3707ft)
Maps	OS Explorer OL39; OS Landranger 50; Harvey *Trossachs North*
Parking	Dalrigh car park is free

Apart from the long track through Glen Cononish and a helpful, rocky route down from Ben Lui, this walk is largely pathless and requires some careful navigation as well as grassy route-finding between crags, particularly up the imposing northern face of Ben Lui. It's harder work than the Dubhchraig, Oss and Lui circuit (Walk 22) and rather than bagging three Munros, you only collect one, along with a Corbett (Beinn Chuirn) and the nothing-in-particular summit of Beinn Dubh.

So, why bother? Well, this route won't be for everyone, but it has a sense of adventure that's hard to find on the popular Munros, there are spectacular views of Ben Lui's most impressive north side as well as the Highlands laid out further north, and a comfortable grassy ridgeline leads along the very edge of the national park between Beinn Chuirn and Beinn Dubh.

If it's taking longer than you thought, or conditions look unfavourable for route-finding up Ben Lui, a simple escape route leads back to the safety of the track out through Glen Cononish.

Leave **Dalrigh** car park in the direction of the main road, but before you get there, turn off left down past a few houses and onto a track marked 'Mine Vehicles on Track' heading south-west. Keep to the main track as it bears left down to a bridge

Descending Beinn Chuirn towards Beinn Dubh

over the Crom Allt just above its confluence with the River Fillan. Cross the bridge and turn right onto a track. At the junction 160 metres afterwards continue ahead, bearing left (west). Keep heading west along this track for another 680 metres to a railway bridge, passing two cattlegrids and ignoring the West Highland Way leading off to the right.

Go under the **railway bridge** and immediately take the right fork at a junction. Continue west along the track through **Glen Cononish** for 3.3km to **Cononish Farm** with a couple of cute white houses and some large barns. Beinn Chuirn rises in a picturesque fashion behind the farm, while Ben Lui looms at the end of the glen. Continue along the track past the farm, now heading south-west. Keep to the track for a further 1.2km passing through a gate, ignoring a sign for Eas Anie waterfall, and going through another gate adjacent to the west corner of a patch of forest.

The ascent of Beinn Chuirn begins unobviously at the Corbett's south-eastern foot: 330 metres past the last gate near the west corner of the small forest, look out for a few stones in a pile (NN 292 279) and some slightly trodden ground leading uphill to the right. This is as good a starting point as any, avoiding the crags around Eas Anie waterfall and the gold mine area, to which entry is prohibited.

Cononish orebody was first drilled in 1985 and, a few years later, a tunnel was dug along the vein into the southern slopes of Beinn Chuirn. Today the gold contained is said to be worth £200 million, but several companies have already tried and failed to extract significant amounts. Operations stopped in 2023 but are due to restart since the mine was bought by a South African mining technology group in early 2025.

WALKING LOCH LOMOND AND THE TROSSACHS

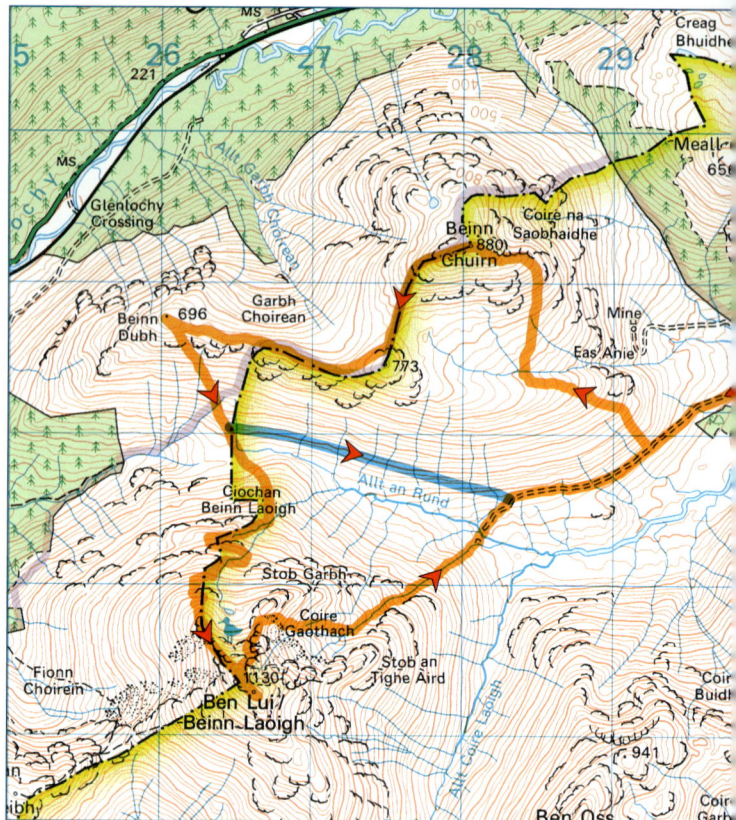

Climb directly uphill (north-north-west) for 300 metres to around the 480m elevation point, then bear left (west-north-west) for a further 700 metres to reach 650m and avoid losing any unnecessary height as you cross Allt Eas Anie. Cross this burn (NN 284 284), then head just east of north for 700 metres, aiming for the south-east shoulder of Beinn Chuirn. Turn left and walk west along rocky slabs and moss, with crags dropping off into **Coire na Saobhaidhe** to the right, to reach the cairned summit of **Beinn Chuirn** (880m).

To descend, follow old fence posts west-south-west for 400 metres, then south-south-west for a further 560 metres, then contour around the north-west

WALK 23 – BEN LUI VIA CHUIRN AND DUBH

side of an unnamed high point between Beinn Chuirn and Beinn Dubh. Continue to Beinn Dubh along a broad, level, grassy ridgeline with great views back to Beinn Chuirn as well as the intimidating northern face of Ben Lui. Climb a short way to the flat summit of **Beinn Dubh** (696m), where a small cairn marks a place that might be the highest point.

From Beinn Dubh, descend south-east down grassy slopes to a boggy col at the head of **Allt an Rund**, aiming just left of a couple of small pools. For a quick escape, follow the valley east, walking along above Allt an Rund, until you reach the track leading north-east out through Glen Cononish. The north face of Ben Lui ahead is high and complex. Immediately above are the **Ciochan Beinn Laoigh**; slant up left below this crag and continue south for 190 metres towards the next crag band, where Allt Coire an Lochain drops over in a waterfall.

A few metres to the right of the waterfall, climb a ramp of grass bypassing the steep rock. Now, turn right to walk up a grassy little valley for 400 metres west-south-west, passing below a smaller waterfall. Just before you reach a small pool, head back up left to gain the top of the next crag and cross the smaller waterfall stream as a rough path forms briefly. As you reach Allt Coire an Lochain once again, continue upstream then bear off right (south-west) across grass to gain Ben Lui's north-western ridge on the west side of Coire an Lochain with its pools.

Continue south-east up the ridge, which is joined by a path. It is grassy then rocky with a short scrambling move (good holds and not exposed) before arriving at **Ben Lui**'s north-west top. Walk a further 200 metres south-west to the summit (1130m) with its large cairn.

Return to the north-west top, then descend north-north-east on a small, rocky path along the ridge between Ben Lui and the slight rise of **Stob Garbh**. Coire an Lochain with its pools is on the left and the more dramatic Coire Gaothach drops down to the right. At the low point between Ben Lui and Stob Garbh, there is a small cairn. Turn right here and follow the continuing path as it descends into **Coire Gaothach**.

Continue east across the coire to a junction marked with another small cairn next to Allt Coire Ghaothaich and turn left to continue descending. Follow the path as it runs down to left of the burn towards the valley floor below. At the bottom, continue past a ruined building and ford the **Allt an Rund** to the beginning of a track.

Follow the track back out through **Glen Cononish**. After 1.3km it rejoins your outward route. Retrace your steps to the car park.

Climbing the south-east shoulder of Beinn Chuirn

WALK 24
Beinn Challuim and Two Corbetts

Start/finish	Auchtertyre Farm car park (free) NN 352 290
Alternative start	Tyndrum
Time	7hr 30min; walking in from Tyndrum via the West Highland Way adds 45min each way
Distance	17km (10.6 miles); walking in from Tyndrum adds 3.4km (2.1 miles) each way
Total ascent	1345m (4410ft)
Terrain	Pathless grassy slopes and hill path
Max altitude	Beinn Challuim 1025m (3363ft)
Maps	OS Explorer 377; OS Landranger 50; Harvey *Trossachs North*

Beinn Challuim is a mountain of some majesty, with a steep broken north face. This route approaches it by a natural horseshoe over two Corbetts: the grassy Beinn Chaorach (appropriately, 'Sheep Hill') and the rugged Cam Chreag ('Crooked Crag'). This leads to a rocky mountain spur at the back of Beinn Challuim. The long grass slope that provides the standard up-and-down for Munro-baggers then supplies a comfortable path for most of the descent.

Well-grazed, the going is not too tough despite most of the route being pathless; however, the descent of Cam Chreag and ascent of Beinn Challuim are rather steep.

From **Auchtertyre Farm** car park continue towards the farm then cross a bridge over the Allt Auchtertyre then take the first left following a sign, 'All abilities path to waterfall'. (Note: this site was changing hands at the time of research, so be prepared for alterations to signs/buildings around the farm and wigwams.) Walk on a track beside the river upstream for 110 metres, past a hydroelectric powerhouse, then turn off left onto a small path following the same sign. Shortly afterwards, take a left fork to stay by the river, pass a waterfall and continue beside and above the river.

After 370 metres, climb steps up to a viaduct, go under the bridge on a track and through a gate. Follow the track as it climbs for about 70 metres, then leave to the left (north) to follow the line of a double fence on the right of a forest.

WALKING LOCH LOMOND AND THE TROSSACHS

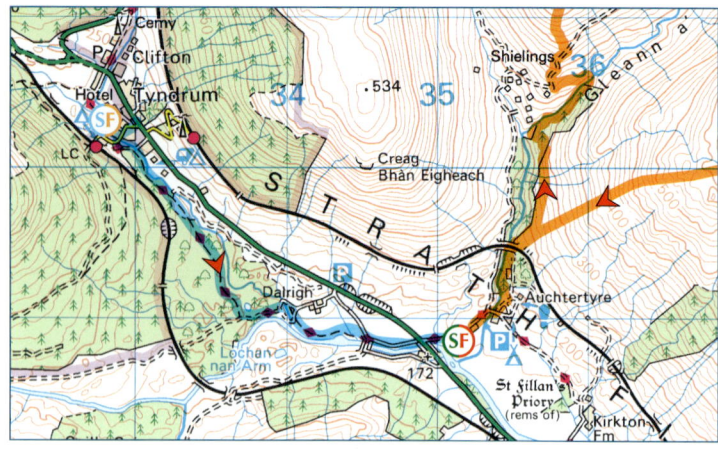

Continue north outside the fences for 650 metres to a stile on the left and an old sign for 'Lower Gorge Woodland'. Cross the stile and head north-north-west to a wooden walkway and overgrown path down to **Allt Gleann a' Chlachain**. At the riverbank, turn right to walk upstream along an overgrown path for 530 metres to a bridge below a weir.

Cross the bridge and head up through a gate on a track. Where this joins a higher track at a T-junction after 280 metres, turn up right for a further 290 metres

Descending to the saddle between Beinn Chaorach and Cam Chreag

WALK 24 – BEINN CHALLUIM AND TWO CORBETTS

following a couple of zigzags. The stone ruins of some old shielings are just south and west of this junction. As the track contours off to the right, continue straight up the grassy spur of **Beinn Chaorach**, crossing a fence at a low point, and continuing to climb up to the trig point on its top (818m).

Continue along a gentle ridge that leads down northwards, with the low posts of a derelict electric fence. Then, from the saddle, follow a narrow path along a line of old fence posts up grassy slopes which lead north-east, then east, to **Cam Chreag**. The first knoll of the ridge is the 884m summit.

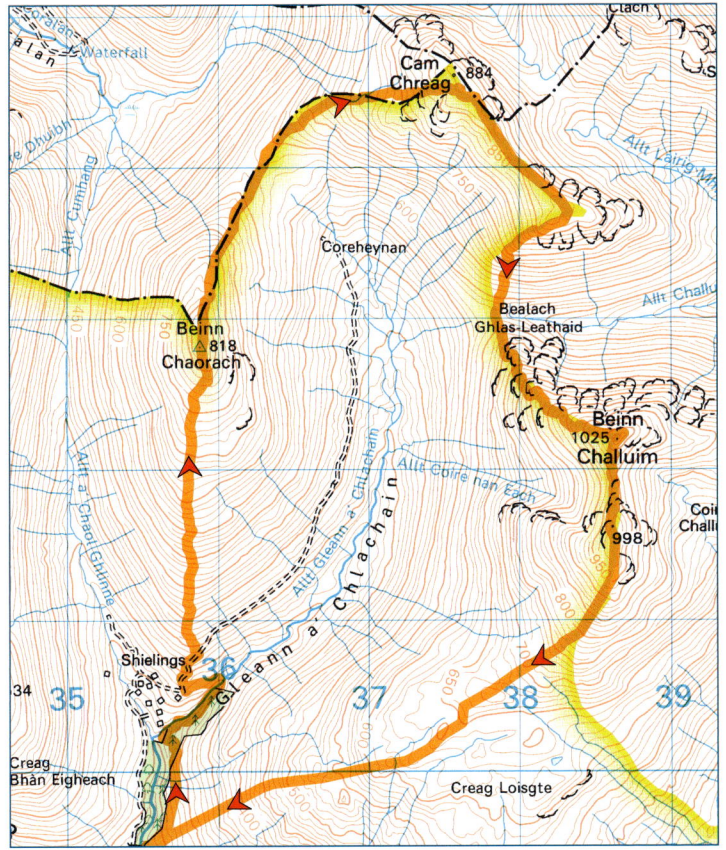

Now follow the bumpy ridgeline south-east, with steep drops on the left and Beinn Challuim looming large on the right. The final summit of Cam Chreag (875m, NN 384 337) has a quartz vein running up it. Here turn sharp back right, past a couple of pools, to a knoll at the corner of the plateau. Head down a spur, south-west, soon with a ruined fence and wall to guide you down to the col, **Bealach Ghlas-Leathaid** (575m).

The fence posts continue up the steep north-west ridge of Beinn Challuim. Continue along them until, at about 750m, they end below craggy slabs. About 30 metres to right of the fence top a grassy groove runs up the slabs, with a move or two of low-grade scrambling. Otherwise, the obstacle can be bypassed on grass slopes to the left (east). Above this, a knobby outcrop can be bypassed on the right.

Now at 800m, the ridge changes its character, becoming smooth and stony to **Beinn Challuim**'s summit cairn (1025m).

To descend, depart south-west, soon picking up the well-worn path. This turns south, and follows a subsidiary mini-ridge to pass to right of the 998m south top. As the ground steepens, continue as the worn path follows old fencing down south-west, to cross a small rise 698m (NN 378 305).

Just beyond this, where the fence takes a left turn, continue to follow it for 110 metres to the sad remains of a stile (NN 376 303) on the right. Cross this onto a very small path south-west. Continuing on the main path would lead down beside fences to a level crossing just above Kirkton Farm, for a finish along the West Highland Way. Follow the new path as it crosses one fence and continues to reach a second one. Turn downhill alongside this, with the path gradually fading. At a junction with contouring fence, head straight downhill on rough grass to the viaduct above **Auchtertyre farm**.

Pass under the viaduct and retrace your outward steps to the car park.

PART 6 CRIANLARICH TO INVERARNAN

Taking a break on Parlan Hill with Beinn Chabhair in the background (Walk 26)

Both the villages of Crianlarich and Inverarnan are very small indeed, although Crianlarich – at the convergence of Strath Fillan, Glen Dochart and Glen Falloch, as well as roads A82 and A85 – has a train station, shop and a few places to eat or sleep. This section focuses on the scattering of Munros between them, south-east of Glen Falloch and the A82. The peaks of An Caisteal, Beinn a' Chroin and Beinn Chabhair have narrow, winding paths, which lead between rocky knolls and crags with a scattering of pretty lochans, grassy glens and views out to the north end of Loch Lomond or the continuing mountain range east; the Munros above Inverlochlarig (Beinn Tulaichean, Cruach Ardrain, Stob Binnein and Ben More) are covered in Part 3 instead.

WALKING LOCH LOMOND AND THE TROSSACHS

WALK 25
An Caisteal and Beinn a' Chroin Horseshoe

Start/finish	A83 lay-by just south-west of Keilator NN 369 238
Time	6hr 30min
Distance	14.7km (9.1 miles)
Total ascent	980m (3220ft)
Terrain	Grassy slopes and pathed ridges, a couple of minor scramble moves
Max altitude	An Caisteal 995m (3264ft)
Maps	OS Explorer OL39; OS Landranger 56; Harvey *Trossachs North*
Public transport	No convenient bus stop
Parking	Free

Caisteal, meaning 'Castle', refers to the rocky lump north of the summit that shows so well from the roadside. Chroin means 'Danger', although this hill is no riskier than any other of its height. These are not particularly proud or outstanding summits, and no huge crags surround them. Even so, they are some of the most enjoyable in the Southern Highlands. Their green and friendly ridgeline, broken by rocky outcrops, occasionally offers a short scramble with spectacular views east to Stob a'Choin, Beinn Tulaichean and Cruach Ardrain (see Part 3). This is the standard route up these two Munros, with a narrow path winding between the summits.

A lay-by car park, part of the former road, is on the south side of the **A82** beside the corner of plantations. Start through a small metal gate in a fence onto a gravel track. Follow it as it curves to the left and then bears right under a railway bridge. Cross a bridge over the **River Falloch** by a small building and follow the track uphill, south-east, with the river on your left.

Follow the track past felled plantations, soon passing a metal sheepfold on your left. After walking 1.3km from the road, when the track splits, stay right (straight) towards a gate. Go through the gate and immediately after a rough path turns off to the right into bog: take this. Continue south-south-west then south as the trodden boggy path through moor grass leads up onto **Sròn Gharbh** (709m).

WALK 25 – AN CAISTEAL AND BEINN A' CHROIN HORSESHOE

A little scrambling on the An Caisteal ascent

Sròn Gharbh translates as the 'Rough Nose', although *sròn* is the usual Gaelic word for a hill's shoulder.

Here continue south as a path runs along the ridgeline, dodging around the occasional outcrop; **Twistin Hill** provides 2km of attractive walking on a pleasant dirt/rock path. Follow the path as a slight scramble crosses a crevasse-like landslip notch in the ridge. A rocky knoll with a cairn at 950m can be scrambled along its crest, or a path runs on the left along the foot of the rocks. Cross a slight drop and continue along the path to **An Caisteal**'s summit (995m), which has two cairns.

For the descent, follow a path south-south-west then south-east down the knolly ridge. If you reach the top of a 6m steepish down-scramble with rather

WALKING LOCH LOMOND AND THE TROSSACHS

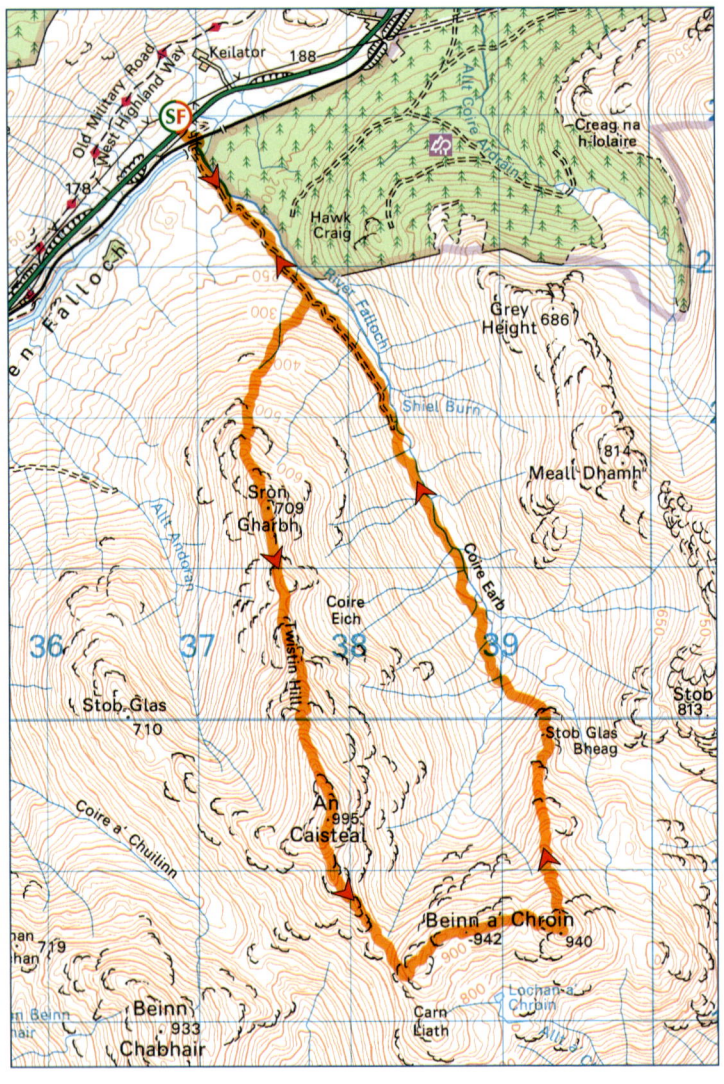

poor holds, you can turn up right to cross the ridgeline, and find a path below the crag round to the foot of the obstacle. Continue as the path then descends steeply, slanting right to a wide col, the Bealach Buidhe (805m).

A band of rock blocks the slope ahead up Beinn a' Chroin. There are various ways to avoid this; the well-trodden – and quite exciting – path route takes a grassy ramp up from its right-hand end.

The path across the Bealach Buidhe might be lost in mist as it splits apart: a compass bearing (147° magnetic) is useful. At the far south-east side of the col, the path has to get past the end of the band of rock, so it climbs quite steeply among rocks and up a grassy ramp slanting to the right; follow it, then continue as the path contours across the steep western slope of the mountain with crags above. After about 200 metres it turns sharply left, uphill, and zigzags up to a 2m scramble on good holds, but which is somewhat exposed. Further erosion of the overlying grass would extend the scrambling here. Above this you emerge on a grass platform. Cross this to another short rise eastwards, to pass through a notch onto the summit plateau. Just to your right is a small, uncairned knoll at 938m, the south-west top of Beinn a' Chroin.

Head east, on a path, to the west top, also 938m, marked by a cairn and a distinctive blocky rock (NN 385 185). Slightly higher is a bare rock beside the cairn.

Continue east over a small step before climbing to **Beinn a' Chroin**'s summit (942m, NN 387 185). Follow the path as it then runs down to a dip, with a scramble move down to bog and stream, after which the path crosses down to the left of the true col. From here an airy little path contours out left, a shortcut onto the descent ridge.

Instead, if you like, take the right fork, which climbs to the east top (940m). Just below the cairn the path divides. Turn up right for a few metres to the cairn. The cairn was taken to be the main summit until 2000, when someone noticed a 940m contour ring on the Harvey map 800 metres to the west. It has a good view to the east.

Return for a few steps and take a path heading down roughly north. Ill-defined at first, it soon becomes clear and a bit eroded as it descends the well-defined north ridge. Near its foot this ridge becomes lumpy, and the path winds from side to side, before you reach the grassland of the valley floor.

Here, follow the path as it bends left, north-west, passing a dead tree to reach a burn. There's a place to cross below small, tree-lined falls, just above a confluence. Hop across the water here, and the second stream, before heading north along the path, which leads down the glen on the left side of the **River Falloch**. It is mostly clear, with many boggy bits. After about 1.5km you reach a small hydro intake; from there the track runs down the valley to rejoin the outward route.

WALK 26
Beinn Chabhair

Start/finish	Beinglas Campsite NN 321 187
Time	7hr; out-and-back route: 5hr 30min
Distance	13.4km (8.3 miles); out-and-back route: 12.3km (7.6 miles)
Total ascent	1010m (3310ft); out-and-back route: 900m (2950ft)
Terrain	Rough path and pathless grassy moorland
Max altitude	Beinn Chabhair 933m (3061ft)
Maps	OS Explorer OL39; OS Landranger 56; Harvey *Trossachs North*
Public transport	There's a bus stop served by Citylink just south of The Drovers Inn (Inverarnan); from here follow the pavement north alongside the A82 for 470 metres, then turn right over the bridge to Beinglas Campsite
Parking	Beinglas Campsite offer day parking in exchange for a donation to their local mountain rescue team; you can pay in their shop or café, or email to check out of season: info@beinglascampsite.co.uk

Chabhair is awkward for English speakers to pronounce: it's 'CHA-wihr,' with the Gaelic CH at the start (as in 'loch') – the internet-famous outdoor swimmer Calum Maclean and Loch Lomond and The Trossachs National Park Authority collaborated to produce a great pronunciation video entitled 'How would you say Beinn Chabhair?' towards the end of 2023, which is worth looking up online.

Beinn Chabhair, at 933m, is a small Munro; this route heads up beside the impressive Beinglas Falls, wanders along a lively little burn and then rambles around some minor summits before mounting the knolly ridgeline, making a wide loop around Lochan Beinn Chabhair.

If you aren't enthused by the pathless section up Parlan Hill and Creag Bhreac Mhòr, the straightforward out-and-back route it also described.

From **Beinglas Campsite** car park, pass to the right of the café and follow a track uphill between cabins to find the start of a steep path on the left of **Ben Glas Burn**. Follow this narrow path as it climbs east up a series of zigzags, keeping

Walking across a broad moorland valley on the approach to Beinn Chabhair

north of the burn. After 150 metres, cross a high stile (severely broken at the time of research: take care) and continue along the path 250 metres to **Beinglas Falls**.

Return to the path (slightly north of the falls) and continue for 150 metres to a second stile. Cross the stile and ignore a steep left turn to continue along the path near Ben Glas Burn. Follow the path south-east then east for 1.2km, ignoring a left turn onto a track and always keeping left of the burn; the path gradually veers away from the burn's bank and is then intersected by a substantial track (NN 335 180). Cross the track and continue roughly east following a network of minor paths across moorland and crossing a few side streams – the easiest route soon returns to the northern bank of Ben Glas Burn. After 1.7km of this upper valley, you reach the outflow of **Lochan Beinn Chabhair**, a wide peaty pool.

Out-and-back route

Continue briefly to the left of the loch, before turning left, up into a grassy gully towards the ridgeline. (The top of this gully is Bealach Garbh, the 'Rough Pass', on the Harvey map.) About halfway up, keep to the path as it bears up right onto the lumpy ridgeline of **Meall nan Tarmachan**, skirting around the south side to avoid the minor summit at 719m. Continue as the path dips east into a col, then heads up the ridgeline south-east with many windings around knolls and a couple of brief dips on the way up to **Beinn Chabhair** summit (933m). Return the same way.

Main circular route

Cross the outflow of Lochan Beinn Chabhair on stepping stones (sometimes underwater, but the stream is small) and cross peaty ground south onto Parlan

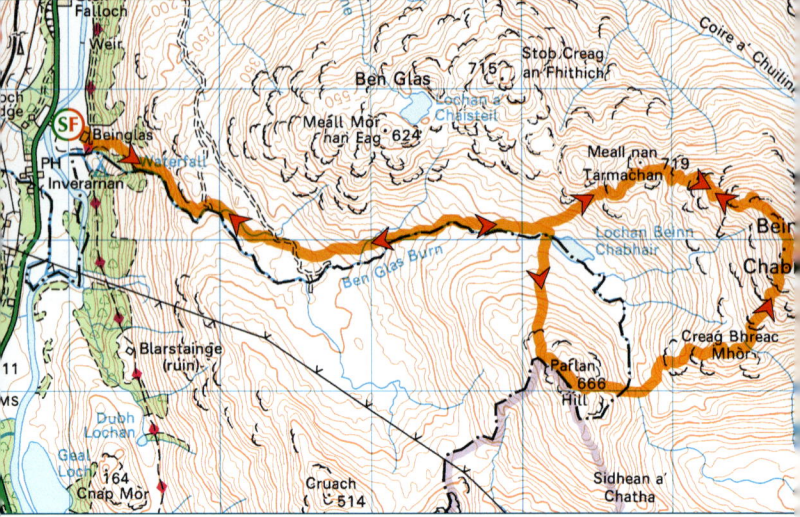

Hill, where the going is over short grass and bare rock. An old fence joins from the south; you can follow this south-east for the final section onto the summit plateau. The broad col south of Parlan Hill was used by Rob Roy as well as by cattle being taken from Loch Katrine to the drove road at Inverarnan. Climb to the summit of **Parlan Hill** (666m), then descend east towards the low ground between Parlan Hill and Creah Bhreac Mhòr, skirting to the right of some small crags on the way down – survey your next ascent on the way.

To climb Creah Bhreac Mhòr, slant up leftwards past the lowest crag, then back up right above it. From **Creag Bhreac Mhòr** (742m) head east down a dip, then continue to climb roughly north-north-east around small crags with plenty of grass. A path forms for the last few steps to the summit cairn of **Beinn Chabhair** (933m).

To descend, follow a much more obvious path that continues down the ridgeline ahead, north-north-west, along the Munro's many knolls. Keep going as the path drops to cross a col, and 200 metres later passes right to left through another small col with a pool. Skirt to the left (south) of **Meall nan Tarmachan**, then descend south-west to the outlet of **Lochan Beinn Chabhair**. Here, rejoin your outward route and roughly follow the course of **Ben Glas Burn** back down to the campsite. Take your time over the final descent, which feels much steeper than it did on the way up.

LOCH LOMOND

Balmaha from the boatyard (Walk 30)

PART 7 LOCH LOMOND EAST

Descending from Conic Hill towards Loch Lomond with the islands of Inchcailloch on the left and Inchfad on the right (Walk 29)

Of all Scotland's freshwater lochs, Loch Lomond has the largest surface area, but the charm of its east bank is found in the trees. Gnarled old oaks shade the shoreline, while swathes of young birch trees are colonising the lower slopes of the hills. This area has rewarding shorter walks: Conic Hill is a popular choice for views across Loch Lomond's southern islands, but a couple of easy, low-level options are suggested here too.

At the centre of the national park, Ben Lomond is an extremely popular Munro. The mountain's proximity to Glasgow, along with having the most straightforward path in the region, makes it an obvious starting point for anyone looking to get into hillwalking or bagging the Munros. The summit views – over the loch to the Arrochar Alps, south to the islands and north towards the Highland's more serious mountain ranges – are nothing short of spectacular.

WALK 27
Ben Lomond

Start/finish	Ben Lomond car park, Rowardennan NS 360 986
Time	5hr; Ptarmigan Ridge ascent and main path descent: 5hr 30min
Distance	12.4km (7.7 miles); Ptarmigan Ridge ascent and main path descent: 12.1km (7.5 miles)
Total ascent	925m (3030ft); Ptarmigan Ridge ascent and main path descent: 935m (3070ft)
Terrain	Obvious hill paths with a steep section on Ptarmigan Ridge
Max altitude	Ben Lomond 974m (3196ft)
Maps	OS Explorer OL39; OS Landranger 56; Harvey *Loch Lomond & The Trossachs*
Toilets	Free toilets and water refill at information building
Public transport	Very limited waterbus sailings from Tarbet or Luss. Summer weekends only. See: www.cruiselochlomond.co.uk
Parking	Ben Lomond car park is pay and display – cash, card or app

Vying against Ben Nevis for the title of most popular Munro in Scotland, Ben Lomond is many people's first mountain. Attempted by over 50,000 people a year – most of whom succeed – it's the country's most southerly Munro, with spectacular views over Loch Lomond and its islands, as well as the rest of the national park.

The main path is wide and well constructed, leaving little opportunity for navigational confusion in summer conditions, so the straightforward out-and-back route is explained here for those looking to gain hillwalking experience. An alternative ascent via Ptarmigan Ridge is also described; in comparison, this route is less obvious and steeper towards the summit, but it still ranks among the easiest Munro ascents in the national park.

Whichever route you choose, it's still important to be properly prepared: severe weather can take you by surprise at 974m and snow can linger until the beginning of May. Check weather forecasts and conditions in advance and pack accordingly.

WALKING LOCH LOMOND AND THE TROSSACHS

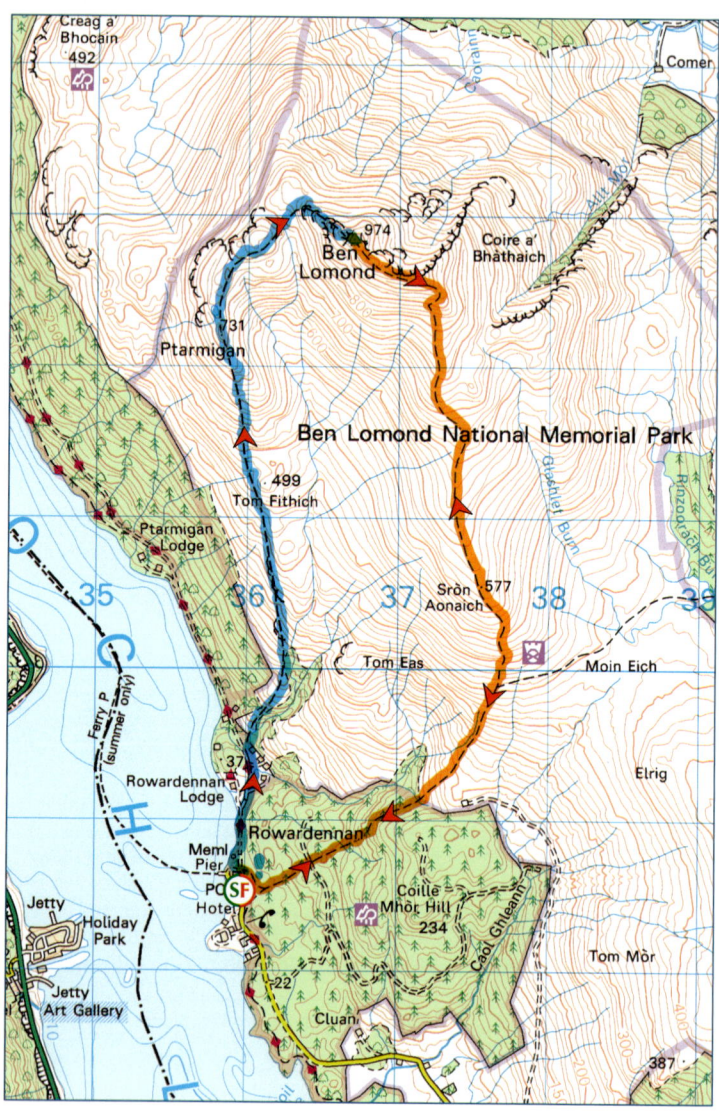

Main path ascent

To take the main path ascent, begin through the information building (where there are toilets), walk past a water-refill station on the other side and go straight across an intersecting track. Head along the Ben Lomond path, which heads initially south-east through mature oaks for 160 metres then veers to the left (north-east) for a further 170 metres to a kissing gate in a deer fence.

> The **oak trees** in this area were planted around 200 years ago when their bark was used as a source of tannin and the wood often made into charcoal. Tannins were used to treat animal skins for leather, while charcoal was used for processes needing a very high temperature. At that time, charcoal was made on level clearings where wood would be stacked and covered with soil before being set on fire.

Go through the gate and continue for 200 metres, then cross a forest road. Continue along the path north-east for nearly 1km through regenerated birchwood – with occasional views to Ben Lomond and Loch Lomond – to another kissing gate at the edge of the trees. Go through the gate and continue on the path across open moorland now heading north-north-west. After 900 metres, go through a kissing gate at 400m elevation. North-west across Loch Lomond are the distinctive horns of The Cobbler (Walk 33) in the Arrochar Alps.

Keep to the path as it heads roughly north up a broad moorland shoulder called **Sròn Aonaich**. After about 2.5km, there is a cairn at 790m; continue as the path veers a little more steeply left, right and then left again coming up to a dramatic view of the steep cliffs of **Coire a' Bhàthaich** which plummets down on the right. Continue west-north-west for 400 metres to the **Ben Lomond** summit trig point at 974m. To keep this route straightforward, return the same way (this is also described at the end of this route, after the instructions for the Ptarmigan Ridge ascent).

> From Ben Lomond, the **views** are spectacular. On a clear day, you can see as far as Ben Nevis to the north, as well as the Munros, Corbetts and lochs to the north and east of the national park. The distinctive Arrochar Alps are north-west, while the view down over Loch Lomond is also spectacular with its islands laid out to the south.

Ascent via Ptarmigan Ridge

The ascent begins at the Loch Lomond side of Ben Lomond car park. Walk north along the loch shore on a wide path that passes a granite ring war memorial. A short distance further, beside a small beach, turn left/ahead onto the West

A small beach on Loch Lomond at the start of the Ptarmigan Ridge route

Highland Way to continue north. After 280 metres, at the entrance track of **Rowardennan Youth Hostel**, fork right (following signs for the West Highland Way, Ben Lomond Bunkhouse etc), then continue for 100 metres before keeping left at another fork (following the same signs).

Follow the main track for a further 190 metres to a junction at a sign, 'Welcome to Ben Lomond'; here, carry on straight ahead, passing a white house called Ben Lomond Cottage with (hopefully) Ben's Bakes honesty box stall set up outside. Cross Adress Burn via a bridge, then take a right turn onto a path leading up beside the river. Continue uphill for 180 metres, ignoring a left turn and passing a waterfall, to a junction beside the moss-covered remains of a longhouse; here, bear left (uphill) onto a substantial gravel path. Pass a stone sheepfold with an enviable loch view, then continue up to a gate.

This is the fence boundary of **Lower Ptarmigan Natural Woodland Regeneration Project**, which aims to protect young trees from grazing animals and establish a more natural treeline to about 400m.

Continue north up the path for 1.2km, ignoring a stile on your right, to another gate at 430m, which exits the regeneration project on the slopes of **Tom Fithich**. Keep to the path as it veers slightly left and crosses a small burn. As the path continues, it is narrow but well repaired with zigzags (please don't shortcut as this will create stream lines that erode the path). Look and listen out for ptarmigan – they often make strange grunting noises like high-pitched pigs – Ben Lomond is thought to be their southernmost breeding ground in Scotland.

WALK 27 – BEN LOMOND

At 600m altitude the path finally reaches the spur line of **Ptarmigan Ridge**; follow it over some pleasant hummocks and past a lochan with glorious views across the north of Loch Lomond to the Arrochar Alps. Keep to the ridgeline as it bends round to the right, running north-east, to a shoulder called Bealach Buidhe at 750m below Ben Lomond's steep north-west ridge.

Climb up the clear zigzag path, which heads up this steep-sided, rocky spur. At 850m the ridge steepening is aided by good handholds in rocks alongside the path – this part is sometimes referred to as 'scrambling' in tourist literature, but the holds are more of a reassurance than a necessity. The emergence at **Ben Lomond** summit (974m) is sudden, with the trig pillar a few metres ahead.

Descent route

To descend via the main path, continue south-east along the almost level ridgeline ahead, with steep drops left into **Coire a' Bhathaich**, then follow the wide path just down to right of the crest. After 500 metres, follow the path as it heads down a steepish slope on the right to the broad moorland shoulder below. At 790m, there is a cairn, then follow the well-built and usually busy path as it descends the gentle slopes of **Sròn Aonaich** southwards; at 550m the path steepens somewhat.

At 400m pass through a kissing gate, then continue for another 900 metres to pass through a second kissing gate which leads into woodland. Continue 1km south-west through young birchwood, then cross a forest road. In a further 200 metres, go through a kissing gate in a deer fence. Finally, follow the path back to the visitor centre and car park through mature oak trees.

Looking north from the base of the steep final ascent of Ptarmigan Ridge before the summit of Ben Lomond

WALK 28
Ardess Hidden History Trail

Start/finish	Ben Lomond car park, Rowardennan NS 359 986
Time	1hr
Distance	3.1km (1.9 miles)
Total ascent	70m (230ft)
Terrain	Woodland paths
Max altitude	Lower Lomond slopes 81m (266ft)
Maps	OS Explorer OL39; OS Landranger 56; Harvey *Loch Lomond & The Trossachs*
Toilets	Free toilets and water refill at information building
Public transport	Very limited waterbus sailings from Tarbet or Luss. Summer weekends only; see: www.cruiselochlomond.co.uk
Parking	Ben Lomond car park is pay and display – cash, card or app

The shortest walk in this book, Ardess Hidden History Trail has been set up by National Trust for Scotland to highlight the rich archaeology and historical context of the oak woods and moorland fields at the foot of Ben Lomond. The walk is signposted and easy to follow, pointing out old stone ruins and the traces of past communities, but it also has great views of Loch Lomond. If some of your party are climbing Ben Lomond and others need a more gentle way to pass the time, combine this little walk with a loch-shore picnic or extend it by strolling further north up the West Highland Way.

Start from the **Loch Lomond** side of Ben Lomond car park. Walk north along the loch shore on a wide path that, after 100 metres, passes a granite ring **war memorial**. A short distance further, beside a small beach, turn left/ahead onto the West Highland Way to continue north. After 280 metres, at the entrance track of **Rowardennan Youth Hostel**, fork right (following signs for the West Highland Way, Ben Lomond Bunkhouse etc). After 100 metres, at the next junction, keep left following the same signs.

Continue along the main track for a further 190 metres to a junction at a sign, 'Welcome to Ben Lomond' – turn right here and pass a 'Welcome to Ardess Lodge' information board. Walk through a gate on the left to pass to the left of

WALK 28 – ARDESS HIDDEN HISTORY TRAIL

the ranger centre and Ardess Lodge. Continue on a grassy track past a restored Cruck Frame Barn. Used from the 13th century onwards, a crooked timber frame would have supported the roof, while the walls were made from earth and turf on a stone base.

Go through a gate and follow the track around to the right as it climbs gently. Just past a sign about oak woods and industry, the track bends round to the left – leave it here and go through a small wooden gate on the right marked with a white arrow. Follow a narrow path as it weaves through woodland, purple with bluebells in spring, and continue as it crosses a tiny burn before climbing stone steps. There's a view down to the remains of a stone ruin over the burn, then the path begins to climb more steeply to the sign indicating traces of some rig-and-furrow cultivation under old oaks.

Go immediately through a wooden gate, then turn right onto a wider path uphill; exit the woodland through a kissing gate onto open hillside. Go straight ahead, bearing right, crossing a small burn and continuing past more old rig-and-furrow cultivation. In a further 20 metres, at a fork, follow an arrow bearing left, uphill.

Follow the path as it bends round to the left to 'The Head Dyke' remains of a wall and a bench overlooking Loch Lomond. The head dyke would have prevented livestock from grazing further down the hill in summer, so crops had a chance to grow.

A restored cruck frame barn

Continue along level ground north-north-west for just over 100 metres to Bloomery Mound, a site used in the 16th and 17th centuries for iron smelting. From here, bear left and walk downhill to a gate at the edge of woodland. Go through the gate and follow a narrow, winding path, which crosses a burn before climbing again. Pass the site of an old working platform and a bench with views between the trees to Loch Lomond, then continue past the scant remains of an 1800s mud and thatch building, once home to a woodcutter and his wife.

Continue to a bench overlooking Ardess Burn and cross it by a bridge; there's a small waterfall just below. The ruin of Tigh an Eas, meaning 'house by the waterfall' is just beyond, then you come to the remains of an 18th-century settlement called Ruskenach (now shown as Rowchnock on modern maps). Rob Roy owned Ruskenach and Ardess between 1711 and 1713 before he was outlawed.

Follow the path left (west) to the grass-covered traces of an oval longhouse. From here, at a junction, continue downhill (south) past a little waterfall. Keep alongside Ardess Burn, bearing left and downhill at minor junctions, until you come out onto the main track. This is the West Highland Way – if you want to extend this walk, turn right and continue north along Loch Lomond for as long as you like. The return route simply follows the West Highland Way south. To return to the car park, turn left here, crossing the large burn over a bridge. Walk past Ben Lomond Cottage (look out for Ben's Bakes honesty shed cakes) and continue to the junction at the 'Welcome to Ben Lomond' sign. Here, keep ahead and retrace your steps 720 metres through woodland on the banks of **Loch Lomond** to the car park.

WALK 29
Conic Hill

Start/finish	Balmaha Visitor Centre car park NS 421 909
Time	2hr 15min
Distance	6.3km (3.9 miles)
Total ascent	340m (1110ft)
Terrain	Predominantly very good path with some potentially muddy sections
Max altitude	Conic Hill 361m (1184ft)
Maps	OS Explorer OL38; OS Landranger 56
Public transport	Balmaha has a bus stop
Parking	The Stirling Council-operated pay and display parking at Balmaha remained frustrating throughout the period of this book's research; payment is via cash or the RingGo app (not card), but there's limited phone signal to download the app and only one of three ticket machines was functional – bring cash, download the app in advance or, where possible, catch the bus.

In terms of an effort to reward ratio, the view from this small hill perched above Balmaha is pretty hard to beat, and climbing it is understandably popular. In the far south of the national park, it's easily accessible and the views out over Loch Lomond are nothing short of spectacular.

Conic Hill is an obvious part of the Highland Boundary Fault Line – looking west from the hill's crest, it's clear how the ridge continues across Loch Lomond as a line of islands. In geological terms, the ridge and narrow terrace just north are Lower Old Red conglomerate and sandstone, while the northern flank of the ridge and the low ground along its base are formed from Highland Border Complex serpentine and the Gualan Fault (a branch of the Highland Boundary Fault). The modern visitor centre at the start provides further information.

The ascent described here follows an impressively well-made and carefully maintained path, with excellent signage; the alternative descent requires marginally more care, but nevertheless keeps to trodden paths across unchallenging terrain.

Following the trodden path to the true summit

Walk to the back (north end) of the **Balmaha Visitor Centre** car park and turn right onto a path signposted for Conic Hill. Follow the path through Balmaha Plantation for 280 metres, then take a signposted left onto wide, smooth path. This path contours round the flank of Tom nan Oisgean up a series of impressive stone steps to Bealach Ard. There is a great viewpoint over Loch Lomond just off to the right here. Turn left (north-west), following another sign and the obvious path, to continue uphill. Keep to the path as it bends round to the right (north-east), climbing up with the ridge of Conic Hill on your right. Ignore a left fork onto the West Highland Way and continue to climb up the well-made path to a summit at 358m. Inchcailloch (Walk 30), Torrinch, Creinch and Inchmurrin ('St Mirren's island') form a line stretching south-west across Loch Lomond in a continuation of the Highland Boundary Fault.

The view from this minor summit is unsurpassed, but to continue to **Conic Hill**'s true summit (361m), leave the well-made path behind and descend to the north-east following a narrow trodden path, which winds along the lumpy ridge-line and up to the final peak 300 metres north-east.

Retrace your steps for 150 metres back to the last dip, then bear right onto a narrow path, which heads north-west to the West Highland Way 110 metres away. Turn left onto the **West Highland Way** and follow it south-west for 800 metres as it rejoins your outward route. Don't follow the main path as it turns left to descend

WALK 29 – CONIC HILL

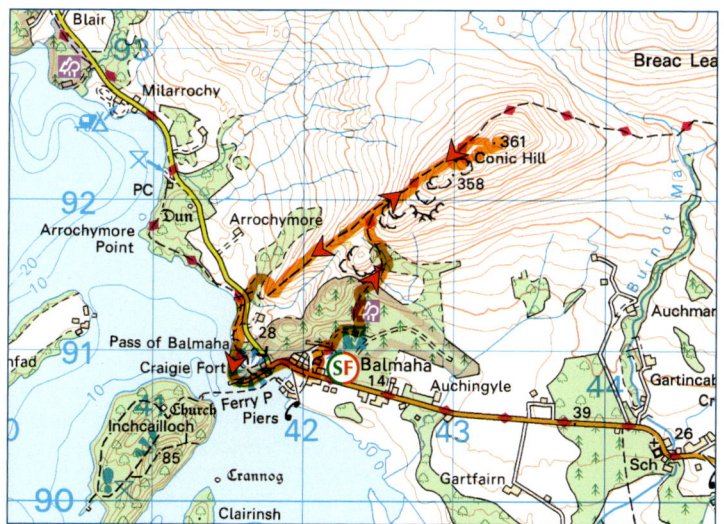

back to Bealach Ard, but instead look for a junction where a fingerpost reads 'Conic Hill Summit ½ mile/0.8km'. Here (NS 425 919), follow a vague, grassy path down the wide ridgeline which continues south-west down Druim nam Buraich.

> There's a good view over the houses, pier and jetty over on Inchfad ('Long Island'). In the 18th and early 19th centuries, **Loch Lomond** was known for having many illicit whisky stills – this was stopped by the government in the mid-19th century, and a legal distillery was built on Inchfad. Slightly further west is Inchcruin ('Round Island'); this wooded spit of land was used as an asylum for the insane at around the same time.

Continue down the grassy ridge for 870 metres (it splits and rejoins heading the same direction), then follow the path as it descends into Coille Ghlas woodland and emerges to a road through a gate. Cross the road, turn left and walk south for 30 metres, then go through a gate on your right into an open field. Cross the field and go through another gate onto a path running along the bank of **Loch Lomond**. Turn left onto the path and follow it along the lochside back to **Balmaha**, ignoring a left turn where the West Highland Way climbs up Craigie Fort. Continue onto a roadside path, which leads east back to the village and visitor centre.

WALK 30
Inchcailloch and Balmaha

Start/finish	Balmaha Boatyard NS 419 908
Time	Inchcailloch: 1hr 30min; Balmaha: 1hr 15min
Distance	Inchcailloch: 3.1km (1.9 miles); Balmaha: 4.1km (2.5 miles)
Total ascent	Inchcailloch: 100m (330ft); Balmaha: 65m (210ft)
Terrain	Woodland paths
Max altitude	Tom na Nigheanan 85m (279ft)
Maps	OS Explorer OL38; OS Landranger 56
Public transport	Balmaha has a bus stop. The passenger ferry from Balmaha Boatyard to Inchcailloch island usually only runs between late April and the end of September. Check annual dates and prices at www.balmahaboatyard.co.uk. It's also possible to reach Inchcailloch south pier or Balmaha from Luss, see: www.cruiselochlomond.co.uk
Parking	There is free parking at Balmaha Boatyard for ferry passengers; pay and display at Balmaha Visitor Centre (see 'Parking', Walk 29)

These two wee walks can be enjoyed separately or linked together by a short trip on one of the traditional wooden passenger ferries run by Balmaha Boatyard.

The wooded isle of Inchcailloch forms part of the Highland Boundary Fault and is run by NatureScot as part of the small Loch Lomond National Nature Reserve. It's 1.25km long and just over 600m wide, with no permanent residents, but it does have a small, seasonal campsite. Inchcailloch's predominantly oak woodland is carpeted with bluebells in spring and the island forms important habitat for wildlife including seasonally visiting migrating wildfowl.

The picturesque village of Balmaha is synonymous with Loch Lomond and therefore the whole national park; it hosts the national park authority's main visitor centre, has a few pleasant cafés and is a popular stop along the West Highland Way. The suggested walking route here climbs the viewpoint of Craigie Fort before meandering along the shoreline to Arrochymore Point.

WALK 30 – INCHCAILLOCH AND BALMAHA

Returning from Inchailloch to Balmaha on the ferry

Inchailloch

To reach Inchailloch, catch a passenger ferry from Balmaha Boatyard. You arrive at the island's north pier. Climb a series of steps up into woodland to an information board at a path junction. Turn left here, following a sign for 'Summit Path' and a narrow path, which weaves through bluebell woods then begins to climb a series of wooden steps.

> As you climb there is some exposed **puddingstone** on the right. This conglomerate – round white pebbles set in a matrix of red sandstone – is about 420 million years old and part of the Old Red Sandstone sedimentary rock sequence.

Follow the path as it ascends with a few hairpin bends to the island's summit (85m), which has a bench with a glorious view north up Loch Lomond. This hill is called Tom na Nigheanan, which means 'Hill of the Daughter'. Descend the opposite side of the hill (south-west) and continue along the path for 350 metres to a junction. Here, turn left following a sign for 'Port Bawn'.

Walk south-south-west along this path down to a pretty sandy beach and picnic benches at Port Bawn, which also has Inchcailloch's southern pier. Boat passengers from Luss arrive at the southern pier. To continue around the island, walk north-west past compost toilets and continue north following a low-level path along the western shore of Inchcailloch. After 700 metres, turn left to a stone ruin and a side path down to the shoreline where there is a view north to Ben Lomond. The ruin is thought to be a deserted farmstead, likely from the 17th century.

Return to the main path and continue, now heading south-east, for 220 metres. When you reach a junction keep ahead (left fork) to visit the ruined **St Kentigerna's Church** and burial ground.

> ### ST KENTIGERNA
>
> St Kentigerna was an Irish saint who settled on Inchcailloch and died here in 733 – the church is named after her. One story recounts that she set up a nunnery and that the name of the island, which translates to something like 'the island of the old women', is a reference to this community; there is no evidence of a nunnery, however, and a second explanation is that the name just refers to St Kentigerna herself. Built in the late 12th or early 13th century, the church was abandoned in 1621, although the burial ground remained in use until the 20th century. The site was the traditional burial ground of Clan MacGregor and has the gravestone of Gregor MacGregor, chief of the clan and cousin of the famous Rob Roy.

Walk the short distance back to the last junction and turn left. At the next junction, just afterwards, turn left again. Continue north-east for 320 metres back to the north pier.

Balmaha

The Balmaha part of this walk begins in the centre of the village: if you're coming from Balmaha Boatyard, return to the main **B837** road and turn left along the pavement; if you're coming from the main Visitor Centre car park, walk down to the B837 and turn right. Follow the path around Tom Weir's Rest picnic area, which has a statue of the well-loved figure and a lovely view of the boats bobbing around in the harbour.

> **Tom Weir** (1914–2006) was a Scottish climber, explorer, author and broadcaster. He served in the artillery during World War II, then worked as an Ordnance Survey surveyor, before making his hobbies professional with a regular column in *The Scots Magazine* for over 50 years. In the 1950s, he was part of the first post-war Himalayan expedition and was one of the first mountaineers to explore the previously closed mountain ranges of Nepal, east of Kathmandu. In his will, he left over £2,000 to the conservation and heritage charity Friends of Loch Lomond.

WALK 30 – INCHCAILLOCH AND BALMAHA

Walk west past the harbour and continue around the pavement along the loch shore. As the B837 road turns a sharp right corner at a junction, continue ahead past pretty blue and white Passfoot Cottage onto a minor road, which is part of the **West Highland Way**.

The name **Balmaha** comes from the Gaelic *Bealach Mo-Cha* meaning the 'Pass of Saint Mo-Cha'. This refers to the narrow route between the hills at the north end of the village (now named The Pass of Balmaha), which the B837 now travels through.

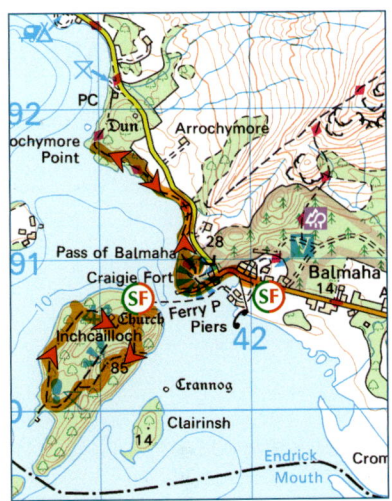

Follow this road along the loch for 230 metres. Ignore the first set of stone steps on your right marked for the West Highland Way, but take the second set, which are indicated as part of Balmaha's Millennium Forest Trail (with a symbol of trees).

Climb up the steps through birch trees then, at the first junction, keep left on a larger path with rocks underfoot. At the next junction, take a quick detour left to a great viewpoint over Inchcailloch island. Return to the path and continue to the next junction where you should continue up (left fork). Soon you emerge at the top of **Craigie Fort**. There was once an Iron Age fort here.

The network of minor paths at the top is confusing, but keep to the most substantial strand, which leads down the opposite side of the small summit and descends stone steps with a view of Ben Lomond ahead. Continue down to the shoreline, where there is a little beach, and turn right to continue along the loch.

After 200 metres, you come to a long shingle beach with views north to Arrochymore Point. This makes a good spot for a picnic, or continue for 900 metres to the point itself where there are minor side trails to tiny coves and views out to Inchfad and Inchcailloch islands. From **Arrochymore Point**, before the main path bends back round to the east, return the same way.

Retrace your steps along the **West Highland Way** for 1.1km, then ignore the turning for Craigie Fort and instead continue around the shoreline. Cross a metal footbridge over a small beach and walk past a pier, then continue for 500 metres back to the road junction and along the lochshore pavement into the village.

PART 8 LUSS

The trig point on Doune Hill with the Arrochar Alps beyond (Walk 31)

Busy little Luss is popular with tourists. The pretty village church, from 1875, is said to be built on the site of an earlier one, established when the Irish Saint Kessog brought Christianity to Luss in AD510. At that time, nestled in the shadows of the hills, the village was called *Clachan Dhu* (Dark Village). A popular story explains how Kessog was martyred and had his body embalmed with herbs; the herbs then grew up from his grave and the village changed its name to Lus (Gaelic for 'plant' or 'herb') in his honour.

The hills in this region are small and pleasant underfoot – the grass is short for easy striding and there are lovely views over the south end of Loch Lomond to Ben Lomond, Conic Hill and across all the islands. To the north, the Arrochar Alps look close and impressive, guarding the Highlands beyond.

WALK 31
Luss Hills: Beinn Dubh, Doune Hill and Beinn Eich

Start/finish	Luss Village car park/bus stop by Luss filling station NS 359 931
Time	8hr 30min; Beinn Dubh only: 4hr
Distance	20.1km (12.5 miles); Beinn Dubh only: 11.9km (7.4 miles)
Total ascent	1430m (4690ft); Beinn Dubh only: 700m (2300ft)
Terrain	Grassy ridges and hilltops, some with small paths. Quiet road for exit.
Max altitude	Doune Hill 734m (2408ft)
Maps	OS Explorer OL39; OS Landranger 56; Harvey *Arrochar Alps*
Parking	There are two car parks in Luss: one in the village centre near Luss filling station and one in the south. For a stay of this length, it is cheaper (but still expensive) to park in the village; you might also choose to use free, indicated parking lay-bys on either side of the village on the A82 and walk in or, preferably, get the bus.

The Luss hills are grassy-green, and don't even reach the Corbett height of 2500ft (762m), so many walkers ignore them. This may be a mistake; the Luss heights have an atmosphere all their own, made up of elegant ridgelines and deep winding hollows sprinkled with oak trees.

For baggers of summits, Luss also has one unique feature. Here a strong walker can achieve eight Grahams (over 2000ft/610m) in a day without any interference from higher Corbetts and Munros. Here we tackle three, in a walk which is quite long enough for most people.

Climbing busier Beinn Dubh alone makes for a pleasant afternoon stomp without encountering any difficult terrain – this route is also described.

Walk out west from the car park between the filling station and the village shop, then turn left onto the Luss link road (former A82). Walk 80 metres south down the road, then turn right into a short cul-de-sac with an ancient signpost for Glen Luss. When the road ends, next to Luss Primary School, continue up steps leading up to a footbridge over the **A82**.

WALK 31 – LUSS HILLS: BEINN DUBH, DOUNE HILL AND BEINN EICH

Keep ahead to join a gravel path, then turn right to follow a wooden sign for 'Beinn Dubh hill path' through a kissing gate (NS 357 931) onto the grassy base of Beinn Dubh. Follow a trodden path north up to another kissing gate, where a wide track leads up through bracken. At about 300m the ridge levels off and becomes boggy; keep to the path, well-trodden, as it continues north-west up the broad ridge. When a fence reaches the ridgeline, continue as the path runs up to the left of it, then cross it through a gap by a broken stile. From the first **Beinn Dubh** summit (642m) – where there is a small cairn – continue north-west along the flat peaty plateau as the Arrochar Alps come into view ahead. After 900 metres, bend round left to reach the second and main Beinn Dubh summit (657m), named as **Coire na h-Eanachan** on some maps; this summit has two cairns. A small path descends south-west for 400 metres onto the shoulder called **Mid Hill**.

Here the ridge and path turn left. For a shorter day just follow that ridge path down south-east towards Glenmollochan farm, then turn left onto the road to return to Luss.

To continue to Doune Hill, leave the path as you reach the lower saddle of Mid Hill: turn off down to the right, north-west, onto a lower spur on the south-west side of **Coire Carlaig**. Continue north-west as this steepens with a few peat hags to reach the broad glen, and a few scattered trees, between Beinn Dubh and Doune Hill.

Cross the small burn that winds down the glen. The odd little groove and crag formation north, presumably a landslip, is named Sìth Mòr or the 'Big Fairy' – find a good line across steep ground to head up to the left of this, then cross above it to find a shepherds' path running up Doune Hill's eastern spur (the path begins towards the right-hand/north side of the ridge, NN 309 973). Head up onto the **north-eastern top** (unnamed, 701m), then continue west-south-west as a path leads down into a col (Bealach an Dùin), and up to the trig point on **Doune Hill** (734m).

Various **MoD structures** in the hollow to the north-west are not marked on maps. The UK's nuclear submarines are based a few miles away at Faslane on Gare Loch.

Descend the grassy ridge south-west to the slight rise of **Beinn Lochain** (698m). Follow the path south-east along the charming grass ridge, with the elegant cone of Beinn Eich rising ahead. The ridge becomes still more shapely up to **Beinn Eich**'s summit (703m), which has a tiny quartz cairn.

Continue east-south-east as the path continues down the spur to a stile (NS 320 941) over a wall at the junction between a wall and a fence, directly above **Edentaggart Farm**. Cross the stile and slant slightly left to a ladder stile 200 metres

Looking down to Loch Lomond and to Ben Lomond from Beinn Dubh

GRAHAMS

As a footnote to the history of hill lists, the 2000–2499ft-ers (610–762m) are named Grahams after Fiona Graham who allowed her list of these hills to be subsumed into a pre-existing list compiled by Alan Dawson. Among her stipulations were that the list be named after her not him, and that this 657m Graham summit be named in Gaelic not English. Normally a nameless hill takes over the nearest bit of writing on the map, 'Mid Hill' being the shoulder to the south-west, but here it borrowed 'Beinn Dubh' from the more distant, but Gaelic, south-eastern outlier – hence the two Beinn Dubh summits you'll see marked on some maps.

to the left of the farm. Cross this and follow a rough path, which leads down to another stile onto the access track below the farm.

Turn left down the track, which becomes a tarred lane at the next stream. The 'Beinn Dubh only' route joins this lane just after the stream. Follow the lane for 3km. Approaching Luss and the A82, turn left/ahead at a junction opposite large posts carved with birds of prey to return over the road bridge from the start of the walk. Cross and continue down the steps into the village.

If you have a little time left at the end of your hike, walk down to **Luss Pier**, which has a beautiful view north along the loch to Ben Lomond. A short distance south, the historic **Luss Parish Church** sands on the bank of Luss Water.

THE WEST

The trig point at the summit of Strone Hill, looking down Loch Long (Walk 43)

PART 9 ARROCHAR ALPS

Hikers on top of The Cobbler's North Peak (Walk 33)

Direct comparisons with the Alpine countries' spikey, snow-laden summits are not particularly helpful here, but the craggy Arrochar Alps do have a distinctly mountainous feel. While there are broader definitions, this part of the book deals with the compact mountain range at the head of Loch Long, using Glen Croe (and the A83) as a south-western border, Glen Kinglas and Strath Dubh-Uisge to the north-west and Loch Lomond to the east.

There aren't any short walks in this section, but the straightforward routes up The Cobbler, Beinn Narnain and Beinn Ìme are good starting points for anyone looking to get into Scottish hillwalking. The other four – covering Ben Vorlich, Ben Vane, A' Chrois and alternative ways to climb those previously mentioned – include pathless terrain, short sections of scrambling or are simply very long, so are best left to hikers with some experience.

WALK 32

Ben Vorlich and the Little Hills from Ardlui

Start/finish	Ardlui train station NN 317 155
Time	6hr
Distance	12.5km (7.8 miles)
Total ascent	1040m (3420ft)
Terrain	Rough grassy hillside, pathless or with small paths
Max altitude	Ben Vorlich 943m (3094ft)
Maps	OS Explorer OL39; OS Landranger 56; Harvey *Arrochar Alps*
Public transport	Train station in village
Parking	Some parking opposite Ardlui train station, east side of the A82
Note	This is the Ben Vorlich beside Loch Lomond; for the other Ben Vorlich, above Loch Earn, see Walk 17

Halfway up the Little Hills, you'd be forgiven for renaming them the Wee Bastards; it's a rough, lumpy, pathless ascent, which is steep at times and feels rather relentless. As the view begins to open up along Loch Lomond, looking south across Ben Lomond and the islands in the loch, or north to the mountains around Tyndrum, it all begins to make sense.

The terrain covering the remainder of the climb from the twin peak Little Hills up the Munro, Ben Vorlich, is comparatively delightful with short grass providing less arduous walking. A broad ridge with a well-worn path provides pleasant, level respite along the Munro itself, before the route becomes less clear again for a rambling descent.

This is not the easiest or quickest route to climb Ben Vorlich (that's from Inveruglas via the Loch Sloy dam road), but it provides the most varied views and more of an adventure.

Starting at **Ardlui train station** Ardlui is pronounced 'ard-loo-ee' walk south along the **A82** for 390 metres to the second bridge (marked '85') where you can walk under the railway – be careful of road traffic along this stretch, as there is not much space. If the gate under this railway bridge remains locked, climb over it (at the hinged end), and at once turn left onto a rough path following field bottoms south-south-east. After 250 metres, go through a gate some 50 metres above and west of the railway, cross a river over stepping stones and follow a track to another gate above a grey house. Go

Walking Loch Lomond and the Trossachs

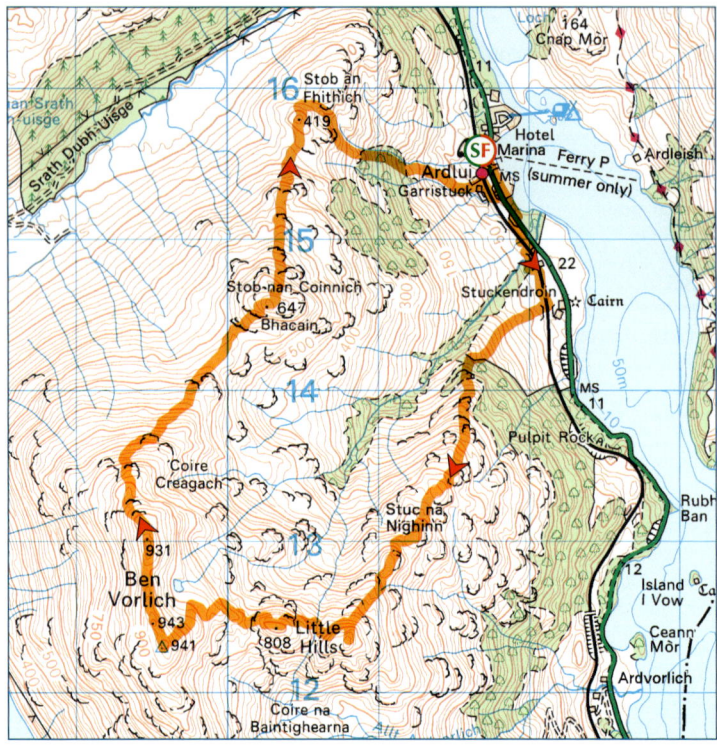

through this gate, still heading roughly south, and cross a field to a stone sheepfold. Go through the sheepfold and turn right onto a track, which emerges from another railway bridge at **Stuckendroin**, marked 'Access Ben Vorlich'.

Head south-west, uphill for 640 metres, first on the track and then traces of a track across rough pasture towards the foot of the Little Hills ridge, which rises to the left in steep humps. When you reach the base of the hills, avoid the first lump on the right and go through a gate to head up to the saddle between the first and second lumps. Cross a flattened section of fence on the loch (east) side of a boulder growing a tree and begin to climb the hills steeply heading south. Start by heading up on the Loch Lomond side, then go round to the right of the next lump to avoid small crags. Continue, doing your best to stay along the crest of the bumpy ridgeline; after some sharp little rises the going gets gentler.

Walk 32 – Ben Vorlich and the Little Hills from Ardlui

At about 500m altitude the views open down the length of Loch Lomond, and just get better as you climb. Pass the cairned knoll at 640m and to the first of the two Little Hills (793m, NN 308 123). For those descending this route in mist, this is a crucial change of direction; they can identify this lower Little Hill by the perched boulder on its top. Steep little crags surround the knoll, and it's a great perch for a prolonged pause in the upward progress.

Now head west. The second **Little Hill summit** (808m) is grassy and smooth on top. Continue west to pick your way around rocky crags for about 600 metres to the view of a pretty lochan below Ben Vorlich's northern summit. From here, climb south-west for 300 metres to **Ben Vorlich**'s trig point and accompanying cairn (941m).

Turn right (north) on a path for 200 metres to **Ben Vorlich's summit cairn**, perched at 943m on a west-facing crag top. The continuing Arrochar Alps look dramatic to the south-west. Continue north along the smooth summit ridge for 500 metres, to a slight rise with a large cairn (931m).

From here a little care is needed to avoid tumbling into Coire Creagach (ahead right). Descend slightly west of north for 400 metres to an ill-defined puddly col. Now turn north-east, down a humpy ridgeline with traces of a path. The ridge, gently angled on the whole, has scattered small crags, and the path heads down, rather than around, a couple of these, giving two scrambly moments. If you want to avoid scrambling due to icy conditions or personal preference, keep further to the west. Continue descending to the col (NN 300 143) between Ben Vorlich and Stob nan Coinnich Bhacain.

Looking back from the eastern slopes of Ben Vorlich towards the Little Hills with Loch Arklet beyond

From the col, a path heads down to the right. It's aiming for a steep direct descent to Bridge 85, but the continuation over Stob nan Coinnich Bhacain (described here) is more scenic. Stob nan Coinnich Bhacain means 'Point of the Mossy Peatbanks', although it is a bit rocky as well. Climb over **Stob nan Coinnich Bhacain** (647m), then continue north along a gentle grassy ridge, which descends to the slight rise of Stob an Fhithich (with crags on its right). Stob an Fhithich, meaning 'Peak of the Raven', matches Maol an Fhithich on the opposite side of Loch Lomond.

Climb over **Stob an Fhithich** (419m) and descend north onto a flat, boggy bit of ridge, then at once turn down right (south-east) into a grassy hollow. Follow a burn down as it develops, keeping on its left to descend – you might be able to find traces of a path, but the area is much overgrown with small trees and bracken. After 600 metres, you should reach an old stile (NN 310 156); cross this and continue south-east on the inside of a fence line. Cross the burn where it becomes more sensible to do so, then when (250 metres after the stile) you reach a fence cutting across the burn, turn right to find a gate 20 metres south (NN 313 155). Here, join a rough track, which heads to the right of a tall shack (a hide?). Continue on the track for 300 metres to another gate, go through this and head towards the barns at **Garristuck** (conspicuous from above and the only buildings above the railway). At the barns, turn right along the track and follow it past a couple of houses. Continue as it bends to the left to pass under a railway bridge. Turn left onto the **A82** and walk 170 metres back to **Ardlui** train station.

An infinity lochan north of Stob nan Coinnich Bhacain

WALK 33
The Cobbler

Start/finish	Glenloin car park two, near Succoth on the A83 NN 294 049
Time	4hr; simple return route: 4hr 30min
Distance	11.5km (7.1 miles); simple descent route: 12.3km (7.6 miles)
Total ascent	840m (2760ft); simple return route: 840m (2760ft)
Terrain	Obvious rocky mountain paths with easy Grade 1 scrambling on descent, which can be avoided by descending the way you came up. Optional exposed Grade 2 scramble on the 'true' Central Peak.
Max altitude	The Cobbler 884m (2900ft)
Maps	OS Explorer OL39; OS Landranger 56; Harvey *Arrochar Alps*
Public transport	Buses into Arrochar. If catching the train to Arrochar and Tarbet station, it's a 2.3km (1.4-mile) walk through the forest to Arrochar. Come down from the platform and turn right under the bridge (left leads to the A83 and Tarbet), follow a path uphill ahead for about 100 metres to a junction, then turn left. The path climbs west then turns north before a junction leads left down into Arrochar, coming out opposite the fish and chips shop.
Parking	Expensive pay and display parking (card/cash) at Glenloin car park

The Cobbler (also known as Ben Arthur) is Loch Lomond and The Trossachs' most instantly recognisable mountain. Shaped like a cartoon Viking helmet, its distinctive rocky horns are visible from as far away as Ben Ledi, on the opposite side of the national park. The mountain's three peaks, when viewed from the east, are said to look like a cobbler bending over his work (the Central and North peaks) with the stooped back of the pyramidical cobbler's wife on the left.

This route heads up the easiest way through the forest and along the course of the Allt a' Bhalachain to Lochan a' Chlaidheimh – from there a good path heads up to The Cobbler's summit plateau; the easiest descent is straight back, but a more direct and rockier alternative is also described. Included at the end is a description for climbing the North Peak, or 'Thread the Needle' – an exposed scramble to the 'true' Central Peak, said to be the most technically difficult to reach summit on the Scottish mainland.

Approaching The Cobbler from Coire a' Bhalachain in winter (photo: Peter Edwards)

On the opposite side of the **A83** from the south end of the car park, take a wide path signposted for The Cobbler and Beinn Narnain leading south-west. Follow this path up through forest for 850 metres until you reach a junction with an intersecting track. Turn left onto this, walk for 50 metres and then turn off right onto a path, which continues climbing up through the forest. After 1.5km you will emerge from the trees, then continue for a further 1.7km north-west following the course of the **Allt a' Bhalachain**. Pass the **Narnain Boulders** on your right and, when the path splits at Coire a' Bhalachain, ignore the left fork that crosses Allt a' Bhalachain and heads directly towards The Cobbler, but instead continue north-west for 1km up to the bealach between The Cobbler and Beinn Narnain just past **Lochan a' Chlaidheimh**. Here routes join from the Ben Vane and Beinn Ìme circuit (Walk 35), as well as connecting to the straightforward ascents/descents of Beinn Narnain and Beinn Ìme (Walk 34).

Turn left onto an obvious path which climbs steeply up The Cobbler's north shoulder. Follow this path up (passing a detour to its North Peak on your left – see below), until you reach the mountain's highest Central Peak. The view from **The Cobbler**'s summit plateau is spectacular (although in dry conditions a confident scrambler with a good head for heights might want to attempt the vertigo-inducing 'true' Central Peak, which is a few metres higher – see below).

WALK 33 – THE COBBLER

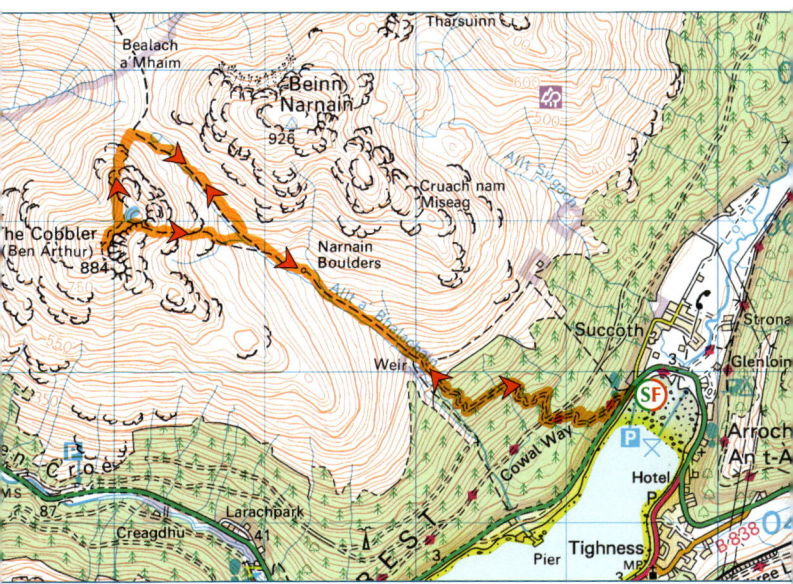

Ours are not the first generations of walkers and mountaineers to find inspiration on **The Cobbler**. From Victorian times until World War II walkers flocked to see this craggy mountain by bus, bicycle and steamship out of Glasgow. The first Scottish climbing club, The Cobbler Club, was founded by experienced alpinist Professor George Ramsay in 1866, and two of Scotland's finest mountain writers – Alasdair Borthwick and WH Murray – had their first mountain experiences on The Cobbler within 10 months of each other in 1933 and 1934.

The simplest descent route from the summit plateau is to return the way you came.

For a quicker but steeper descent route east, retrace your steps to the col between the Central and North peaks, then find and follow a path on the right leading steeply downhill and below the imposing wall of the North Peak, before heading generally east for about 1km with some short sections of easy scrambling.

Reaching Coire a' Bhalachain, turn right onto the main path which leads down to the forest. After 3km the path is intersected by a track, turn left onto this and walk for 50 metres before taking the path on your right, which leads back to the start.

North Peak

A sharp left from the main ascent route takes in the North Peak. In good conditions it's an uncomplicated ascent – a rather rocky walk rather than a climb or scramble. It's only after you come down that you realise that what you've been standing on is basically empty air, with a thin shelf of schist sticking out over the top of it.

From North/Central col, the path leads to the bottom left corner of bare slabs. Walk up these to reach the flat summit. If you don't fancy the slabs, perhaps because they're iced over, there's also an off-rock alternative. From the lowest slab, a narrow ledge out left reaches broken ground where you can turn up right to North Peak.

'True' Central Peak (the Argyll Needle)

The Cobbler's true top is a balanced rocky tower hanging out over the void, reached by a scary Grade 2 scramble. The crucial ramp has smooth, sloping holds; schist is slippery when wet. It's not demeaning to use a rope (15m minimum, plus two long slings) – or if it is, better demeaned than deceased. As is usually the case, getting down can be harder than getting up.

Clamber over boulders to the front left corner of the tower. Pass to the right through a hole (the Eye of the Argyll Needle) to arrive on a ledge above a drop. Walk left along the ledge, which is comfortably wide. At its end a ramp leads up towards the tower's outer end. For the less experienced it's a good idea to reverse the step onto the ramp immediately after making it, to familiarise yourself with the holds for the descent. Then ascend the ramp on smooth footholds to a nook below the perched boulder at the tower's outer end. For the roped, here is a secure stance and belay.

The Cobbler's 'True', central summit

Scramble onto the boulder above, and thence to the 884m **summit**. Given the necessary ancestry, you could now become Chief of Clan Campbell.

Descend by the same route.

WALK 34
Straightforward Beinn Narnain and/or Beinn Ìme

Start/finish	Glenloin car park two, near Succoth on the A83 NN 294 049
Time	Both Munros: 8hr; Beinn Narnain only: 5hr 30min; Beinn Ìme only: 6hr 30min
Distance	Both Munros: 17km (10.6 miles); Beinn Narnain only: 13km (8 miles); Beinn Ìme only: 15km (9.3 miles)
Total ascent	Both Munros: 1260m (4130ft); Beinn Narnain only: 900m (2950ft); Beinn Ìme only: 980m (3220ft)
Terrain	Rocky paths
Max altitude	Beinn Ìme 1011m (3317ft)
Maps	OS Explorer OL39; OS Landranger 56; Harvey *Arrochar Alps*
Public transport	Buses to Arrochar. If catching the train to Arrochar and Tarbet station, see Walk 33 for connecting walk
Parking	Expensive pay and display parking (card/cash)
Note	Climbing two Munros in a day is never going to be easy, but this route is uncomplicated with paths to follow and no scrambling or particularly difficult ground. If you're bagging Munros, it's the quickest way to go, but climbing one of these peaks is also a good introduction to the Arrochar Alps for anyone looking to gain experience

The flat summit of Beinn Narnain looks down over Loch Long stretching out towards the sea, while Beinn Ìme is the highest mountain in the Arrochar Alps, with great views over to Ben Vane and out across the national park.

Just be aware that – as in all Scottish mountains – there are no signposts at the higher altitudes, and poor weather, falling darkness, snow or ice can make for difficult or dangerous conditions if unprepared. It's only a beginners' route in good, summer conditions.

On the opposite side of the **A83** from the south end of the car park, take a wide path signposted for The Cobbler and Beinn Narnain leading south-west. Follow this path up through forest for 850 metres until you reach a junction with a forest track. Turn left, walk for 50 metres, then turn off right onto a path which continues climbing up through the forest. After 1.5km you leave the forest behind; continue

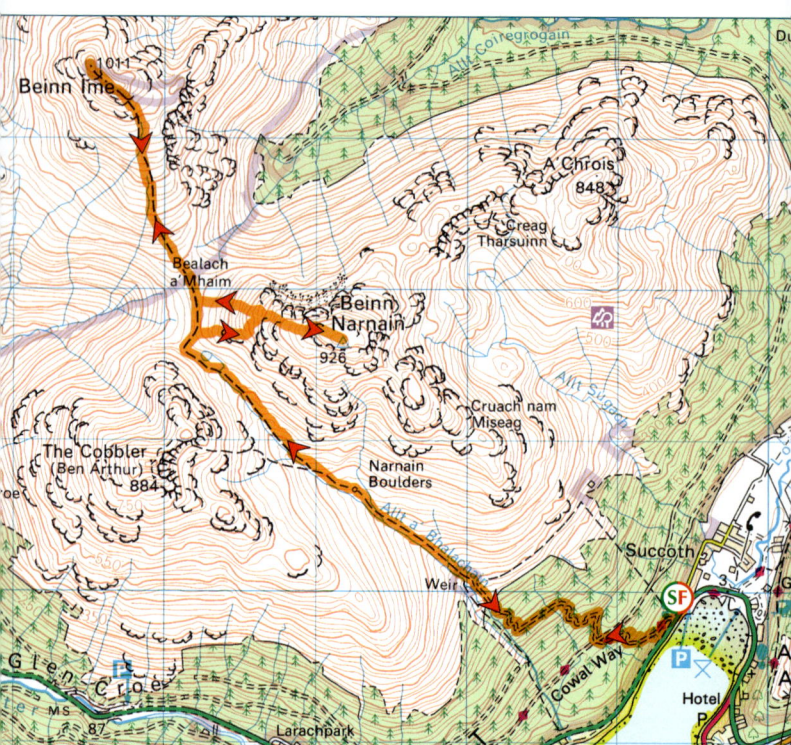

north-west for a further 1.7km following the course of the **Allt a' Bhalachain**. The Cobbler (Walk 33) dominates the view ahead. Pass the large **Narnain Boulders** on your right and, when the path splits at Coire a' Bhalachain, ignore the left fork that crosses Allt a' Bhalachain and heads towards The Cobbler. Continue north-west for 1km past **Lochan a' Chlaidheimh** up to the bealach between The Cobbler and Beinn Narnain.

When the path splits at the northern base of The Cobbler, ignore the steep left turn and continue for 140 metres north-east on a roughly level path to the west side of Beinn Narnain where there is a junction. To climb Beinn Ìme without Beinn Narnain, continue north for 200 metres, then continue the instructions from 'Walk north-north-west, crossing Bealach a' Mhaim' three paragraphs below.

Walk 34 – Straightforward Beinn Narnain and/or Beinn Ìme

To climb Beinn Narnain, turn right and follow a path leading west then north-west for 530 metres. When you reach a junction, turn right to continue uphill. Follow the path east for about 600 metres; it climbs across a patch of boulders then leads past a couple of cairns, to the summit trig point of **Beinn Narnain** (926m).

Return 600 metres to the last junction. To return to Arrochar from here, retrace your outward steps. To climb Beinn Ìme, turn right here and follow the path west for 420 metres to a T-junction at the flat bealach, then turn right.

Walk north-north-west, crossing **Bealach a' Mhaim** towards the base of Beinn Ìme. Go through a gate and follow the obvious path up **Beinn Ìme**. Ignore one right turn marked with a small cairn and continue to the summit (1101m).

Descend the same way and return to the col between Beinn Ìme, Beinn Narnain and The Cobbler. Walk back towards the northern base of The Cobbler. You could go on to climb The Cobbler from here (see Walk 33). Then follow your outward route down the valley, along **Allt a' Bhalachain** and into the forest.

Narnain Boulders with The Cobbler in the distance

WALK 35

Arrochar to Ben Vane and Beinn Ìme

Start/finish	Arrochar, head of Loch Long, just east of the road bridge over Loin Water NN 298 050
Time	9hr; including the Cobbler: 10hr
Distance	20.2km (12.6 miles); including the Cobbler: 21.1km (13.1 miles)
Total ascent	1455m (4770ft); including the Cobbler: 1665m (5460ft)
Terrain	Wide valley path, small steep ridge path, pathless grassland, a good hill path and final descent by a gentle path
Max altitude	Beinn Ìme 1011m (3317ft)
Maps	OS Explorer OL39; OS Landranger 56; Harvey *Arrochar Alps*
Public transport	Buses to Arrochar. If catching the train to Arrochar and Tarbet station, see Walk 33 for connecting walk
Parking	Expensive pay and display parking (card/cash)

The well-trodden, rocky paths up Munros Ben Vane and Beinn Ìme stand in stark contrast with the pathless, fertile glen between them. This is the best sort of Arrochar wild country. High slopes of grass are interrupted by waterfalls, small gorges and overhanging outcrops; a green banked burn meanders down the valley floor, with glimpses of Loch Lomond, Loch Arklet and Loch Katrine leading off into the distance.

The day – probably long enough on its own – can be rounded off by an ascent of The Cobbler; otherwise, it's a gentle descent down by the Buttermilk Burn (Allt a' Bhalachain).

Just east of the road bridge over Loin Water, take a tarred track alongside the river marked, 'No unauthorised vehicles'. Walk along with the river on your left and after 240 metres turn right onto a footpath following a sign for the Loch Lomond and Cowal Way. The walk will follow the Loch Lomond and Cowal Way as far as the Coiregrogan track. Follow the path as it crosses the valley floor into woods on the west slope of **Cruach Tairbeirt**. At a path T-junction turn left, signposted for Inveruglas and **Glen Loin**.

WALK 35 – ARROCHAR TO BEN VANE AND BEINN ÌME

Follow the path north up the glen alongside a gravel road and two sets of pylons. After 2km, continue as the path crosses a wooden footbridge and then begins to climb. In a further 600 metres, go through a kissing gate and follow the path across the gravel road and into birch trees on the other side. After crossing the valley head under a pylon, follow the path as it descends northwards into a wide tree gap. Continue alongside trees on the left, then follow the path as it veers left to enter forest for 500 metres. Soon Ben Vane comes into view.

Follow the path as it bends right, across a field, to a gate where it joins a track near Coiregrogain. Turn right, over **Inveruglas Water**, to join a tarred access track at a waymark post.

Turn left up this private road (it goes to Loch Sloy Dam). After 600 metres turn left onto a track across a bridge and around the base of Ben Vane. Ignore the left turn to Coiregrogain and after 480 metres, below Ben Vane's east spur, the track crosses a small stream.

A path sets off to the right just before the stream, but continue for 30 metres to the start of a well-built stone path on your right. Take this as it heads up to the left of a small, wooded crag at the bottom of Ben Vane's steep east ridge.

Loch Sloy Dam

WALKING LOCH LOMOND AND THE TROSSACHS

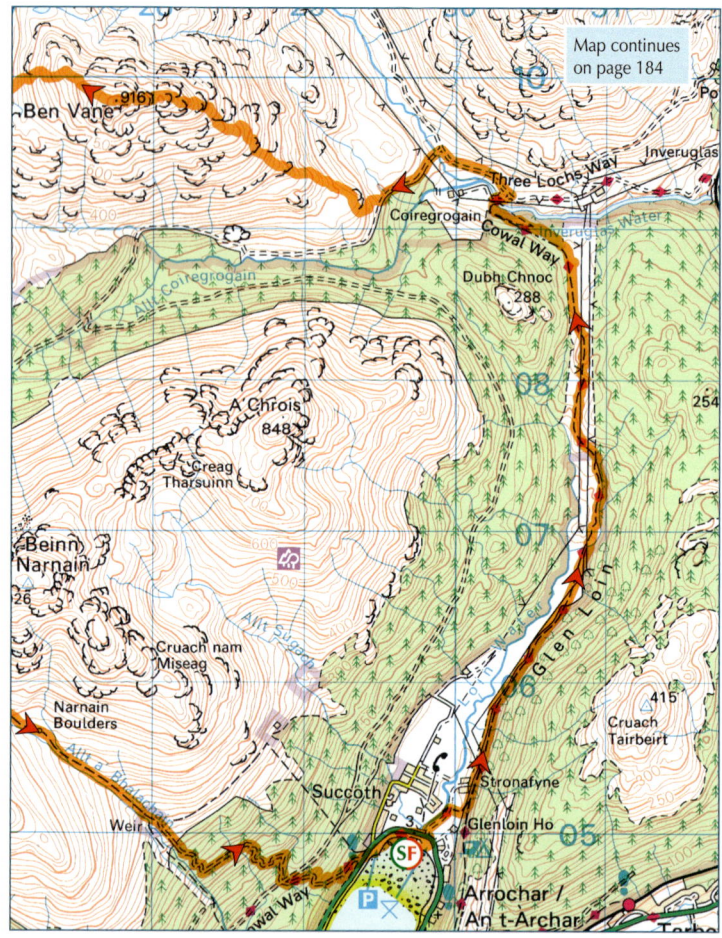

The massive, pioneering **Loch Sloy Dam** and hydroelectric scheme was the first project of a new North of Scotland Hydro-Electric Board formed in 1943. Construction began in 1945, but serious issues arose due to post-war shortages of materials and in the workforce. By late 1945, construction was employing 45 British men and 398 German prisoners of war. Further problems arose with access and weather, but the scheme was finally completed in 1950.

Walk north-east along the path, which now climbs the steep, bumpy ridge. It's eroded to bare rock in places and weaves from side to side of the ridge, passing below dripping crags. There are a few, unexposed scrambling moves and a false summit before you arrive at the sudden summit cairn of **Ben Vane** (916m).

A small pool is just beyond, and a second cairn. Head down generally westwards on pathless grass. Pass to the right of a swampy plateau at the 700m level. Don't shortcut to the left towards the broad, grassy saddle between Vane and Ìme – any such shortcutting leads to crag tops, so keep down west. There's a short crag band to work down through to reach a broad level ridge with pools, which leads left (south-west) to the glen between Bens Vane and Ìme. Named on recent OS maps as Lag Uaine, green hollow.

Ahead, three streams come down the side of Beinn Ìme. The left-hand one is larger, and runs down through a gorge, so ignore that. To the right, two parallel streams run down out of the col **Glas Bhealach** that's between Ìme and the almost-Corbett Beinn Chorranach. Follow either of these two streams, which both give easy passage through the band of broken ground at the slope top. The Glas Bhealach col is just above. Looking down on the valley is beautiful from above and Loch Lomond, Loch Arklet and Loch Katrine can be seen in the distance.

Turn left up the fairly steep slope of Beinn Ìme. It has broken crag in its left lower half. You can head straight up on a vestige of a path or, more excitingly, pass to the left onto a grass ledge through the crags, and zigzag back right up more grass, to the top of this craggy section. Stony slopes lead up to **Beinn Ìme's summit cairn** (1011m), perched on a little rock platform. The cairn contains remnants of a former trig point.

Descend south-east on a clear path that skirts down to the right of the nearby south-east top. Or you could cross it, to visit the crag-ringed far east top down beyond. Ignore a left turn marked by a cairn and continue south as the slope becomes broad and grassy, eventually reaching a gate (NN 262 071) at the **Bealach a' Mhaim**. Pass through the gate and continue into the wide, complex col between Ìme, Narnain and The Cobbler. Continue south on the path (ignoring two left turns to Beinn Narnain) to the Narnain/Cobbler col near **Lochan a' Chlaidheimh**. Here, the path joins a corner of The Cobbler's well-built ascent path. Here you might decide to take the detour path onto the Cobbler (Walk 33).

Otherwise keep ahead on the smooth, gentle path through the col and down the Buttermilk Burn (**Allt a' Bhalachain**), keeping to left of the stream. After 1.5km pass the two Narnain Boulders on your left.

WALKING LOCH LOMOND AND THE TROSSACHS

Continue down the main path, which descends into forest, for a further 2.4km until the path is intersected by a forest road. Turn left here and walk 50 metres before taking the continuing path on your right. Follow the zigzags down to the **A83**, cross the road, and follow the shoreside path around the head of **Loch Long** back to the start of the walk (or whichever car park/bus stop you might have started from).

WALK 36
Beinn Narnain and The Cobbler with optional extension to Beinn Ìme

Start/finish	Glenloin car park two near Succoth on the A83 NN 294 049
Time	6hr; including extension to Beinn Ìme: 8hr
Distance	11.4km (7.1 miles); including extension to Beinn Ìme: 15.2km (9.4 miles)
Total ascent	1140m (3740ft); including extension to Beinn Ìme: 1490m (4890ft)
Terrain	Rocky mountain paths with easy Grade 1 scrambling
Max altitude	Beinn Narnain 926m (3038ft); Beinn Ìme 1101m
Maps	OS Explorer OL39; OS Landranger 56; Harvey *Arrochar Alps*
Public transport	Buses to Arrochar. If catching the train to Arrochar and Tarbet station, see Walk 33 for connecting walk
Parking	Expensive pay and display parking (card/cash)
Note	For a more challenging scrambling on The Cobbler, see Walk 33.

Popular for different reasons, these two mountains are usually climbed individually: The Cobbler (884m) is one of Scotland's favourites for its true mountain feel and unique silhouette, while Beinn Narnain (926m) is an accessible Munro and good place to start for those wanting to complete a round. Regarding the experience of walking them, it's hard to choose a favourite, so this route visits both with the option of adding a second Munro: Beinn Ìme.

This isn't Beinn Narnain's easiest ascent: for that, see Walk 34. Here, though, the initial damp slog up the Munro's lower reaches is quickly rewarded with expansive views over Loch Long and the Luss Hills, as well as the dramatic, crumbling horns of The Cobbler. The peak of Beinn Narnain itself, with its imposing rock buttress, The Spearhead, isn't visible until you're nearly upon it, with a final steep, rocky ascent.

After descending to Lochan a' Chlaidheimh, a good path heads up to The Cobbler's summit plateau. The final descent described here heads west via An t-Sron before joining a well-made valley path.

Cross the **A83** from the south end of the car park and take a wide path signposted for The Cobbler and Beinn Narnain leading south-west. After a very short distance, notice where the path crosses a small stream, and 25 metres later look out for the start of a much less distinct path on your right – take this, heading north-west through the forest. It can be boggy underfoot.

After 250 metres, the path is intersected by a track; cross this and find where the path ascends steeply on the opposite side. Continue heading roughly north-west, ignore a left turn after 225 metres, and 500 metres further you'll reach a T-junction: bear right and continue uphill.

Leaving the forest, the path winds around rocks as you climb over Creag an Fhithich – with views over Loch Long and the Luss Hills – and on to **Cruach nam Miseag** where The Cobbler suddenly appears to the west. Finally, Beinn Narnain's summit comes into view ahead.

From the highest point of Cruach nam Miseag, The Spearhead rock buttress and precipitous rocks around Beinn Narnain's summit look intimidating, but follow the path as it descends before climbing, initially around to the left, weaving around sharp boulders. After passing below The Spearhead, the most obvious

Looking down Loch Long from Creag an Fhithich, Beinn Narnain

Walk 36 – Beinn Narnain and The Cobbler with optional extension to Beinn Ìme

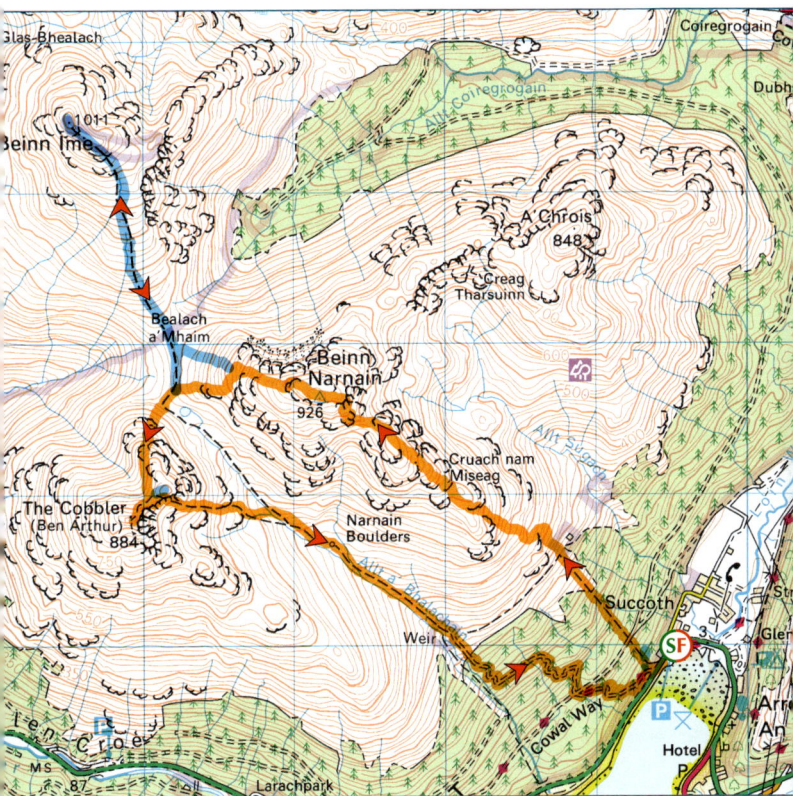

route is to scramble up the gully on its right-hand side, but easier ground can be found by continuing a little further before turning left.

Upon reaching the **Beinn Narnain** summit plateau, turn left and walk to the trig point at 926m. Looking south, you might catch a glimpse of Arran and Ailsa Craig on a clear day, while Ben Lomond breaks above the skyline to the east.

From the trig point, head towards the north-western shoulder of Beinn Narnain, where Beinn Ìme dominates the view, passing a couple of cairns and finding a path that begins to descend. Walk over a short section of small boulders before continuing on a grassy path heading west-north-west.

Roughly 600 metres from the summit trig, the path splits (NN 266 069).

Extension to Beinn Ìme

To climb Beinn Ìme, turn right here and follow the path west-north-west for 420 metres to a T-junction. Turn right (north-north-west), crossing **Bealach a' Mhaim** towards the base of Beinn Ìme. Go through a gate and follow the obvious path north-north-west up Beinn Ìme. Ignore one right turn marked with a small cairn and continue to the **summit** (1101m). Descend the same way and return to the col between Beinn Ìme, Beinn Narnain and The Cobbler. Walk towards the northern base of The Cobbler and continue to follow the instructions skipping one paragraph below.

Main route

To continue to The Cobbler, go left, heading in a more southerly direction on stone steps, descending gently towards **Lochan a' Chlaidheimh**. As you reach the lower ground between Beinn Narnain and The Cobbler, turn left at the first junction, walk along the path for 140 metres south-west, and then turn right towards The Cobbler.

Follow the obvious path up **The Cobbler**, passing a detour to its North Peak on your left (see the end of Walk 33 to climb this), until you reach the mountain's Central Peak. The view from the summit plateau is superb, but confident scramblers might want to attempt climbing the 'true' summit (see the end of Walk 33).

From the summit plateau, retrace your steps to the col between the Central and North peaks, then find and follow a path on the right leading steeply downhill and below the imposing wall of the North Peak, before heading generally east for about 1km with some short sections of easy scrambling.

Reaching Coire a' Bhalachain, turn right onto the main path which leads down along **Allt a' Bhalachain** and into the forest. After 3km the path is intersected by a track; turn left onto this and walk for 50 metres before taking the path on your right, which leads back to the start.

WALK 37
A' Chrois, Beinn Narnain and The Cobbler

Start/finish	Glenloin car park two near Succoth on the A83 NN 294 049
Time	7hr 30min; without The Cobbler: 6hr 30min
Distance	15.2km (9.4 miles); without The Cobbler 14.1km (8.8 miles)
Total ascent	1245m (4080ft); without The Cobbler: 1025m (3360ft)
Terrain	Tracks, paths and grassy ridge, but with very rough, steep grass up A' Chrois
Max altitude	Beinn Narnain 926m (3038ft)
Maps	OS Explorer OL39; OS Landranger 56; Harvey *Arrochar Alps*
Public transport	Buses to Arrochar. If catching the train to Arrochar and Tarbet station, see Walk 33 for connecting walk
Parking	Expensive pay and display parking (card/cash)
Note	For some challenging scrambling on The Cobbler, see Walk 33.

There's no getting around the fact that the unpathed, rough grass ascent of A' Chrois is arduous – perhaps defeatingly so in mid-summer. But when you finally reach the summit and the view opens to show the continuing ridge, your efforts are proved worthwhile.

On lawn-like grass, the lumpy ridgeline wanders around the broad, craggy corrie east of Beinn Narnain. There's drama in all directions: Ben Vane and Beinn Ìme dominate the north, while the rocky Sugach Buttress crumbles away south.

This route is recommended outside of July or August, avoiding the most vicious vegetation. There's no real scrambling, but careful and competent route-finding is required to navigate between crags on the steep upper slopes of A' Chrois – it's not advised in poor visibility, as you need to judge your line of ascent by eye.

If the weather is still on side, it's a pointless self-deprivation not to include The Cobbler at the end.

Cross the **A83** from the car park and take a lane towards **Succoth**. After 500 metres the lane bends right, over the Allt Sugach burn. Take a path up to the right of the stream – starting with a short stretch of fence on your left and an old stone wall on the right – past some small waterfalls and a concrete water tank.

At a forest road cross 20 metres to the right, where a narrow, mossy path resumes with a rocky step into a plantation. Follow the path, which soon veers right (somewhat unclear in one section) up to a higher forest road.

Here, turn right and walk north-north-east for 1.58km. Pass a turning place for forestry trucks, then reach a substantial passing place just after a small rocky waterfall, where there is a clear view of hills ahead. At this point, a rough track zigzags up to the left (NN 302 071). Follow it north-west up to the forest top at 300m. (From here the track runs south along the forest top for another 300 metres, making it easier to hit if descending off the hill.)

Where it first reaches the forest top, leave the track (NN 299 075) as it turns to the left and levels out, and turn up left, stepping over a broken rusty fence after about 10 metres. The initial slope is steep, with long grass and some bracken, making it arduous (especially in high summer). Ascend roughly north-north-west, choosing a good line and keeping to vegetated sections around the crags and boulders, towards the east ridge of A' Chrois. At 400m the going gets less severe, steadily improving from then on up. Once on the knolly ridgeline turn uphill, west. Quite soon you'll be confronted with the ridge hump at 590m, which has a drop beyond it defended by an overhanging crag. This is disconcerting, but it can be bypassed by taking a few steps down to its left (south) or right then circling round into the col below.

Sugach Buttress and Creag Tharsuinn with Ben Vane in the distance

WALK 37 – A' CHROIS, BEINN NARNAIN AND THE COBBLER

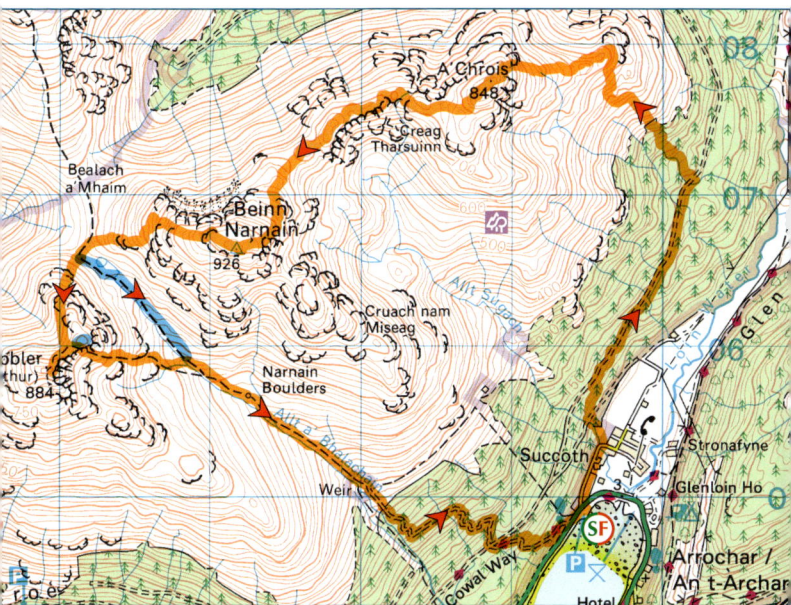

Continue as the ridgeline steepens, up to the band of broken ground defending A' Chrois. At the base of this broken ground (NN 291 078) a grassy gully slants up slightly to the right, its foot divided by a small crag. Pass up to left of the small crag and continue up the grassy gully. As the ground gets steeper, turn up left, on grassy slopes between small crags, to arrive at the northern point of the summit plateau (NN 289 077). Head south-west for 50 metres to **A' Chrois** cairn (849m – or 848m on some maps).

CORBETT TOPS

While A' Chrois is high enough to be counted as a Corbett (something your legs will be well aware of by now), this much-neglected mountain's lack of prominence above the connecting ridgeline with its neighbouring Munro classifies it as a 'Corbett top of Beinn Narnain'. Corbett tops are summits of within the same height range as Corbetts (762–914m), but with a drop of at least 30m on all sides rather than the 152.4m required for Corbett classification. There are 450 Corbett tops in Scotland.

The reward for the tough ascent is the grassy wander along the continuing ridgeline. Head south-west for 400 metres and drop off A' Chrois onto the grassy wide ridge below. Continue west along the ridge, on its narrow path. The path contours round left of the first knoll. This gives views down into the huge corrie east of Beinn Narnain. Then pass along above **Creag Tharsuinn** (781m), going over the small knolls to retain your views, rather than following the path as it tries to save effort on the northern flank. The ridgeline turns south-west to the base of the final slope of Beinn Narnain.

Head up the open slope. At its top, bypass a fringe of crag by heading to its left side, then clambering up the right-hand side of a gully filled with boulders. Emerging from the gully, you reach the flat summit plateau of **Beinn Narnain**. Continue to the Munro's summit trig point (926m).

From the trig point, head towards the north-western shoulder of Beinn Narnain, passing a couple of cairns and finding a descent path. Walk over a short section of small boulders before continuing on a grassy path heading west-north-west.

Roughly 600 metres from the summit trig, the path splits (NN 266 069); go left, heading roughly south-west on stone steps to **Lochan a' Chlaidheimh**. As you reach the lower ground between Beinn Narnain and The Cobbler, turn left at the first junction, walk along the path for 140 metres south-west.

Escape route

If you have had enough here, or the weather is unfavourable, keep ahead on the smooth, gentle path through the col and down **Allt a' Bhalachain** (Buttermilk Burn) south-east towards Arrochar. Walk past the dam and follow the well-made path into the forest. When the path is intersected by a track (NN 283 047), turn left onto this and walk for 50 metres before taking the continuing path on your right.

Main route

To continue up to **The Cobber**, turn right where the path splits at its northern base, and climb up following the obvious path. Ignore the left turn to the North Peak and continue to the Central summit plateau. (See Walk 33 for scrambling the summit and climbing the North Peak.)

From the summit plateau, retrace your steps to the col between the Central and North peaks, then find and follow a path on the right leading steeply downhill and below the dramatic North Peak crags, before heading generally east for about 1km with some short sections of easy scrambling.

Reaching Coire a' Bhalachain, turn right onto the main path which leads down along **Allt a' Bhalachain** and into the forest. After 3km the path is intersected by a track; turn left onto this and walk for 50 metres before taking the path on your right, which leads back to the start.

PART 10 GLEN CROE TO LOCH GOIL

Climbing over the northern shoulder of Cnoc Coinnich with Beinn an Lochain and its surrounding hills behind (Walk 39)

Just west of the Arrochar Alps – and included within them by some definitions – a small collection of craggy hills looms over the forests of Ardgartan and Rest and Be Thankful pass. Beinn an Lochain, The Brack and Ben Donich (two Corbetts and a Munro) each have one well-trodden path, which you could use for their ascent and descent, but the routes suggested here are longer, rambling circuits with better views and a sense of adventure. The third route, Argyll's Bowling Green, leaves the rumble of the A83 far behind, meandering through peaceful mountain glens without chasing the summits at all – the group's third Corbett, Cnoc Coinnich, is an optional addition.

WALK 38
The Brack and Ben Donich

Start/finish	Car park off B828, 480m south-west of Rest and Be Thankful NN 228 070
Alternative start	Ardgartan Forestry and Land Scotland car park (NN 270 037) could be used as an alternative starting point, with straightforward navigation along forest tracks to begin. This adds a total of 3.4km (2.1 miles), 125m (410ft) ascent and 45min.
Time	7hr; Ben Donich without The Brack: 4hr 30min; The Brack without Ben Donich: 5hr 30min); starting at Ardgartan car park: 7hr 45min
Distance	13.2km (8.2 miles); Ben Donich without The Brack: 9.7km (6 miles); The Brack without Ben Donich: 10.4km (6.5 miles); starting at Ardgartan car park: 16.6km (10.3 miles)
Total ascent	1085m (3560ft); Ben Donich without The Brack: 650m (2130ft); The Brack without Ben Donich: 740m (2430ft); starting at Ardgartan car park: 1210m (3970ft)
Terrain	Steep grass slopes, grassy ridges, rocky path, track
Max altitude	Ben Donich 847m (2779ft)
Maps	OS Explorer OL39; OS Landranger 56; Harvey *Arrochar Alps*
Public transport	There are bus stops at Rest and Be Thankful and Ardgartan
Parking	The car park off B828 is free, as is Rest and Be Thankful

A double Corbett hike: The Brack is superbly rugged, grass giving way to rock in unexpected ways; Ben Donich is smoother, but higher and has interesting rock chasms on the northern descent ridge. There are great views to the less commonly seen southern aspects of the Arrochar Alps across Glen Croe with The Cobbler dominating the scene to the north. The sprawling Cowal peninsula stretches seaward, out to the south-west.

The described ascent of The Brack is relentlessly steep, but life gets easier for the remainder of the walk, with a more comfortable ascent of Ben Donich's eastern shoulder.

WALK 38 – THE BRACK AND BEN DONICH

The Arrochar Alps from Ben Donich

From the car park, walk 190 metres south along a forest track. When you reach a junction, take the left turn marked '**Glen Croe**'. Walk east then south-east along this forest track for 830 metres, then when you reach a track junction, take the right fork, which keeps to higher ground.

Ben Donich only

To climb Ben Donich excluding The Brack, follow the forest road for a further 1.7km looking out for a wooden post with a white symbol indicating a hiker on the right (NN 241 048). Take this path up into the forest and follow it south-south-west for 280 metres to a stile with a tall white pole. Cross the stile and follow a path marked by white poles uphill for 320 metres to the base of Ben Donich's east flank (NN 241 042). Turn right and continue the instructions from 'To climb Ben Donich', halfway through this route.

Main route to The Brack

Continue on the track through forest for 3.17km from the track junction. Look out for a wooden post on the right marked 'Hill Access to The Brack' (NN 252 040) – take this right turn onto a narrow path, which runs up to the left of a stream with waterfalls. The path is extremely steep, especially at the start, and seriously eroded by both feet and water. It reaches a fence and a place where a stile is missing at the forest's top (NN 252 037 – 50 metres east of where the stream enters the trees – there is a white pole here, not easily seen by descenders from above). Step either over or under the fence depending on your stature.

After 100 metres follow the path as it turns right, and crosses the stream between two waterfalls, then continue uphill just to the right of the stream. This leads into a shallow corrie under the broken final face of The Brack (NN 249 032). One big boulder in this corrie has space under to shelter a couple of people, with a fine view across to The Cobbler.

From here easy slopes lead up left to a col, but a steep grass gully up to the right offers a more direct and interesting way towards the summit. Following the gully, from 550m altitude (NN 248 032) take a small path, which weaves among fallen blocks before reaching the Brack's north ridge just below the summit. Head south for 100 metres to **The Brack**'s summit (787m).

From the summit, descend north-north-west through Elephant's Gully, with steep drops on the right; then swing slightly further north-west into the wide boggy col between The Brack and Ben Donich (Bealach Dubh-lic). Cross a fence (NN 241 041), which runs across the low point of the col. In another 100 metres, a path with white-topped poles also runs across. For an easy escape bear right on this path, down rough grass to a marked stile into the trees. A path leads down to the forest track below.

To climb Ben Donich

Head up the wide, gentle ridge following a faint path up Ben Donich's east flank. At the 570m knoll (NN 233 043) there's a conspicuous cairn on the right among crag hollows and overhangs. The main ridgeline passes to left of this cairn. The cairn makes a lunch spot and a foreground feature for photos in several directions.

Continue up the ridgeline to reach a mossy plateau, where you will come to a well-trodden path; turn left onto this path and **Ben Donich** summit (847m) is 400 metres to the south-west.

To descend, return across the mossy plateau, and bear left to descend the north ridge of Ben Donich where there is a well-trodden path. At the 650m contour the ridge rises slightly in a mass of crag and landslip, with strange deep cracks; the path has a fine moment passing through and over the blocks. Beinn an Lochain and Loch Restil (Walk 40) make a picturesque scene ahead. After this,

WALK 38 – THE BRACK AND BEN DONICH

the ridge gets grassy again. Continue to follow the path north-north-east to a gate (NN 229 065); go through this and follow the obvious path into trees. Keep to this well-surfaced path for 380 metres until you reach a junction with a forest track which runs through **Gleann Mòr**. Turn right onto this and walk roughly north for 370 metres back to the car park.

WALK 39
Argyll's Bowling Green

Start/finish	Ardgartan Forestry and Land Scotland car park NN 270 037
Time	5hr; including Cnoc Coinnich: 6hr 30min
Distance	15.6km (9.7 miles); including Cnoc Coinnich: 17.9km (11.1 miles)
Total ascent	655m (2150ft); including Cnoc Coinnich: 895m (2940ft)
Terrain	Forest track and paths, valley path and hillside slopes with one short section of arduous ground in a felled forestry area
Max altitude	Argyll's Bowling Green 500m (1640ft); Cnoc Coinnich 764m (2506ft)
Maps	This route annoyingly straddles OS Explorer OL37 and OL39; OS Landranger 56; Harvey *Arrochar Alps*
Public transport	There is a bus stop just south on the A83
Parking	Free at Ardgartan Forestry and Land Scotland car park, which also has toilets

Argyll's Bowling Green is a poorly defined and entertainingly named area between Loch Long and Loch Goil. A corruption of the Gaelic *Baile na Greine* or 'Sunny Hamlet,' the term is sometimes stretched to include the whole Ardgoil peninsula including The Brack – the region is far from flat.

This route muddles together forest tracks, mountain glens, open hillside and a peaceful stretch of Loch Long's shoreline to create a pleasing circle. There are mountain views without really needing to climb any, but if you've chosen a good day, it seems a shame to miss the nearby Corbett, Cnoc Coinnich, which only adds 240m of ascent.

Starting at the Forestry and Land Scotland car park, cross the **River Croe** and turn right passing a further car park and following a cycle path sign going uphill onto a wide dirt track. Continue north-west then west on this for 1.8km to a T-junction; turn right here to continue up Glen Croe. There are views through the trees to the slopes of The Cobbler.

Walk up this new track for 1.57km, ignoring the turning for The Brack hill path on your left shortly after the junction; look out for a white pole on your right. Continue for 15 metres past the pole to a left turn onto a smaller path marked with a large wooden post and a hiker symbol (NN 241 048). Now heading south-west, climb up the rocky path through a mossy forest floor for 200 metres to emerge from the trees. Continue straight ahead towards a white pole and a stile with the slopes of Ben Donich on your right.

Ben Donich beyond a stile and gate on the Cowal Way

Cross the stile and continue ahead (south) following more sporadically placed white poles and a narrow, boggy path, which climbs to 400m to cross Ben Donich's eastern foot. Reaching the high point, walk between a distinctive, pointed boulder and a wooden stick on its left, then head south-west down the valley between The Brack and Ben Donich keeping to the west side of **Allt Coire Odhair**, with a fence running parallel some 70 metres to your left.

Continue for 1km, crossing several small burns, until the path meets a fence in line with the edge of a forested area. Here, cross a stile (indicated with a white post, NN 233 034) and then a burn over a plastic pipe to join a narrow path through felled forest. After 150 metres, keep to the path as it crosses another small burn and continues through an area of young trees.

After another 400 metres, turn left at a junction with a wide forest road and cross a bridge over the Allt Coire Odhair. Follow the track as it bears right and continues south-west for 1km rising to a good view of the hills beyond Loch Goil. Ignore one intersecting track and continue to the forest road's abrupt end.

At the end of the track, continue ahead (south-west) following a rough path over an area of felled trees for 400 metres (this terrain, which is also boggy in parts, makes for very irritating walking, but is thankfully short-lived). When you meet a sign for the **Cowal Way** (NN 221 018) turn left, uphill, onto a much better path where you will soon meet a bench and a sign for Coilessan. Continue uphill with plantation trees on your right and a felled area on the left for about 200 metres, then follow an arrow directing you to bear right, and marker poles, which lead to a stile (NN 224 016) by a bench.

WALKING LOCH LOMOND AND THE TROSSACHS

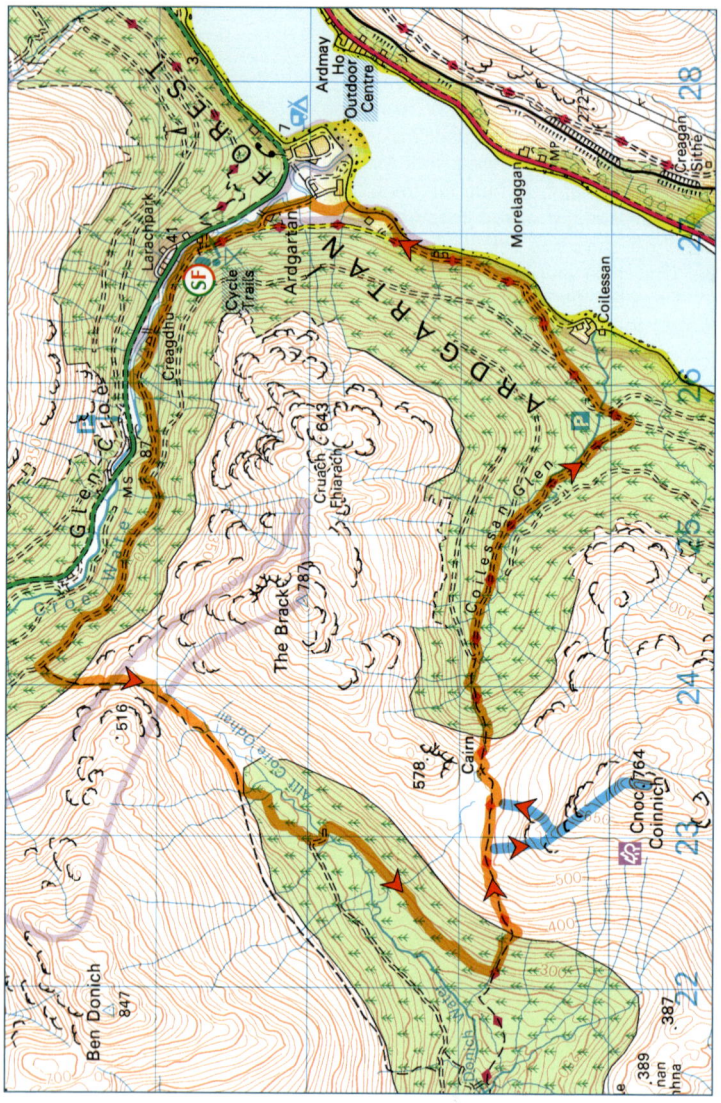

Cross the stile and bear left (east-north-east), following a few more marker posts to cross Argyll's Bowling Green and the saddle between The Brack and Cnoc Coinnich at around 500m. Ben Lomond looks majestic ahead.

To climb Cnoc Connich

Bear off to the right (south-east) here and ascend the fairly clear ridgeline, past some perched boulders and then with crag drops on the left, to **Cnoc Coinnich** summit cairn (764m). Descend the same ridge until just past the perched boulders, at 600m altitude. Now follow grassy slopes down to the right (north) to rejoin the marked path.

Main route

Cross a low bridge over a burn and continue east to reach a substantial signpost (missing its arrows at the time of research, but at the point of a cairn marked on the 1:25,000 OS map, NN 234 019) at the brow of the hill overlooking **Coilessan Glen**. Descend bearing right (not crossing a fence below/left to a stile (NN 237 018) and gate into forest.

Cross the stile and turn left onto a path, which descends through trees. After 330 metres, cross a forest road and continue along a narrow path, which soon crosses two footbridges. When you reach a second junction with the forest road, join it and continue ahead downhill. After 900 metres, bear right at the next junction, continuing downhill. In a further 440 metres, cross a road bridge over **Coilessan Burn**, then continue straight/downhill at the junction just afterwards. Continue south-east for a further 670 metres to a T-junction above Loch Long. Turn left here and walk north-east. Ignore a road joining from the right, cross another bridge over Coilessan Burn, and pass a parking area on the left, continuing downhill. Pass some stone ruins and at the next junction bear right, downhill, following a sign for car park and toilets.

Continue for a further 1.2km passing a couple of houses and a small waterfall. Just 240 metres past the houses, look out for an arrow post to a smaller path on the right; follow this to walk along the loch shore. Keep to this path for 440 metres, passing a small house with a swing on the shoreline then, when the path splits 100 metres before the massive Ardgartan Hotel, leave the loch shore and turn left onto a path through woodland.

Follow the woodland path for 300 metres, then turn left onto a minor road following an arrow for the Cowal Way. Walk upstream beside the **Croe Water** river, passing a stone ruin and a pink house. After 270 metres, don't cross the bridge but continue straight (left fork), then at the T-junction just afterwards turn right following a sign for the car park and toilets. Walk a final 370 metres, then cross the bridge back to the car park where this route began.

WALK 40

Beinn an Lochain

Start/finish	Car park off B828, 480m south-west of Rest and Be Thankful NN 228 070
Time	3hr 30min
Distance	6.6km (4.1 miles)
Total ascent	635m (2080ft)
Terrain	Steep pathless hillside, pathed ridge and rough grassland
Max altitude	Beinn an Lochain 901m (2956ft)
Maps	OS Explorer OL37; OS Landranger 56; Harvey *Arrochar Alps*
Public transport	Bus stop at Rest and Be Thankful
Parking	The car park off B828 is free, as is Rest and Be Thankful

Beinn an Lochain was originally classed as a Munro. Early hillwalkers of the Scottish Mountaineering Club reached the 840m south summit and worked out its height by sighting on neighbouring hills; but they then ascended into mist, and badly overestimated the extra ascent to the main summit. The correction came in 1974 – 901m Beinn an Lochain being, now, the lowest ex-Munro.

It doesn't feel like a Munro; perhaps because of the 250m start-point, but it is blessed with a fine north-east ridge, sharpened by landslips on the northern side, so the path is actually a little exposed. To create a loop, this route uses a very steep, pathless ascent of the south-eastern flank before descending that good ridge – a straightforward up and down from the lower, car park (NN 234 089 by Easan Duch Fall, north of Loch Restil) is more popular.

Start out from the car park by turning left on the **B828** for about 30 metres, then cross the road and ditch to find some vehicle tyre marks and old wooden posts, which briefly aid the first ascent north-west. Head uphill to the right of a plantation for 300 metres, then bear left and skirt around the top of the forest south-west for 200 metres or so before beginning a direct ascent north-west on a steep slope of wet grass. Aim for the east side of Beinn an Lochain's southern summit.

Along the western bank of Loch Restil

After a tough ascent, weaving among small outcrops, you arrive suddenly and satisfyingly at the top. Continue north along a path, which runs past a pretty lochan and along a pleasant ridge to **Beinn an Lochain**'s main summit (901m).

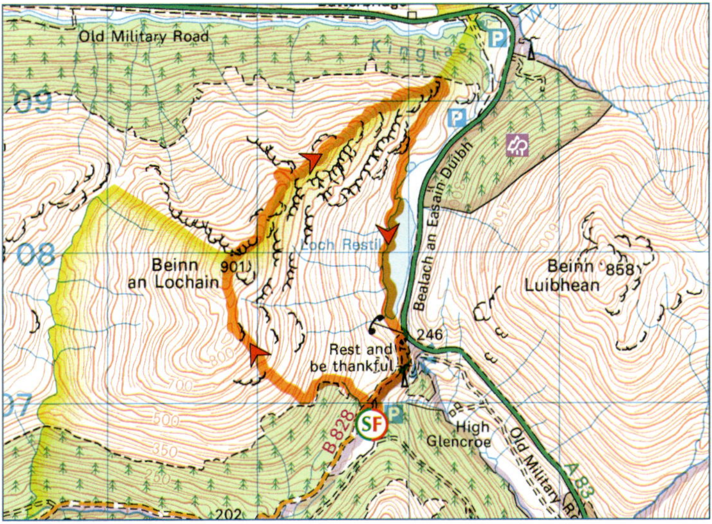

WALKING LOCH LOMOND AND THE TROSSACHS

Now the splendid ridge runs down north-east, with crags dropping to the right. On the opposite side you look down into the mass of broken rock where half the ridge has collapsed towards Loch Fyne. Follow the small, rather exposed path as it zigzags down; it's steep, but does not require anything that really counts as scrambling.

At the foot of the ridge the path drops off to the right, onto moorland, where it passes between two boulders. To walk back along the west bank of Loch Restil, leave the path at the two boulders, and contour to the right (south) with imposing crags above. The ground is rough but there are traces of paths, leading to a small dam at the outflow of **Loch Restil**. Continue south as path traces lead along the loch's western shore to **Rest and Be Thankful** car park, viewpoint and – if you're lucky – snack van.

> Built in response to the Jacobite uprisings, the original road here was built between 1747 and 1749 by 450 soldiers and civilians, who inscribed a stone set into a turf seat at the high point, **'Rest, and Be Thankful'**.

From here, follow the narrow **B828** south then south-west back to the car park at the start.

The winding path down Beinn an Lochain's northern ridge

PART 11 COWAL

An intermittent path follows the grassy ridgeline between Creachan Mòr and A' Chruach (Walk 41)

Quite separate from the rest of the national park, the Cowal peninsula splinters off into the sea. Cowal (pronounced 'cow-ul') is *Comhghall* in Gaelic – the name refers to Comgall mac Domangairt, an early sixth-century king of Dál Riata who is thought to have centred his power here. Long saltwater lochs defend this region from the casual tourist, with a few historic villages dotted among the quiet forest and loch shores. Some – not all – of the lower hill slopes are prickly with impenetrable plantations; the steep sides are surprisingly craggy, while the tops above are pathless and coarsely grassy.

In this section, you'll find one rough hillwalk (Walk 41), an easy wander through magical Puck's Glen, and a short but rewarding climb up little Strone Hill, which looks out over the sea – there should be something here for everyone.

WALK 41
Loch Eck and Beinn Mhòr

Start/finish	Car park at Benmore Gardens NS 143 855
Time	7hr 30min
Distance	19.7km (12.2 miles)
Total ascent	880m (2890ft)
Terrain	After the good approach track, the route is predominantly pathless with tussocks, boggy areas, and steep vegetated sections
Max altitude	Beinn Mhòr 741m (2431ft)
Maps	OS Explorer OL37; OS Landranger 56
Public transport	There is a convenient bus stop on the A815
Parking	Free parking at Benmore Gardens (worth visiting in their own right and with an excellent café)

Don't be fooled by the manageable-looking metres of elevation on this route, the rough terrain covered makes for an arduous day's outing, which should not be underestimated. While Argyll has easier hikes to higher summits, the solitude and spellbinding scenery found along this adventurous route make the significant effort involved worthwhile. The peaceful Cowal peninsula has no hill higher than Beinn Mhòr on the western side of Loch Eck, or in the south leading down to the sea. The summit looks out across the national park, with the Arrochar Alps, Ben Lomond and Ben Lui all visible on a clear day; to the south, Goatfell and the outline of Arran are across the Firth of Clyde, and the Paps of Jura peek over Kintyre to the west.

From the car park, take a track marked 'private road' and cross the **River Eachaig** over a bridge. At a track junction just beyond, turn right. Walk north for 300 metres, passing **Benmore Gardens**, then follow the track as it bends left past the buildings of Benmore Farmstead and a clock tower. When you reach a T-junction, turn right onto a lane and walk north. Continue past the foot of **Loch Eck** to a hydroelectricity plant, then go straight ahead through a gate onto a stony track, which leads along the peaceful loch shore. Follow this for 4km north, past the promontory at Coirantee and Rubha Ban Frionais point. Some 400 metres beyond Rubha Ban Frionais, follow the track as it bends left to a junction near **Bernice**. Here, turn left onto a forest track (NS 134 914).

WALK 41 – LOCH ECK AND BEINN MHÒR

Walking above Coire an t-Sìth between Beinn Mhòr and Clach Bheinn

Follow this track up for 70 metres, then leave it behind, turning right (west) onto the rough grassland above to a gate. Go through the gate, then loosely follow a fence line uphill across boggy ground before slanting up right to the edge of a plantation where a gate stands at a fence junction. Go through the gate, turn left and follow a rough path south uphill, avoiding the worst of the bracken, to reach the plantation's corner. Contour around the corner to the plantation's most southerly point, then head directly uphill (south-south-west) across grassy tussocks to **Meall an t-Sìth** (Hill of the Fairies) at around 469m. Here, rocky knolls protrude from shimmering white grass – a miniature landscape above the treeline and loch. There are great views over Loch Eck and Bernice Glen.

Turn right and follow a fence west-north-west up the flank of **Meall Dubh** and across the grassy plateau above. When you reach a fence junction, cross the fence in front of you and continue ahead (west) for 380 metres to the prominent trig point on **Beinn Mhòr** (741m). The views across Cowal, the peaks of the national park and coastal Argyll are superb.

From the summit, return south-east keeping to the higher ground near the fence line. After 500 metres another fence runs roughly south; keep to its left

WALKING LOCH LOMOND AND THE TROSSACHS

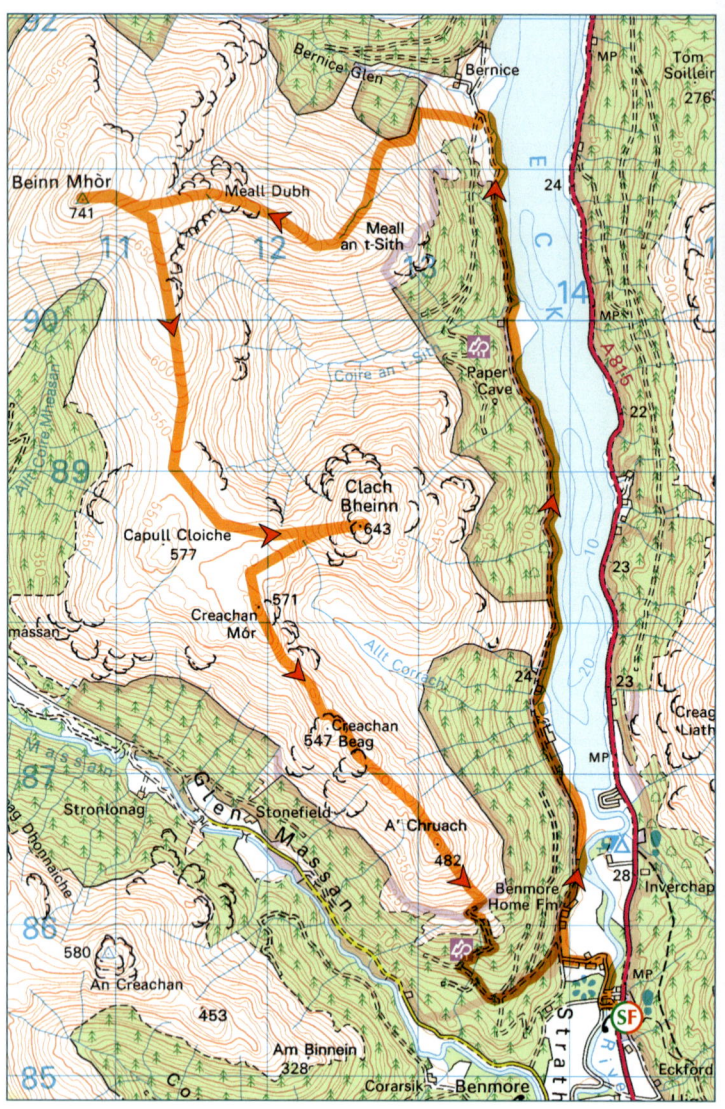

WALK 41 – LOCH ECK AND BEINN MHÒR

following the higher line of the ridge south for 1.6km. There are spectacular views over Coire an t-Sìth below on your left. Descending into a wide, boggy col, contour round left (losing as little height as possible) into the lower col at the south-western side of **Clach Bheinn**, then choose a good line for the steep, grassy climb between crags to the summit (643m). From here, the bulky shape of Beinn Mhòr is more impressive.

Return to the soggy, boggy col and head south-west for 400 metres to the lumpy knoll of **Creachan Mòr** (571m) – be careful not to overshoot west and end up at Capull Cloiche. From Creachan Mòr, follow a grassy ridge south-east with occasional rusty fence posts and sections of path over **Creachan Beag** (547m) to the summit of **A' Chruach** (482m). Descend south-east over more chaotically rough ground where a few old iron posts lead to a rough track and fence above the treeline. Bear right for about 100 metres to find a gateway (NS 134 861) leading into the woodland below.

Go through the gateway onto a narrow, rough track, which leads to the right before weaving down through the trees for 500 metres to join another, more substantial track. Turn left and keep to the largest track ahead as it leads downhill along the top edge of **Benmore Gardens**. Ignore a gate on the right and tracks forking off left. The main track slants downhill and joins the minor road from the outward route. Turn right onto the road to rejoin your outward route via the clock tower to the car park.

Looking over Loch Eck

WALK 42
Puck's Glen

Start/finish	Car park at Benmore Gardens NS 143 855
Time	2hr; excluding the Upper Glen: 1hr 30min
Distance	5.7km (3.5 miles); excluding the Upper Glen: 5.3km (3.3 miles)
Total ascent	225m (740ft); excluding the Upper Glen: 150m (490ft)
Terrain	Paths and tracks
Max altitude	Upper Puck's Glen 230m (755ft)
Maps	OS Explorer OL37; OS Landranger 56
Public transport	There's a convenient bus stop on the A815
Parking	Free at Benmore Gardens (both gardens and café are well worth a visit)

Glowing green with dripping moss and delicate ferns, Puck's Glen is a smoothed, rocky ravine carved out by the Eas Mòr burn. In the 1870s, the new owner of Benmore Estate, James Duncan, added paths, steps and bridges to the gorge so his visitors could soak up the mystical atmosphere. In folklore, the puck are mischievous mythological demons or fairies, also appearing as Puck, a character in Shakespeare's play, *A Midsummer Night's Dream* – the glen seems an appropriate habitat for such creatures.

This popular area is run by Forestry and Land Scotland and is subject to closures as a result of storm damage and forestry work. Alternative marked trails in the area can be found on their website route card for Puck's Glen or in Puck's Glen car park (1.6km south along the A815 from Benmore Gardens).

Start by crossing the **River Eachaig** on a track marked 'private road', then turn left. Follow this track south for 600 metres, then turn left on a path to cross a metal footbridge over the river and join a track at **Uig** village hall; follow this out to the **A815**.

Cross the road onto the track opposite and follow it to a junction with an old road along the glen. Turn right here and walk south 500 metres, passing a green barn and then a sign for Puck's Glen car park. Cross a stone bridge with an iron mile-marker '6 miles from Dunoon Pier', then turn up left, with the stream on your left, following a sign for 'Puck's Glen Gorge and Black Gates Trail', Follow a well-built path south-east inside the little green ravine of **Puck's Glen**.

WALK 42 – PUCK'S GLEN

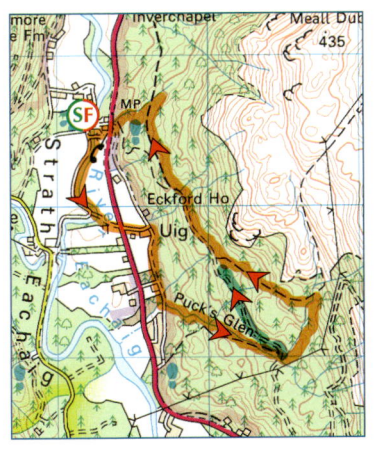

After 400 metres and an uncountable number of small waterfalls, the path rises up the right side of the ravine to a junction. Continue ahead (left fork) on a path dropping back into the glen. Continue upstream, until the path rises to a forest road.

The Upper Puck Loop, ahead, is no longer waymarked as an official path. If necessary, you could just turn left along this forest road – follow it north-west for 2.1km to a turning marked as a cycle route which leads down to Benmore Gardens. If it is open, take this rougher path ahead continuing upstream. After 400 metres, several more waterfalls and a set of stepping stones, it rises up the left-hand side of the stream hollow. Here, at a junction with two wooden markers, turn left onto a smooth, contouring path through conifers.

Follow the path as it passes through open ground with views up the valley, then descends to rejoin the forest road. Turn right on this track, which runs roughly level up the valley. Two signposted trails down left are shortcuts to Benmore Gardens; or continue to a third (marked as a cycle path), just before a stream, which doubles back to the left. It zigzags down to Black Gates, directly opposite the car park at **Benmore Gardens**.

Ferns and moss grow thick in the woodland glen

WALK 43
Kilmun to Strone Hill

Start/finish	Kilmun Pier NS 171 816
Time	3hr
Distance	7.2km (4.5 miles)
Total ascent	380m (1250ft)
Terrain	Forest track and paths, which are steep and occasionally boggy towards the summit
Max altitude	Strone Hill 385m (1263ft)
Maps	OS Explorer OL37; OS Landranger 63 and 56 (only the very summit of Strone Hill on 56)
Public transport	Bus stop at Memorial Graham's Point
Parking	Free at Kilmun Pier and Memorial Graham's Point

While most of the hill walks in this book climb a high point to look out over Loch Lomond and The Trossachs, this one visits the national park's boundary where you can stand on its very edge looking out to sea. The splintered peninsula and sea lochs of Cowal feel far away from the freshwater shores of Loch Lomond or the mighty Munros further north, but the region has a specific, peaceful charm as well as a rich history – this walk provides a brief introduction and a good overview.

The route itself is rewarding and straightforward, although a bit steep and boggy at times approaching the summit.

Starting at **Kilmun Pier**, turn right onto the pavement and walk 430 metres southeast beside the road to **Memorial Graham's Point**, which juts out into Holy Loch with a bus stop, play park and benches.

> The holy origins of the loch are thought to date from the late sixth and early seventh centuries, when the Irish **Saint Munn** (Fintán of Taghmon) landed at Kilmun and founded a monastic community. Kilmun Parish Church and Argyll Mausoleum are said to stand where his church was once located. The village of Kilmun is named after the church, with the Gaelic *Cill Mhunna* meaning 'Munna's Church'.

WALK 43 – KILMUN TO STRONE HILL

Walk around the point and then continue along the road for 130 metres past another bus stop. Turn left up an unmarked road past a large, square, white house called Hillside. Ignore the right turn down Johnston Avenue and continue past Hillside Cottage, which has a defibrillator outside attached to a garage with an arched door – just after this, turn right onto a path past a wooden barrier and follow it as it runs beside a mossy stone wall with ferns, above the row of houses on Johnston Avenue.

Continue along the narrow path as it climbs for 350 metres through mixed woodland, crossing a burn and then meeting a forest track. Turn left onto the forest track and walk a short distance to a junction, then turn right to continue walking east.

Follow the track uphill for 1km as the view opens up over Holy Loch and down the Firth of Clyde. On a clear day, you can see as far as the distinctive island of Ailsa Craig from here. When you reach a large four-way junction, take a small path up sharp left (there was a tiny arrow on a wooden post at the time of research). Follow the path as it swings round to lead north into dense spruce forest with a mossy carpet. When the path splits at an old stone wall after 400 metres, do not cross the wall, but instead turn left uphill – the route now roughly follows the course of this wall north-west to the summit. When the path splits again and gets steep, keep left heading directly up (do not cross the wall here); if you meet a rusty fence, head left for a few more metres to rediscover the path heading north-west. This section can be boggy. Follow the path as it bends back to the right towards the wall and continues on its left side. After 150 metres, cross the wall at

Ardnadam and Dunoon, where Holy Loch joins the Firth of Clyde

the corner of a fence (again marked with a tiny arrow on a post) and continue up on the right-hand side of the wall.

A few hundred metres further you emerge from the trees onto heathery moorland. Continue along the course of the path beside the wall until it ends as another wall arrives from the east (make a mental note of which wall to follow back down!). Almost immediately the summit trig point of **Strone Hill** comes into view. Continue to the top (385m) where there's a view over Loch Long and into the national park, as well as across the east of Cowal, across Dunoon to the Isle of Bute, Arran and Great Cumbrae Island.

Return the same way.

APPENDIX A
Munros and Corbetts by route number

Munros
- An Caisteal (995m) – Walk 25
- Beinn a' Chleibh (916m) – Walk 22
- Beinn a' Chroin (942m) – Walk 25
- Beinn Chabhair (933m) – Walk 26
- Beinn Dubhchraig (978m) – Walk 22
- Beinn Ìme (1011m) – Walk 34, 35 and 36
- Beinn Narnain (926m) – Walk 34, 36 and 37
- Beinn Tulaichean (946m) – Walk 12
- Beinn Challuim (1025m) – Walk 24
- Ben Lomond (974m) – Walk 27
- Ben Lui (1130m) – Walk 22 and 23
- Ben More (1174m) – Walk 13
- Ben Oss (1029m) – Walk 22
- Ben Vane (916m) – Walk 35
- Ben Vorlich, Loch Lomond (943m) – Walk 32
- Ben Vorlich, Loch Earn (985m) – Walk 17
- Cruach Ardrain (1046m) – Walk 12
- Meall Glas (959m) – Walk 19
- Sgiath Chùil (921m) – Walk 19
- Stob Binnein (1165m) – Walk 13
- Stùc a' Chroin (975m) – Walk 17

Corbetts
- Beinn a' Choin (770m) – Walk 6
- Beinn an Lochain (901m) – Walk 40
- Beinn Chaorach (818m) – Walk 24
- Beinn Chuirn (880m) – Walk 23
- Beinn Each (813m) – Walk 9
- Beinn Odhar (901m) – Walk 21
- Ben Donich (847m) – Walk 38
- Ben Ledi (879m) – Walk 5
- Benvane (821m) – Walk 5
- Cam Chreag (884m) – Walk 24
- Cnoc Coinnich (764m) – Walk 39
- Creag Mac Rànaich (809m) – Walk 16
- Meall an t-Seallaidh (852m) – Walk 16
- Stob a'Choin (869m) – Walk 11
- The Brack (787m) – Walk 38
- The Cobbler (884m) – Walk 33, 36 and 37

APPENDIX B
Access information

Since 2005 Scotland has a legal right of access to almost all open country and farmland (the main exceptions being growing crops and land around buildings). Walking and cycling are included, but the provision does not apply to motor vehicles. Access also includes wild camping, but within the national park specific restrictions – Camping Management Zones – apply to popular loch shores and roadsides between March and September (see 'Camping and accommodation' in the introduction to this book). For information about your access rights and responsibilities, see the Scottish Outdoor Access Code www.outdooraccess-scotland.scot.

Deer stalking

Part of the public's specified responsibilities include avoiding disturbance to deer stalking. Deer management can take place during many months of the year, but the most sensitive time is the stag stalking season (usually from 1 July to 20 October, but with most stalking taking place from August onwards). During this season, you can help to minimise disturbance by taking reasonable steps to find out where stalking is taking place, following signs and by taking account of advice on alternative routes. Most of the routes in this book are unaffected by stalking, but you should check the Scottish Outdoor Access Code website page 'Heading for the Scottish Hills' for up-to-date information and estate contact details. Sections 6 (Central Highlands) and 7 (Southern Highlands) cover this area. Hill routes most likely to be affected include those around Ben Lui, east of the Ben More and Stob Binnean ridge, and Meall Glas.

APPENDIX C
Gaelic in the landscape

The national park authority (www.lochlomond-trossachs.org) produces an invaluable guide to Gaelic place names called 'What's in a name?' – the best version comes as a paper leaflet, but the 'Our Gaelic culture' pages of the website are also very helpful. While Gaelic has over 100 words which imply a type of hill, some crop up repeatedly. The following is a list of common Gaelic landscape features and words that appear frequently in place names, along with their approximate pronunciations and definitions.

allt – 'owlt' – burn, stream

àrd/àird – 'aarsd' – tall/promontory, headland, height

beag – 'beg' – small

bealach – 'BYALuch' – a mountain pass

beinn (often Anglicised to *ben*) – 'bayn' – mountain or big hill

càrn – 'karn' – cairn

cnoc – 'krochk' – hill

coire – 'KORuh' – corrie

creag – 'krayk' – crag

druim – 'DROOim' – ridge

gleann – 'GLEH-own' – glen, valley

maol – 'moeul' – bare hill, mountain

meall – 'myowl' – lump-shaped hill, mountain

mòr – 'moar' – big

sìthea/sìdhean – 'SHEEhun' – knoll (related to the 'sìthichean' or fairies)

sròn – 'stron' – nose, point or the end of mountain ridge

stob – 'stop' – a high rocky hill like a pointed stick

taigh/tigh – 'tuh-ee' – house

tom – 'town' – hillock

APPENDIX D
The long routes

West Highland Way
The West Highland Way runs 154km from Glasgow to Fort William and is Scotland's most popular long walk. It is wide, waymarked, and well-provided with accommodation. The scenery is very fine, although it's often within sight and sound of the A82, so more adventurous walkers might find it too tame.

It does provide the romantic, and environmentally sound, approach from Glasgow to Loch Lomond and The Trossachs. This book also uses sections of it along the east of Loch Lomond and around Tyndrum.

Loch Lomond and Cowal Way
The Loch Lomond and Cowal Way (previously and still sometimes marked as 'Cowal Way') runs for 90km from Inveruglas, north Loch Lomond, to Portavadie, at the mouth of Loch Fyne. It traverses the south-west of the national park, before following Loch Riddon and the Kyles of Bute to the sea, crossing hill passes, moorland, forest, woodland and loch shores through the splintered peninsula of Cowal. The (somewhat haphazard) waymarking also takes you a variety of picturesque villages, historic sites and waterfalls, while some sections include more forest track and quiet road than strictly ideal. Walk 39 visits one of its most rewarding sections at Argyll's Bowling Green, while Walk 35 uses it as an approach.

Rob Roy Way
This 128km route runs north-east from Drymen to Pitlochry crossing the far east of the national park through Aberfoyle, Callander, Strathyre, Lochearnhead and Killin. The route is low-level with long stretches of forestry track and shared cycle paths. Pleasant sections are used on Walk 3 (Menteith Hills, return leg), Walk 8 (Three Callander Bridges) and around Lochearnhead.

The Great Trossachs Path
A 48km route through The Trossachs from Callander to Inversnaid on the north-east bank of Loch Lomond. Launched in April 2015, it follows and celebrates the Great Trossachs Forest NNR created the same year, passing scenically above Loch Venachar, then along the shores of Lochs Achray, Katrine and Arklet. The walking is very easy going and paved along Loch Katrine, but it takes in some spectacular scenery. Walk 6 utilises two particularly beautiful sections for its approach and return, while it also features briefly in Routes 1, 5 and 8.

Three Lochs Way
Skirting just along the outside of the national park for much of its course, this 55km route starts in Balloch (far south Loch Lomond) then heads to Helensburgh, Gaelochhead and up to Arrochar on Loch Long before finishing at Inveruglas. It follows minor roads, hard tracks and footpaths with good public transport links.

John Muir Way
This 215km coast-to-coast route just dips into the south of the national park, but doesn't feature in any of this book's routes.

APPENDIX E
Further reading

Other relevant Cicerone guidebooks

Bailey, Dan, *Scotland's Mountain Ridges*, first ed. 2006 reprinted 2022

Kew, Steve, *Walking the Munros Volume one – Southern, Central and Western Highlands*, fourth ed. 2021 reprinted 2024.

Marsh, Terry, *The West Highland Way*, fifth ed. 2024 reprinted 2025

Turnbull, Ronald, *Not the West Highland Way*, second ed. 2025

General

Humble, BH, *On Scottish Hills*, Chapman & Hall Ltd, 1946

Murray, WH, *Mountaineering in Scotland*, Vertebrate Publishing, 2022 (first ed: Dent, 1947)

Murray, WH, *Rob Roy Macgregor: His Life and Times*, Canongate, 1991

Ransom, PJG, *Loch Lomond and The Trossachs in History and Legend*, John Donald Publishers, 2004

Scott, Walter, *Rob Roy*, 1817

Turnbull, Ronald, *Granite and Grit: a Walkers' Guide to the Geology of British Mountains*, Frances Lincoln, 2009

Wrightham, Mark and Nick Kempe (editors), *Hostile Habitats: Scotland's Mountain Environment*, Scottish Mountaineering Trust, first ed. 2006

Online

Butterfly Conservation, www.butterfly-conservation.org

Forestry and Land Scotland, www.forestryandland.gov.scot (search 'Queen Elizabeth Forest Park' or 'Argyll Forest Park')

Historic Environment Scotland, www.trove.scot

Loch Lomond and The Trossachs National Park Authority, www.lochlomond-trossachs.org

Mountaineering Scotland, www.mountaineering.scot

National Nature Reserves, www.nnr.scot

National Trust for Scotland, www.nts.org.uk

NatureScot, www.nature.scot

RSPB, www.rspb.org.uk

Scottish Geology Trust, www.scottishgeologytrust.org

Scottish Mountain Rescue, www.scottishmountainrescue.org

Scottish Outdoor Access Code, www.outdooraccess-scotland.scot

The Great Trossachs Forest NNR, www.thegreattrossachsforest.co.uk

VisitScotland, www.visitscotland.com

Woodland Trust, www.woodlandtrust.org.uk

DOWNLOAD THE GPX FILES

All the routes in this guide are available for download from:

www.cicerone.co.uk/1240/GPX

as standard format GPX files. You should be able to load them into most online GPX systems and mobile devices, whether GPS or smartphone. You may need to convert the file into your preferred format using a conversion programme such as gpsvisualizer.com or one of the many other such websites and programmes.

When you follow this link, you will be asked for your email address and where you purchased the guidebook, and have the option to subscribe to the Cicerone e-newsletter.

www.cicerone.co.uk

LISTING OF CICERONE GUIDES

BRITISH ISLES CHALLENGES, COLLECTIONS AND ACTIVITIES

Great Walks on the England Coast Path Map and Compass
The Big Rounds
The Book of the Bivvy
The Book of the Bothy
The Mountains of England and Wales
  Vol 1 — Wales
  Vol 2 — England
The National Trails
Walking the End to End Trail
Cycling Land's End to John o' Groats

LAKE DISTRICT

Bikepacking in the Lake District
Cycling in the Lake District
Joss Naylor's Lakes, Meres and Waters of the Lake District
Lake District Winter Climbs
Lake District: High Level and Fell Walks
Lake District: Low Level and Lake Walks
Mountain Biking in the Lake District
Outdoor Adventures with Children — Lake District
Scrambles in the Lake District — North
Scrambles in the Lake District — South
Trail and Fell Running in the Lake District
Walking The Cumbria Way
Walking the Lake District Fells
  — Borrowdale
  — Buttermere
  — Coniston
  — Keswick
  — Langdale
  — Mardale and the Far East
  — Patterdale
  — Wasdale
Walking the Tour of the Lake District

NORTH-WEST ENGLAND AND THE ISLE OF MAN

Walking the King Charles III England Coast Path: North West
Walking the King Charles III England Coast Path: North West
  — Cumbria Map Booklet
  — Lancashire and Merseyside Map Booklet
Cycling the Pennine Bridleway
Walking the Pennine Way
Walking the Pennine Way Map Booklet
Isle of Man Coastal Path
The Lune Valley and Howgills
Walking in Cumbria's Eden Valley
Walking in Lancashire
Walking in the Forest of Bowland and Pendle
Walking on the Isle of Man
Walking on the West Pennine Moors
Walking the Ribble Way
Hadrian's Wall Path
Hadrian's Wall Path Map Booklet

The Coast to Coast Cycle Route
The Coast to Coast Map Booklet
The Coast to Coast Walk

NORTH-EAST ENGLAND, YORKSHIRE DALES AND PENNINES

Walking the Dales Way
The Dales Way Map Booklet
Cycling the Reivers Route
Cycling the Way of the Roses
Cycling in the Yorkshire Dales
Great Mountain Days in the Pennines
Mountain Biking in the Yorkshire Dales
The Cleveland Way and the Yorkshire Wolds Way
The Cleveland Way Map Booklet
The North York Moors
Trail and Fell Running in the Yorkshire Dales
Walking in County Durham
Walking in Northumberland
Walking in Northumberland
Walking in the North Pennines
Walking in the Yorkshire Dales
  — North and East
  — South and West
Walking St Cuthbert's Way
Walking St Oswald's Way and Northumberland Coast Path

DERBYSHIRE, PEAK DISTRICT AND MIDLANDS

Cycling in the Peak District
Dark Peak Walks
Scrambles in the Dark Peak
Walking in Derbyshire
Walking in the Peak District
  — White Peak East
  — White Peak West

SOUTHERN ENGLAND

20 Classic Sportive Rides in South East England
20 Classic Sportive Rides in South West England
Bikepacking — South East Gravel
Cycling in the Cotswolds
Mountain Biking on the North Downs
South West Coast Path Map Booklet
  — Vol 1: Minehead to St Ives
  — Vol 2: St Ives to Plymouth
  — Vol 3: Plymouth to Poole
Suffolk Coast and Heath Walks
The Cotswold Way
The Cotswold Way Map Booklet
The Kennet and Avon Canal
The Lea Valley Walk
The Lea Valley Walk
The North Downs Way
North Downs Way Map Booklet
The Peddars Way and Norfolk Coast Path
The Pilgrims' Way
The Ridgeway National Trail

The Ridgeway Map Booklet
The South Downs Way
The South Downs Way Map Booklet
The Thames Path
The Thames Path Map Booklet
The Two Moors Way
Two Moors Way Map Booklet
Walking Hampshire's Test Way
Walking in Essex
Walking in Kent
Walking in London
Walking in Norfolk
Walking in the Chilterns
Walking in the Cotswolds
Walking in the Isles of Scilly
Walking in the New Forest
Walking in the North Wessex Downs
Walking on Dartmoor
Walking on Guernsey
Walking on Jersey
Walking on the Isle of Wight
Walking the Dartmoor Way
Walking the Jurassic Coast
Walking the Sarsen Way
Walking the South West Coast Path
Walks in the South Downs National Park

WALES AND WELSH BORDERS

Cycle Touring in Wales
Cycling Lon Las Cymru
Great Mountain Days in Snowdonia
Hillwalking in Shropshire
Mountain Walking in Snowdonia
Offa's Dyke Path
Offa's Dyke Map Booklet
Scrambles in Snowdonia
Snowdonia: 30 Low-level and Easy Walks
  — North
  — South
The Cambrian Way
The Pembrokeshire Coast Path
Pembrokeshire Coast Path Map Booklet
The Snowdonia Way
The Wye Valley Walk
Walking Glyndwr's Way
Walking in Carmarthenshire
Walking in Gower
Walking in Pembrokeshire
Walking in the Brecon Beacons
Walking on Gower
Walking the Severn Way
Walking the Shropshire Way
Walking the Wales Coast Path

SHORT WALKS SERIES

15 Short Walks in Dumfries and Galloway
15 Short Walks in Perthshire North — Pitlochry, Aberfeldy and Dunkeld
15 Short Walks in the Scottish Borders
15 Short Walks in the Trossachs — Callander and Aberfoyle
15 Short Walks on the Isle of Mull
15 Short Walks on the Isle of Skye

15 Short Walks on the Orkney Islands
15 Short Walks on the Shetland Islands
15 Short Walks Hadrian's Wall
15 Short Walks in the Lake District
— Keswick, Borrowdale and Buttermere
— Windermere Ambleside and Grasmere
— Coniston and Langdale
15 Short Walks in Arnside and Silverdale
15 Short Walks in the Ribble Valley
15 Short Walks in Nidderdale
15 Short Walks in Northumberland — Wooler, Rothbury, Alnwick and the coast
15 Short Walks in the Yorkshire Dales
— Grassington, Skipton, Malham and Ilkley
— Sedbergh, Kirkby Lonsdale and Ingleton
15 Short Walks in the Peak District — Bakewell and the White Peak
15 Short Walks in the Peak District — Edale and the Hope Valley
15 Short Walks on the Malvern Hills
15 Short Walks Cheddar and the Mendips
15 Short Walks in Cornwall
— Newquay and the North Coast
— Falmouth and the Lizard
— Land's End and Penzance
15 Short Walks in Norfolk — Broads and Coast
15 Short Walks in South Devon — Salcombe, Brixham and the coast
15 Short Walks in the South Downs — Brighton, Eastbourne and Arundel
15 Short Walks in the Surrey Hills
15 Short Walks on Dartmoor North — Okehampton and Chagford
15 Short Walks on Dartmoor South — Ivybridge and Princetown
15 Short Walks on Exmoor
15 Short Walks on the Isle of Wight
15 Short Walks Winchester
15 Short Walks in Bannau Brycheiniog — Brecon Beacons
15 Short Walks in Pembrokeshire — Tenby and the south
15 Short Walks in the Forest of Dean

SCOTLAND

Ben Nevis and Glen Coe
Cycling in the Hebrides
Cycling in the Hebrides
Cycling the North Coast 500
Great Mountain Days in Scotland
Mountain Biking in Southern and Central Scotland
Mountain Biking in West and North West Scotland
Not the West Highland Way: A Mountain High Way
Scotland
Scotland's Best Small Mountains
Scottish Wild Country Backpacking

Skye Munros
Skye's Cuillin Ridge Traverse
The Borders Abbeys Way
The Hebridean Way
The Hebrides
The Isle of Skye
The Skye Trail
The Southern Upland Way
The West Highland Way
West Highland Way Map Booklet
Walking Ben Lawers, Rannoch and Atholl
Walking in the Cairngorms
Walking in the Pentland Hills
Walking in the Scottish Borders
Walking in the Southern Uplands
Walking in Torridon, Fisherfield, Fannichs and An Teallach
Walking Loch Lomond and the Trossachs
Walking on Arran
Walking on Harris and Lewis
Walking on Jura, Islay and Colonsay
Walking on Mull, Coll and Tiree
Walking on Rum and the Small Isles
Walking on the Orkney and Shetland Isles
Walking on Uist and Barra
Walking Rum and the Small Isles
Walking the Cape Wrath Trail
Walking the Corbetts
Vol 1 — South of the Great Glen
Vol 2 — North of the Great Glen
Walking the Fife Pilgrim Way
Walking the Galloway Hills
Walking the Great Glen Way
Walking the Great Glen Way Map Booklet
Walking the John o' Groats Trail
Walking the Munros
Vol 1 — Southern, Central and Western Highlands
Vol 2 — Northern Highlands and the Cairngorms
Winter Climbs in the Cairngorms
Winter Climbs: Ben Nevis and Glen Coe

ALPS CROSS-BORDER ROUTES

100 Hut Walks in the Alps
Alpine Ski Mountaineering Vol 1 — Western Alps
Hiking the Tour of Monte Rosa
The Karnischer Höhenweg
The Tour of the Bernina
Trail Running — Chamonix and the Mont Blanc region
Trekking Chamonix to Zermatt
Trekking in the Alps
Trekking in the Silvretta and Ratikon Alps
Trekking Munich to Venice
Trekking the Tour du Mont Blanc
Tour du Mont Blanc Map Booklet
Walking in the Alps

FRANCE, BELGIUM AND LUXEMBOURG

Camino de Santiago — Via Podiensis
Chamonix Mountain Adventures
Cycling London to Paris
Cycling the Canal de la Garonne

Cycling the Canal du Midi
Mont Blanc Walks
Mountain Adventures in the Maurienne
Short Treks on Corsica
The GR5 Trail — Through the French Alps
The GR5 Trail — Vosges and Jura
The Moselle Cycle Route
Trekking in the Vanoise
Trekking the Cathar Way
Trekking the GR10
Trekking the GR20 Corsica
Trekking the Robert Louis Stevenson Trail
Via Ferratas of the French Alps
Walking in Provence — East
Walking in Provence — West
Walking in the Auvergne
Walking in the Briançonnais
Walking in the Dordogne
Walking in the Haute Savoie: North
Walking in the Haute Savoie: South
Walking on Corsica
Walking the Brittany Coast Path
The GR5 Trail — Benelux and Lorraine
Walking in the Ardennes
The River Loire Cycle Route
The River Rhone Cycle Route
Cycling the Route des Grandes Alpes

PYRENEES AND FRANCE/SPAIN CROSS-BORDER ROUTES

Shorter Treks in the Pyrenees
The Pyrenean Haute Route
The Pyrenees
Trekking the Cami dels Bons Homes
Trekking the GR11 Trail
Walks and Climbs in the Pyrenees

SPAIN AND PORTUGAL

Camino de Santiago: Camino Frances
Coastal Walks in Andalucia
Costa Blanca Mountain Adventures
Cycling the Camino de Santiago
Mountain Walking in Mallorca
Mountain Walking in Southern Catalunya
Spain's Sendero Historico: The GR1
The Andalucian Coast to Coast Walk
The Camino del Norte and Camino Primitivo
The Camino Ingles and Ruta do Mar
The Mountains Around Nerja
The Mountains of Ronda and Grazalema
The Sierras of Extremadura
Trekking in Mallorca
Trekking in the Canary Islands
Trekking the GR7 in Andalucia
Walking and Trekking in the Sierra Nevada
Walking in Andalucia
Walking in Catalunya — Barcelona
Walking in Catalunya — Girona Pyrenees
Walking in the Picos de Europa
Walking La Via de la Plata and Camino Sanabres
Walking on Gran Canaria
Walking on La Gomera and El Hierro
Walking on La Palma
Walking on Lanzarote and Fuerteventura

Walking on Tenerife
Walking on the Costa Blanca
Walking the Camino dos Faros
Portugal's Rota Vicentina
The Camino Portugues
Walking in Portugal
Walking in the Algarve
Walking in the Algarve
Walking on Madeira
Walking on the Azores
Cycling the Ruta Via de la Plata

SWITZERLAND
Switzerland's Jura Crest Trail
The Swiss Alps
Tour of the Jungfrau Region
Trekking the Swiss Via Alpina
Walking in Arolla and Zinal
Walking in the Bernese Oberland — Jungfrau region
Walking in the Engadine — Switzerland
Walking in Ticino
Walking in Zermatt and Saas-Fee

GERMANY
Hiking and Cycling in the Black Forest
The Danube Cycleway Vol 1
The Rhine Cycle Route
The Westweg
Walking in the Bavarian Alps
The Elbe Cycle Route

POLAND, SLOVAKIA, ROMANIA, HUNGARY AND BULGARIA
The Danube Cycleway Vol 2
The High Tatras
The Mountains of Romania

SCANDINAVIA, ICELAND AND GREENLAND
Hiking in Norway
 — North
 — South
Trekking the Kungsleden
Trekking in Greenland — The Arctic Circle Trail
Walking and Trekking in Iceland

SLOVENIA, CROATIA, SERBIA, MONTENEGRO AND ALBANIA
Hiking Slovenia's Juliana Trail
Mountain Biking in Slovenia
The Islands of Croatia
The Julian Alps of Slovenia
The Mountains of Montenegro
The Peaks of the Balkans Trail
The Slovene Mountain Trail
Walking in Slovenia: The Karavanke
Walking the Julian Alps of Slovenia
Walks and Treks in Croatia

ITALY
Alta Via 1 — Trekking in the Dolomites
Alta Via 2 — Trekking in the Dolomites
Day Walks in the Dolomites
Italy's Grande Traversata delle Alpi
Ski Touring and Snowshoeing in the Dolomites
The Way of St Francis: Via di Francesco
Trekking Gran Paradiso: Alta Via 2
Trekking in the Apennines
Trekking the Giants' Trail: Alta Via 1 through the Italian Pennine Alps
Via Ferratas of the Italian Dolomites
 — Vol 1
 — Vol 2
Walking Gran Paradiso National Park
Walking in Abruzzo
Walking in Italy's Cinque Terre
Walking in Italy's Stelvio National Park
Walking in Sicily
Walking in the Aosta Valley
Walking in the Dolomites
Walking in Tuscany
Walking in Umbria
Walking Lake Como and Maggiore
Walking Lake Garda and Iseo
Walking on the Amalfi Coast
Walking the Cammino Materano
Walking the Via Francigena Pilgrim Route
 — Part 1
 — Part 2
 — Part 3
 — Part 4
Walks and Treks in the Maritime Alps

IRELAND
The Wild Atlantic Way and Western Ireland
Walking the Kerry Way
Walking the Wicklow Way

INTERNATIONAL CHALLENGES, COLLECTIONS AND ACTIVITIES
Europe's High Points
Pocket First Aid and Wilderness Medicine

AUSTRIA
Innsbruck Mountain Adventures
Trekking Austria's Adlerweg
Trekking in Austria's Hohe Tauern
Trekking in Austria's Stubai Alps
Trekking in Austria's Zillertal Alps
Walking in Austria
Walking in the Salzkammergut: the Austrian Lake District

MEDITERRANEAN
Trekking in Greece
Walking and Trekking in Zagori
Walking and Trekking in Corfu
Walking on the Greek Islands — the Cyclades
Walking in Cyprus
Walking on Malta

HIMALAYA
8000 metres
Annapurna
Everest: A Trekker's Guide
Trekking in the Indian Himalayas
Trekking in the Karakoram

NORTH AMERICA
Hiking and Cycling the California Missions Trail
Hiking the Pacific Crest Trail
The John Muir Trail

SOUTH AMERICA
Aconcagua and the Southern Andes
Hiking and Biking Peru's Inca Trails
Trekking in Torres del Paine

AFRICA
Climbing Toubkal
Kilimanjaro
Walking in the Drakensberg
Walks and Scrambles in the Moroccan Anti-Atlas

NEW ZEALAND AND AUSTRALIA
Hiking the Overland Track

CHINA, JAPAN AND ASIA
Hiking and Trekking in the Japan Alps and Mount Fuji
Hiking in Hong Kong
Japan's Kumano Kodo Pilgrimage
Trekking in Bhutan
Trekking in Ladakh
Trekking in Tajikistan
Trekking in the Himalaya

TECHNIQUES
Fastpacking
The Mountain Hut Book

MINI GUIDES
Alpine Flowers
Navigation

MOUNTAIN LITERATURE
A Walk in the Clouds
Abode of the Gods
Fifty Years of Adventure
The Pennine Way — the Path, the People, the Journey
Unjustifiable Risk?

For full information on all our guides,
books and eBooks,
visit our website:
www.cicerone.co.uk

CICERONE

Trust Cicerone to guide your next adventure, wherever it may be around the world...

Discover guides for hiking, mountain walking, backpacking, trekking, trail running, cycling and mountain biking, ski touring, climbing and scrambling in Britain, Europe and worldwide.

Connect with Cicerone online and find inspiration.

- buy books and ebooks
- articles, advice and trip reports
- GPX files and updates
- regular newsletter

cicerone.co.uk